The New
Art Museum Library

Edited by Amelia Nelson and Traci E. Timmons

ROWMAN & LITTLEFIELD
Lanham • Boulder • New York • London

Published by Rowman & Littlefield
An imprint of The Rowman & Littlefield Publishing Group, Inc.
4501 Forbes Boulevard, Suite 200, Lanham, Maryland 20706
www.rowman.com

6 Tinworth Street, London SE11 5AL, United Kingdom

British Library Cataloguing in Publication Information Available

Library of Congress Cataloging-in-Publication Data

Names: Nelson, Amelia, 1979- editor. | Timmons, Traci E., 1968- editor.
Title: The new art museum library / edited by Amelia Nelson and Traci E. Timmons.
Description: Lanham : Rowman & Littlefield, [2021] | Includes bibliographical references and index. | Summary: "Art museum libraries are thinking about their audiences, object-based learning, and the needs of researchers in the age of digital art history. By embracing changes in technology, research, and a shifting information landscape, these libraries are positioning themselves at the nexus of digital preservation, access, and radical experimentation"— Provided by publisher.
Identifiers: LCCN 2020049951 (print) | LCCN 2020049952 (ebook) | ISBN 9781538135693 (cloth) | ISBN 9781538135709 (epub)
Subjects: LCSH: Museum libraries—Administration. | Art libraries—Administration. | Museum libraries—Case studies. | Art libraries—Case studies.
Classification: LCC Z675.M94 N49 2021 (print) | LCC Z675.M94 (ebook) | DDC 025.1/9768—dc23
LC record available at https://lccn.loc.gov/2020049951
LC ebook record available at https://lccn.loc.gov/2020049952

♾️™ The paper used in this publication meets the minimum requirements of American National Standard for Information Sciences—Permanence of Paper for Printed Library Materials, ANSI/NISO Z39.48-1992.

Contents

Acknowledgments

This is a publication that truly took the Art Libraries Society of North America (ARLIS/NA) village to complete. The editors would like to first acknowledge the members of ARLIS/NA's Museum Division who have contributed over the years to what is now this final publication: Joan M. Benedetti, who kicked off the whole notion of such a book with her book of gathered essays on art museum librarianship in 2007, and Suz Massen and Heather Slania, who initiated the planning for a new publication on the subject in 2014. Following that, a second team was convened that included this book's editors, along with Lauren Gottlieb-Miller, Douglas Litts, Caroline Dechert, and Judy Dyki who were all instrumental in pushing the project forward. In addition to these colleagues who contributed during the development phase, there have been others who stepped up to add their skills in the final stages—including Margaret Huang, digital archivist at the Philadelphia Museum of Art, who was an additional reader; and Natalia Lonchyna, former librarian at the North Carolina Museum of Art, who indexed this publication. We'd also like to extend our deepest thanks to Roger Lawson, executive librarian at the National Gallery of Art, who truly went above and beyond in lending his expert editing skills and extensive knowledge of art libraries—all of which made this publication better.

Amelia Nelson is grateful for the support of colleagues at The Nelson-Atkins Museum of Art and the Spencer Art Reference Library who have been supportive throughout this long process. This book would not have been possible without the kindness, intelligence, and passion of so many members of ARLIS/NA—but especially her coeditor Traci Timmons! Amelia would also like to thank her husband for his unfailing support on this project and so many others.

Traci E. Timmons would like to thank her colleagues at the Seattle Art Museum and her art librarian colleagues in ARLIS/NA and beyond for their encouragement and support of this project. She is grateful to have had the opportunity to work with her coeditor, Amelia Nelson, on this project. Amelia is incredibly gracious, a joy to work with, and very adept at keeping projects on task. She would also like to thank her family who have endured many nights and weekends hearing the phrase, "I'm sorry, I can't, I have to work on the book."

In the spirit of camaraderie clearly evidenced here, the editors will donate any revenue received from this publication in the first five years to ARLIS/NA to support the ongoing work of the diversity committee, which promotes equity, diversity, inclusion, and justice in the field of art librarianship.

Preface

Amelia Nelson, The Nelson-Atkins Museum of Art,
and Traci E. Timmons, Seattle Art Museum

This publication has a long provenance that really began with the success of Joan M. Benedetti's 2007 book, *Art Museum Libraries and Librarianship*. That volume explored art museum librarianship with thoughtful essays on a broad range of topics written by practitioners from art museum libraries of all sizes. This volume was immediately useful as a tool to librarians, offering best practices and expert insight. It became especially useful when art museum budgets were significantly reduced during the 2008 global financial crisis and art museum librarians had to figure out how to do more with less. During this time, librarians were called upon to justify and advocate for staff, budgets, and spaces. The impact and aftermath of this period was documented in the Art Libraries Society of North America (ARLIS/NA) sponsored 2016 white paper, *State of Art Museum Libraries*. The report captures a field struggling with long-term budget cuts, reduced staff, and low morale, but even at that difficult moment many art librarians where forging ahead with the difficult task of fundamentally rethinking the role of a successful art museum library in this new reality. Documenting their work was the catalyst for this new volume focused on art museum librarianship.

In the course of producing this book, another series of crises has emerged. In 2020, museums (and the world) are dealing with the impact of the global COVID-19 pandemic and the public reckoning and social unrest sparked by publicly exposed incidents of police brutality and institutionalized racism targeting Black, Indigenous, and People of Color (BIPOC).[1] Cultural institutions are facing uncertainty in this tumultuous time as they deal with both the revenue collapse from the pandemic and a recognition of the institutional norms within museums that don't fully support the ideals of diversity, equity, and inclusion that are at the core of many institutions' missions and values. Despite the fact that most art museums and art libraries have closed to the public during the pandemic, librarians are still creatively sharing resources with audiences through virtual programs, social media posts, and even digital care packages. This period has also highlighted the need to have a robust digital strategy, quality metadata, and off-site access to resources for staff and public researchers who rely on these materials to do their jobs. In an ever-expanding network of information, art museum libraries are creating access nodes with robust, organized data that ensure resources are available and discoverable for the future. Preservation actions, data migration, and other measures will ensure that future generations of researchers can discover the rich resources art museum libraries have to offer.

Art museums are changing. Art museums and their counterparts across the cultural sector are redefining their purpose. No longer is the focus exclusively on the preservation and display of a museum's collection; now, critical thinking about the "curatorial voice" as well as the perception and impact collected objects and exhibitions have on visitors are important consideration. Forward-looking museums routinely employ new forms of engagement and include multiple perspectives in telling the often-complex histories of collections and objects. Although this re-envisioning is embraced by many in the field, it is an approach that is still being debated—as evidenced in the controversial new definition of "museum" proposed by the International Council of Museums in 2019.[2] The notion of "democrati[z]ing, inclusive and polyphonic spaces for critical dialogue about the past and the future"[3] shifts the focus away from an authoritative voice that reigns over collections toward a more complex, global, and inclusive museum vision. There is also an ever-growing body of research indicating that museums must adapt to remain relevant to new generations who value content creation, relevancy, and personal meaning over a more traditional, and more passive, museum experience.

Although this debate is far from resolved, its effect on art museum libraries is undeniable. When an art museum shifts its mission to community engagement and critical discourse and away from the more traditional research-centered activities, the art museum library must adapt. As the chapters in this volume illustrate, libraries are actively engaged in radical exploration, experimentation, and self-examination in the face of rapid changes in the museum sector and to changes in the information landscape. Traditional functions of the library, including collection stewardship and providing access, are now facets of ever-expanding library work. Embracing changes in technology, research, and the information landscape, many libraries have positioned themselves at the nexus of digital preservation, access, and research within their institutions and the broader community. One of the goals of this publication is to examine how art museum libraries are building on a strong foundation to navigate challenges and embrace new opportunities for experimentation, creative thinking, and new ways to support information access in their own institutions and beyond.

This volume was conceived to share how art museum libraries and staff are adapting and thriving in an ever-changing environment, ensuring that they remain vital to their institutions and community. Each section in this book focuses on different aspects of the profession with an eye toward the future. Kristen Regina sets the stage with her introductory chapter focused on the transformation of art museum librar- ies. She demonstrates how the cornerstones of librarianship are being leveraged to provide greater, more equitable access to collections; how librarians must collaborate with other departments and institutions to achieve library goals; and how library staff roles now routinely demand technical skills traditionally seen in computer scientists. The next section explores some of the ways library staff work with col- lections: developing unique collections, creating and maintaining archives, enacting preservation and conservation strategies, and addressing storage issues. This section also acknowledges an issue that affects all museums and requires even libraries to look inward: addressing institutionalized racism. In her chapter, Courtney Becks critically addresses how art museums, and therefore art museum libraries, have centered white- ness, discusses how art museums have overlooked community and cultural systems of organization, and explores innovative alternative models.

In the next two sections, contributing authors explore how art museum library collections are being shared through advocacy, outreach, systems, collaborations, and programming. Although these initiatives are providing new opportunities for art libraries, they are also shifting the skills required of librarians. Art museum library staffing models vary widely from institution to institution, with libraries staffed by solo librarians with modest budgets to large libraries with numerous staff and large budgets. This section includes chapters that cover personnel considerations for those new to the field or aspiring to enter it, the vital role and management of library volunteers, as well as one institution's ongoing professional development program.

The final section focuses on how art museum libraries have harnessed the potential of technology to expand the impact and reach of local resources. The rise of digital art history, big data, and digitization have created a new interest in and greatly ex- panded the reach of art museum libraries' collections and services. In this section au- thors explore how linked data, Wikimedia, and open source platforms are being used in art museum libraries to make previously siloed collections globally discoverable.

By documenting, celebrating, and encouraging the innovative work of art mu- seum libraries, the hope is that this book will help those who do not have the needed support, funding, or staff to be able to innovate, collaborate, and advocate for what is possible. As the authors of the chapters included in this volume show, when art mu- seum libraries and librarians contribute to the broader missions of their museums, support their colleagues' research needs, and provide services that help museums fulfill their educational missions, they are successful and valued.

NOTES

1. Helier Cheung, "George Floyd death: Why US protests are so powerful this time," *BBC News*, June 8, 2020. Accessed June 23, 2020, https://www.bbc.com/news/world-us -canada-52969905

2. Vincent Noce, "Vote on ICOM's new museum definition postponed: Decision over the controversial update was made at the general assembly in Kyoto on the weekend," *The Art Newspaper*, September 9, 2019. Accessed May 17, 2020, https://www.theartnewspaper.com /news/icom-kyoto

3. Ibid.

Introduction

The Art of Transformation

Kristen Regina, Philadelphia Museum of Art

The key tenets of library, archival, and information management are access, discoverability, and systems of organization. As information managers, we want to provide access to our collections for curators, researchers, other museum staff, and the public. We want to enable our users to have that "a-ha" discovery moment of finding what they wanted and what they didn't even realize they needed. We achieve these goals by creating systems of organization—such as the Dewey Decimal System, the Library of Congress classifications, and so forth. In fact, librarians have been doing this for thousands of years (since the eighth century BCE in Mesopotamia). But what a long way the profession has come since organizing scrolls or even updating a card catalog were common necessary tasks.

With the advent of computers and computer networks, librarians and archivists eagerly moved their practices to the online world. To continue to provide access to data, practitioners train users on how to access information via online catalogs, databases, how to search the internet, and contribute skills to resources beyond single institutions such as the Wikimedia movement, digital art history and open access initiatives, CIDOC-CRM, Linked Art, and more similar broadly collaborative initiatives. The community continues to strive for "a-ha" moments in the online research spaces of libraries, archives, and beyond.

As the digital world arrived and museums' normal business activities expanded from the analog to include digital creations—from day-to-day email and electronic documents to born-digital works of art—so, too, has the art museum library and archive evolved. Around the world, libraries and archives steward analog manuscript and archival collections critical to their institutions' missions and the field of art history in general. In Philadelphia, key collections include John G. Johnson's correspondence with his buyers in Europe as he was assembling the eponymous collection and the letters between artist Marcel Duchamp, the collectors the Arensbergs, and

1

museum director Fiske Kimball as that collection was being given to the museum. Just as these analog materials are stored in a climate controlled, secure facility, now the Philadelphia Museum of Art (PMA) and the wider library and archives community do the same for electronic materials, storing them in secure online repositories. Museum librarians and archivists now capture and preserve such institutional digital files as the email correspondence between curators and living artists, exhibition photography and histories, and archiving important web-based art historical information more broadly so that these contextual references will be available to future generations of researchers and staff.

Many initiatives help support and sustain this work, but an important moment in the evolution of librarianship came from a 2013 pilot program developed by the Institute of Museum and Library Services, in conjunction with the Library of Congress. Called the National Digital Stewardship Residency (NDSR), the program was developed to bridge the gap between existing well-developed library and archives classroom education programs and the need for more direct professional experience in the field. The program served several different populations: students interested in the field of digital stewardship, partnering institutions, and the broader cultural heritage community. The mission of the NDSR was to build a dedicated community of professionals who will advance our nation's capabilities in managing, preserving, and making accessible the digital record of human achievement.

In 2016, the Institute of Museum and Library Services awarded a grant to the PMA, in partnership with the Art Libraries Society of North America (ARLIS/NA), to create an NDSR program for art information professionals (NDSR Art). NDSR Art adapted and expanded the NDSR model by addressing issues of digital preservation and stewardship in relation to the arts, with a particular focus on new media and arts information. The program supported two nationally dispersed cohorts from 2017 to 2019—each consisting of four recent postgraduates embedded in museum and cultural heritage organizations for twelve-month residencies. The goal of the program was to empower art information professionals to apply digital preservation practices already used in the library and archives community to the broader art museum sector by fostering conversations at the host institution, within the local ARLIS/NA chapter, and nationally through ARLIS/NA and other organizations. Projects ranged from examining how to preserve digitized and born-digital publications, artist theses, gallery interactives, and time-based media and works of art.

Museum libraries and archives are also undertaking institution-wide digital asset management by applying the same library principles of access, discovery, and organization to the audio and visual assets made across the institution. The goal is to apply practices historically used to organize books and documents to organizing non-traditional formats such as museum event and non-object photography, videos, conservation photos, audio tours, and other ephemeral materials. Enabling staff to use, reuse, share, and preserve digital assets in a more comprehensive way continues to enable "a-ha" moments.

But how can the museum library and archives field further extend and develop the holistic management of museums' collections-related data—the materials that define, link, and contextualize art collections—beyond just audiovisual assets? In England and the early American colonies, a "commons" was a tract of land owned and used jointly by all the residents of the community. It belonged equally to or was shared alike by everyone. Thus, in this context, the concept of an Art Information Commons is a forum and space for furthering the communities' data strategies, best practices, and tools. With support from the Andrew W. Mellon Foundation, the PMA created the Art Information Commons at the end of 2018. Its goal is to help evolve the holistic management of data, content, and technology within cultural institutions. The project works on analyzing and documenting how art information is created, used, and stored; creating unified vocabulary and data standards; and collaborating with staff to find ways to improve workflows, processes, and leverage the institution's art information.

A museum-wide initiative, the Art Information Commons is led by the Library and Archives because of its expertise in information management. Service, accessibility, training, collaboration, data organization, preservation, digitization, and image and information management have long been the hallmarks of libraries and the services they provide. The library and archives professions have foundations in structured vocabulary work, cataloging, and sharing deep information resources at scale. Information management is different from technical management of systems: it is a discipline rooted in the needs of internal and external users. And it has as its focus establishing consistent practices and vocabularies that will integrate across silos as well as extend to other institutions' data in order to support broad-based cultural heritage scholarship.

When it invests in information management, the community is able to collaborate, share, and make discoverable the information it creates and uses across all of its work more efficiently, and, ultimately, to illuminate the historical and contextual relationships between objects. Through the search mechanisms currently available to the public at the PMA and many museums, users are likely to discover only a fraction of what the institution has to offer. For instance, a popular search term on the PMA's website is "Duchamp." Using this term, researchers would readily discover multiple works of art in the collection. In a separate section of the website that is not searchable in the same manner, they might discover some of the books that the museum has published about Duchamp work. In yet another section of the website, they might find recent exhibitions organized by the museum. If they are already aware of the museum's archival holdings, they could open yet another separate search function for archival finding aids.

Strides have been taken to experiment and think about how to create such integrated connections through other Andrew W. Mellon Foundation supported projects at institutions such as the Milwaukee Art Museum, the J. Willard Marriott Library and the Utah Museum of Fine Arts at the University of Utah, and the Snite Museum of Art and the Hesburgh Libraries at the University of Notre Dame. The Georgia

O'Keeffe Museum developed a collections search that integrates library, archives, and art collection data; the PMA's John G. Johnson digital publication brings together relevant auction catalogs, archival documents, and art objects. Another collaborative project that integrates physically separated collections, sponsored by the National Endowment for the Humanities, is the Duchamp Research Portal.

The Duchamp Research Portal is an international partnership between the PMA, the Centre Pompidou, and Association Marcel Duchamp to make a significant portion of Duchamp's primary source materials and artworks available through a single searchable online interface. The project is making connections between the art and archive collections by building relationships within the data. The Duchamp Research Portal is a significant step forward in showing how to present contextual information resources along with art objects, how art data and archives data are different, but also how they can be integrated.

All of this work requires practitioners to think differently about how the profession catalogs and makes this information digitally accessible. Ultimately, by opening up collections through these new initiatives, the community can continue to fulfill its mission and extend institutional work beyond the walls of the library, archives, and museum. There is the potential to harness the power of technology to approach collections in innovative ways and invite the public to connect with integrated collections as never before.

In April 2019, the world watched in horror as the great Cathedral of Notre Dame burned. *Washington Post* columnist Alexandra Petri compared the fire to a great book burning, "one of the greatest [books] ever written." In her essay, Petri noted,

> There is something luminous about any human document that survives a sufficient length of time. A cave painting, a tablet. Simply by virtue of enduring they acquire new and unlooked-for meanings. Mona Lisa appears on T-shirts, in music, in movies. Shakespeare mutates and transforms and multiplies with the modifications of generations of minds. Things last because they acquire new meaning and they continue to acquire new meaning because they last.[1]

It is the job of the library and archives to help ensure that things last, by making them accessible, discoverable, and organized, whether they are in analog or digital form. It is the proper role of libraries and archives to enable conversations between the living and the dead, between the past and the future, between the object, its creator, and all those who observe it, write about it, or find in it some inspiration or beauty, to continue uninterrupted.

NOTE

1. Alexandra Petri, "The Burning of a Great Stone Book," *Washington Post*, April 15, 2019, https://www.washingtonpost.com/opinions/2019/04/16/burning-great-stone-book/.

I

DEVELOPING, MANAGING, AND CARING FOR COLLECTIONS

1

Shelved Out of Sight

Library Spaces and Archives Storage in Art Museums

Jenna Stout, Saint Louis Art Museum

The library occupies a unique niche within the art museum. Libraries often started alongside the art museums they support. Others developed later in the museum's history with endowments in place to support collection development, programming, and other needs. Library holdings provide context to interpret and understand the art collections. The historical development of library spaces within art museum settings presents opportunities as well as challenges for librarians and archivists. Gallery space is in high demand by curators to display exhibitions, so historically, library spaces may have been relocated to accommodate museum needs and allow for growth. Many were relocated to staff-only or low-traffic areas of the museum; for libraries that are open to the public, this has made access for these users difficult.

Often operating under the library department, art museum archives are poised to alleviate spatial constraints in departments as records are transferred from offices to their holdings. However, as archivists take in large volumes of records, they must consider their own spatial limitations. If the physical plan of the museum has reached capacity, library and archives staff alike may investigate off-site storage as they look for alternate spaces to house print and archival collections. This movement can decrease the load on shelving, allow for collection growth, and enable the accrual of department archival records, but shifting materials to off-site storage also impacts reference service. Rather than having same-day access, users may need to request materials in advance of their visit.

LOCATING THE LIBRARY

The late nineteenth and early twentieth centuries witnessed a heyday of art museum construction. These museums were seen as culturally uplifting spaces; thus, their design often came in the form of grandiose palatial structures. Early American art museums modeled in neoclassical styles conveyed messages of authority, democracy, and cultural refinement to rival their European counterparts. The Cleveland Art Museum, Detroit Institute of Arts, Nelson-Atkins Museum of Art, and Toledo Art Museum exemplify classical influences in their architecture. Some museums' main buildings were built for, or in conjunction with, world's fair expositions. The Philadelphia Museum of Art's charter dates back to the 1876 Centennial Exposition, and the Art Institute of Chicago's building was originally designed for the 1893 Columbian Exposition as the World's Congress Auxiliary Building; the Saint Louis Art Museum's Cass Gilbert Building served as the Palace of Fine Arts during the 1904 Louisiana Purchase Exposition. While the bulk of the world's fair building stock existed solely as temporary structures, a few permanent structures remained at their original sites. The Chicago and Saint Louis buildings were intentionally designed for the purpose of housing art institutions after the expositions closed.

The very architectural characteristics that made the structures stand out during the fair were, in some ways, a hindrance to their uses as welcoming museum spaces. Although intended to benefit the cultural life of their cities, their imposing structures aligned them with the elite rather than the masses. But, museums stood as tangible evidence that a city recognized the significance of public education. A social discourse emerged on the desired type of visitor. In *Museums and American Intellectual Life, 1876–1926*, Steven Conn notes that this discourse played out in different ways, such as the establishment of Sunday operating hours to accommodate working classes. If museums were to be beacons of culture and education, then it was their social obligation to serve the masses rather than the elite.[1] The art museum library, however, was often removed from these discussions because it was not viewed as a space to be visited by the general public.

The art museum library's collections typically developed as a complement to the art holdings and therefore reflected the museum's collecting strengths. Endowed funds helped create some of the first museum libraries, whereas other prominent collectors bequeathed their personal research libraries to the museums. Donors often left legacies in the form of naming rights, conditions driving the display of certain objects such as plaques or book purchases. As originally established, art museum library collections primarily supported the interpretation of the institution's art holdings and secondarily facilitated the broader function of art education. In light of this interdependent relationship, the library's role was understandably upstaged by the art collections. This primacy of the art collections was further communicated in how gallery space is utilized and where the library is housed on the museum campus.

Whether accessible only to in-house staff or open to the general public, the art museum library fills a need by providing access to critical research materials and information services. Although online catalogs and finding aids have significantly increased discoverability, the art museum library is often perceived as off-limits to the general public. While libraries in art museums chiefly support the host institutions' research, they also can serve docents, students, and community members. In a 1997 article, Clive Phillpot touched on the barriers erected to block users deemed not to be serious researchers (i.e., not art historians). Furthermore, he emphasized that by privileging art historical research these libraries missed the opportunity to engage casual visitors or the community at large. The serendipity of freely browsing shelves is absent in libraries where the stacks are closed to the public.[2]

The location of the library within the museum is a manner of organizational politics and space planning. Because art museums prioritize the art collections, space is a valuable commodity within the museum setting. Thus, a long-established library may have adapted nimbly to meet evolving needs as well as to accommodate the growth of the museum's collections. The Saint Louis Art Museum's Richardson Memorial Library opened in April 1915 in three east wing galleries that were redesigned as library space.[3] Muralists Elmer E. and Julian E. Garnsey decorated the entrance to the reading rooms.[4] The library moved to the lower level of the west wing in 1938 as part of the project "to maximize gallery space and increase the efficiency of service areas."[5] It eventually found a long-term home in the new administration wing by 1980.

Moving the library from its original location is often necessary, but it is not always a seamless transition. In his essay "125 Years and Still Waiting: A Museum Library History,"[6] Allen Townsend discusses the struggles of the Philadelphia Museum of Art to renovate the library over the course of the twentieth century.[7] Library space studies help focus attention on the growth potential of the library and where the space is needed. The location of the library greatly varies based on its primary users—public or staff users. If the library has historically occupied an area adjacent to galleries, a move to a new space offers up new potential benefits as well as drawbacks. Is the library open to the public? A more prominent entrance near galleries can enhance the library's public image and increase the library collection's accessibility. Alternatively, if the library is tucked away in the basement, administrative building, or off-campus it will have decreased visibility and less public awareness about its collections. If the library is located on-site, proper signage and maps can provide museum visitors with visual clues for finding the space. Institution-specific accessibility studies can offer in-depth examinations of how patrons interact with spaces and any barriers that hinder usage. Knowledgeable visitor services staff and gallery attendants can also direct first-time visitors to the library. Library orientation sessions for new museum employees is an excellent way to familiarize non-library staff members with the library space and its resources.

Library spaces placed in significant architectural structures must balance historic integrity with modern needs. Can the stacks support the weight of books? In *Museum Librarianship* Esther Green Bierbaum advises that "second floors, particularly in historic houses and buildings, may require bracing or even replacing before bearing the load of a library collection."[8] Are the stacks open to the public or closed? Library stacks also must meet local code standards. Some libraries may allow staff to browse the stacks and restrict external researchers from accessing these areas. This practice helps ensure patron safety and adds an extra level of security to valuable library collections.

A brief orientation for first-time users gives the reference library staff a forum to address the issue of closed stacks and retrieval methods. This also alleviates library anxiety as first-time users may not have visited an art museum library before and may be unfamiliar with the library's policies and procedures. Physical and digital infrastructures in the form of signage, catalogs, finding aids, and databases enable the discoverability of materials; however, library staff members facilitate the patron experience through behind-the-scenes work as well as reference desk duty.

The reading room, sometimes referred to as the research room, is the meeting ground for patrons to use noncirculating materials from the library and archival collections. Security measures will vary depending on the institution. Reading rooms typically have similar rules in place regarding writing utensils, laptops, cameras, phones, food and drink, jewelry such as rings and bracelets, and other outside materials. Researchers may be asked to store personal belongings in a locker or on the floor. The reading room will usually contain oversized tables, viewing equipment (e.g., a microfilm reader), archival accessories (e.g., book cradles, book snake weights, alkaline buffered papers, pencils), scanners, copiers, and computers linked to the library catalog.[9]

Optimum conditions for a reading room may not always be realistic for small library and archive spaces if the reading room is located in an office or processing area. An established appointments-only policy, rather than drop-ins, is one way to alleviate overcrowding and allow staff to pull materials ahead of time. A log that tracks visitors and material use is helpful for reference statistics as well as a safeguard against theft. Quantitative data for the library's usage can justify the preservation of archival collections and help staff advocate for additional resources.

Because archival materials are susceptible to light exposure, it is recommended that these records be housed in folders and boxes when not in active use. Mary Lynn Ritzenthale's *Preserving Archives and Manuscripts* offers practical advice on how to maintain a preservation environment. She specifies that windows are admissible in reading rooms "in part for aesthetic reasons and human comfort and in part because archival materials in these spaces are exposed for relatively brief periods of time."[10]

The reading room may also contain exhibit cases for library exhibitions. Any original archival records on display should be rotated out on a regular basis to prevent light damage. A collection of books and other library resources focused on a certain theme or connected to a current art exhibition is another display option. In "Creating Alternative Art Libraries," Ksenia Cheinman explores how reading rooms have traditionally been the place for the promotion of print collections and offers some innovative ways to bring the library's collections into the galleries.[11] The library's reading room may lack accessibility and, therefore, be hidden from the public eye.

THE ARCHIVES AS LIBRARY SPACE

A 1979 survey of art museum archives gathered data on the current state of archival programs in the United States and Canada.[12] It found that "in over 50% of the instances where the archives is part of another museum department, it is under the library."[13] Librarians expressed that they felt a sense of responsibility to safeguard archival records, hence the common placement of archives within the library department. In December 1979, the Archives of American Art held a three-day conference on museum archives to address recordkeeping practices and advise on archival standards. Guidelines established at the symposium included a section on archival environments. Recommendations included that archival materials be located in a secure, climate-controlled space and that suitable staffing and accommodations are necessary; if these were not available, the archival holdings should be transferred to another repository or held in a consortium.[14] Forty years later, art museum archivists and librarians still strive to maintain optimal conditions in their respective storage spaces.

In smaller institutions, the archives and library may utilize adjacent storage areas for their collections and share the same reading room for researchers. The librarian, at some institutions, assumes archival responsibilities when there is no funding for a full-time staff member. In light of these ongoing interactions, it is important to understand that archival collections require spaces capable of maintaining specific environmental condition for long-term preservation. Collections of mixed paper–based archival materials should be housed in a space with a maximum temperature of 65 degrees Fahrenheit and a set point of 35 to 45 percent relative humidity.[15] Data loggers are an affordable way to monitor storage environments. The data can periodically be retrieved through a USB flash drive and uploaded for analysis. This allows archives staff to track temperature, humidity, and other levels over periods of time; in turn, this statistical data can be used to advocate for new storage facilities; heating, ventilation, and air conditioning systems; and other preservation measures.

Cool storage (range of 35–65 degrees Fahrenheit) and cold storage (below freezing) should be used for unstable materials, like photographic or audiovisual materials. Staff should consider how frequently these materials are used because moving materials in and out of cool temperature storage can be detrimental. Duplicating these materials to produce reference copies is one practical approach. The expense to maintain cool storage systems may present a financial hardship to many institutions.[16] If an archive does not have its own cool storage system, the art museum may have a cold storage environment that archival materials can be housed.

Compact mobile shelving is commonplace in many archives' settings. It holds more collections than stationary shelving and allows for efficient use of space. In addition, for archives in areas with seismic activity, compact mobile shelving contains extra bracing. Art museum library and archives staff should consult with their building managers to choose the shelving that best fits their storage needs. After all, art museum libraries house materials such as oversized folios and uniquely shaped artists' books that do not fit standard bookshelves and require innovative approaches to shelving. For example, flat file storage cabinets are appropriate for architectural drawings, maps, and related materials. Multiple museum departments also utilize shelving; thus, the institution may have a preferred vendor for supply and installation. Ongoing conversations with other departments can inform decisions to adopt new shelving.

SEEKING OFF-SITE STORAGE SOLUTIONS

Inevitably, a library or archive that is actively collecting will eventually run out of space. Art museum libraries with encyclopedic collections may find themselves at a tipping point in which they must move materials to another location; the same can be said for archives housing records of enduring value.

If the construction of a new library and archives facility is a possible option, *Archival and Special Collections Facilities: Guidelines for Archivists, Librarians, Architects, and Engineers* is a useful resource and advocates for collaboration between the library and archives early in the design phase.[17]

Securing funding and maintaining proximity to museum staff may prevent a new facility or addition from becoming a reality. Many librarians and archivists are faced with the decision of whether to send library and archival materials off-site. The physical environment may have reached capacity and not be functional for everyday operations. Off-site high-density storage offers a potential solution to help free up space. The librarian and archivist should weigh a number of considerations regarding their collections, including usage, enduring value, processing time, size, digitization potential, and housing costs for materials transferred to off-site storage. Frequently consulted print and archival collections may be better suited to remain on-site. Archival materials sent to off-site storage should be processed to enable retrieval at a later point.

Soliciting bids from at least three vendors is typical practice at many institutions. Cost, including storage and retrieval prices, should obviously be considered, but it is not the only factor at play. How quickly will the facility retrieve items from off-site storage? Does the storage facility maintain a climate-controlled environment? Does the facility offer a scan-on-demand service? For local vendors, library staff members may be situated close enough to tour the facilities, if possible, to assess the physical conditions. All these factors—rather than just the cost—are essential to the selection process. For libraries considering off-site storage, regional professional listservs are a forum to reach out to colleagues for their own experiences with different vendors serving the area. Art museum staff and public users should also be invited to participate in the planning. Do patrons drop in at the library, or are appointments required to allow for retrievals of materials? Are staff typically on tight project deadlines that require materials to be available with little notice? Will a digital surrogate suffice for research purposes? Gathering input from the art museum library's patron base is critical in helping library staff members weigh user expectations and needs.

The art museum library is still very much a resource heavily dependent on printed materials, despite digital initiatives and the proliferation of online materials. This fact, paired with the prevalence of noncirculating collections at many institutions, makes these spaces mainstays for their institutions. Nonetheless, art museum libraries that have reached their centennial have inevitably transformed over the decades because of collection growth, building modernization, and new technologies. Not only are libraries now equipped with computers, scanners, and Wi-Fi access, reading room tables feature plug-in ports to accommodate laptop usage. The shift from physical slide collections and card catalogs to digital surrogates and online databases have had major physical impacts on libraries' layouts and work routines. As special libraries, art museum libraries must frequently overcome preconceived notions of their patron base as well as physical obstacles in terms of location.

While proximity to the main museum campus is desirable, the library and archives may find long-term solutions in off-site facilities. It is important to document the increasing budgetary cost of off-site storage and retrieval fees for library and archival materials. By providing financial projections for collection growth in third-party, high-density facilities, library and archives staff can make a strong case for the construction of a museum-owned research and storage facility. This advocacy for expansion in turn elevates the library and archives in long-term space planning conversations by museum administration. Art museum libraries and archives are linked in many institutional histories; thus, through close collaboration, librarians and archivists can strategically plan for collection growth, access, and preservation needs.

NOTES

1. Steven Conn, *Museums and American Intellectual Life, 1876–1926* (Chicago: University of Chicago Press, 1998), 204.

2. Clive Phillpot, "The Social Role of the Art Library," *Art Documentation: Journal of the Art Libraries Society of North America* 16, no. 2 (Fall 1997): 25–26.

3. "Richardson Memorial Library," *Bulletin of the City Art Museum of St. Louis* 1, no. 3 (May 1915): 2–5.

4. "Mural Decoration: In the City Art Museum, St. Louis, Mo.," *Art and Progress* 7, no. 2 (December 1915): 58–59.

5. Osmund Overby, "The Saint Louis Art Museum: An Architectural History," *Bulletin (St. Louis Art Museum), New Series* 18, no. 3 (Fall 1987): 22.

6. Allen Townsend, "125 Years and Still Waiting: A Museum Library History," *Art Documentation: Journal of the Art Libraries Society of North America* 20, no. 1 (2001): 4–7.

7. The Philadelphia Museum of Art Library is now located in the Perlman building, which opened in 2007.

8. Esther Green Bierbaum, "Nuts and Bolts: Space, Furnishings, Equipment, and Security," in *Museum Librarianship*, second edition (Jefferson, NC: McFarland & Company, Inc., Publishers, 2000), 61–62.

9. Mary Lynn Ritzenthaler, *Preserving Archives and Manuscripts*, second edition (Chicago: Society of American Archivists, 2010), 264–65.

10. Ibid., 137.

11. Ksenia Cheinman, "Creating Alternative Art Libraries," *Art Documentation: Journal of the Art Libraries Society of North America* 33, no. 1 (Spring 2014): 44.

12. Ann B. Abid, "Museum TOL Column," *ARLIS/NA Newsletter* 8, no. 2 (February 1980): 42–43.

13. Ibid., 42.

14. "Conference on Museum Archives," *Archives of American Art Journal* 19, no. 4 (1979): 25.

15. Ritzenthaler, 115.

16. Ibid., 118.

17. Michele F. Pacifico and Thomas P. Wilsted, editors, *Archival and Special Collections Facilities: Guidelines for Archivists, Librarian, Architects, and Engineers* (Chicago: Society of American Archivists, 2009).

2

Cultivating Wisely

Strategies to Keep the Collection Alive and Evergreen

Doug Litts, The Art Institute of Chicago

Building a collection can be one of the most rewarding aspects of art museum librarianship. As a museum develops its art holdings, its library collects in tandem both to support the mission of the museum as well as to acquire its own treasures. Although museum libraries' collection management practices resemble those of academic or special libraries in many cases, art museum libraries face many unique challenges. This chapter can only offer a survey of the issues surrounding acquisitions and collection development at museum libraries, so I advise those new to the field to seek broader in-depth guides[1] and to consult the first major work on the subject of art museum libraries, *Art Museum Libraries and Librarianship*, edited by Joan M. Benedetti.[2]

THE LIBRARY IN THE MUSEUM, OR KNOW YOUR USERS

Although some museum libraries may have sizeable staffs, most are operated by only a few individuals, thus requiring the librarian to wear many hats. Unless the library is new, one will inherit a collection that reflects the priorities of the museum, the strengths of its art holdings, and the particular research interests of previous curators and collection managers. It is important to spend time at the outset getting to know the collection so you can learn how it has been developed over time and come to know its strengths and deficiencies. Subject expertise is crucial for collection development, and a background in researching and studying art will help prepare one to develop the collection. However, it is just as important to know the museum's mission and the library's role in fulfilling it. Museums that emphasize research and publishing will have different expectations of what their libraries can and should collect than those with other priorities.

As most art museums still focus on objects, their libraries reflect this. Because research typically focuses on works of art, museum libraries do not routinely collect aesthetics, philosophy, and theory. Rather, they may acquire in the areas of anthropology, archaeology, civilization, cultural history, and fashion, for example. Besides supporting the museum's collection, museum libraries must also address other priorities. Upcoming exhibitions often dictate how resources are spent, especially if the subjects have scant material in the stacks already. Even traveling exhibitions may create a need for research material to support docents, museum educators, and programming.

Just as important as subject expertise is user expertise. As curators are responsible for what goes in the galleries and what enters and leaves the art collection, they are the primary focus of the library. Curatorial requests typically guide acquisitions more than any other considerations, and often the heaviest users of the collection are research assistants and interns in curatorial departments. Depending on the museum's priorities, the library may also collect for other populations, such as staff in conservation, education, and possibly even security. Frequently, other departments do not have book budgets and thus rely on the library to purchase on topics such as art law, building code standards, museum studies, and science. Librarians must get to know their patrons from the outset, but they also must guard against assuming they and their needs will not change. Fostering a continual dialogue with users will help avoid spending acquisition funds in a subject area no longer of interest. Conducting ongoing conversations, either informally or through structured liaisons and outreach, will help inform spending and make the most of the library's staff and financial resources.

Other initiatives and priorities of the museum beyond the focus on art and collections may also drive acquisition decisions. For example, in 2017, the American Alliance of Museums convened the Working Group on Diversity, Equity, Accessibility, and Inclusion to address issues of inequality and minority representation in American museums and their leadership. Programs such as the Diversifying Art Museum Leadership Initiative and the Facing Change: Advancing Museum Board Diversity and Inclusion project reflect the need for change in museums and their missions. In addition to the library purchasing content on art subjects by diverse authors and creators in order to serve its users effectively, the library should also provide resources to support such initiatives. Librarians should be engaged with such projects and also work to have on hand resources addressing not only diversity and equity in the arts, but, more broadly, diverse perspectives on societal issues for non-specialist audiences. By actively collecting to support initiatives such as these, the library can continue to find new ways to integrate and support its museum.

COLLECTION POLICIES AND PHILOSOPHIES

Active collection policies, drawing from the mission of the library and its intended users, are also a useful tool for managing holdings. There are many published examples that reflect different levels of detail, methodologies, and focus.[3] A well-written policy provides scope, justifications for acquisitions and deselection, and guidance on what to prioritize when resources are tight. Ideally a collection policy is drafted with input from museum administration to help articulate what the museum expects of the library and what, realistically, can be achieved. This is important in determining the breadth and depth of collecting in subjects. An idealistic policy out of touch with the actual resources available is ineffective. Like other museum policies, the collection development policy should be a living document, reviewed periodically so that it may evolve alongside the institution's priorities.

As many art museums continue to address budget challenges, libraries have looked to alternative options to provide the materials their users need. Several have developed partnerships with larger institutions, such as universities, receiving support for services or collections while building resources to support the mission of both institutions. Other museums have collaborative collection development, working collaboratively with other libraries. The New York Art Resources Consortium is an example of museum partnership, but local public and academic libraries also provide opportunities for coordinating collection development. Another informal strategy is not to purchase items that are available locally from other libraries.

Alternatively, some libraries are moving from a "just-in-case" to a "just-in-time" model. Research libraries, which include some museum libraries, must continue to add to their collections to anticipate both current and future user needs. Many librarians can point to jewels in their collections that were serendipitously acquired without any prescience that they would become important or rare years later. However, with the vast amount of new research resources appearing annually, there are often not enough funds to buy things that *might* be used. As a result, many libraries have adopted a "just-in-time" acquisition policy, purchasing material once it is requested. Patron-driven acquisition for electronic media can also supply immediate user access online; however, this option is often too costly for most museum libraries. Interlibrary loans can also serve to provide access to material as needed, especially for journals and collected works that fall outside of collecting scope. The ability to borrow material that is expensive or hard to find plays a crucial role in purchasing decisions.

Even as they move toward reactive collecting models, librarians must continue to think about the future and the collection that their day-to-day choices are creating. Relying exclusively or primarily on user purchase requests will leave holes in the collection and can result in overrepresentation of certain areas. Every library has its super-users who actively use it, give suggestions, and make requests, and it is a natural tendency to favor those who show support. The responsible collection manager must work to avoid allowing gaps to form in the library's resources, even if some of its user base is silent. For the collection to retain its relevance and usefulness to its museum, it must continue to address all subject areas in the collection development plan.

For those libraries that can pursue a "just-in-case" model, selecting materials for purchase largely depends on resources. Unlike the majority of academic libraries, few museum libraries can use approval plans. Some large museum libraries depend on bibliographers or subject specialists to discover and track down the material most useful to their users. But at most museums, collection development is typically one of the many responsibilities of the librarian, who must find the means and vendors that work for their particular situation. Vendors have consolidated, and few specialist art-book vendors remain. Many libraries rely on electronic notices from vendors to alert them to new titles and important series for which they might want to establish standing orders. Increasingly, libraries also depend on sites like Amazon, which often provide discounted prices and free shipping. However, this route is labor intensive, so one must determine whether the savings outweigh the additional costs in time and labor.

International vendors are crucial for libraries that collect material published abroad. These vendors have expert knowledge of the markets and publishers in the countries they represent and are crucial tools for discovering important resources for the collection. Domestic vendors can only offer a fraction of what is available direct from foreign markets. Yet even international vendors are challenged to provide access to independently published items and books from small museums. Collecting material from developing nations can be even more challenging, as there are few or no mechanisms by which to discover or purchase books produced there.

Those new to collection development for art museum libraries will quickly discover that there is no easy way to find everything one needs. As the art collection of each institution has evolved organically, shaped by its particular history, donors, curators, and mission, there is no one-size-fits-all solution to maintaining and expanding the library collection that supports it. Building an effective resource that is useful both today and in the future is more art than science. It is relatively easy to stay abreast of and purchase the latest releases from large scholarly presses, and often these titles are what libraries with smaller budgets acquire, relying on interlibrary loans as supplements. Unfortunately, this initially must-have material may become the least valuable material in the collection. But items produced in small runs by small museums, independent presses, foreign publishers, and artist's book printers are, in the long run, what make the collection unique and special. Thus, finding a balance among the types of materials purchased will result in a collection best suited to the needs of its users.

WHAT TO COLLECT

The types of materials that art museum libraries collect vary minimally. All collect their own publications and catalogs of exhibitions held in the museum. Libraries usually also prioritize acquiring publications that include information about objects in the art collection. Often, image permission contracts stipulate that the museum that holds an object whose image is reproduced receive a copy of the publication. Books with information about the collection often tend to be the most heavily used.

Publications from other museums are another top priority. Many museums still actively publish many catalogs annually in both print and digital formats. Museum collection catalogs are important to acquire because curators use them heavily. Similarly, exhibition catalogs are valuable for both the scholarship and reproductions they contain. Other museum publications are also targeted for collecting. Museum calendars, bulletins, and member's magazines are increasingly online, but many museums still publish these in print. A smaller number still publish serials in hard copy (e.g., the *Metropolitan Museum Journal*), whereas others appear in electronic format only (e.g., *Stedelijk Studies*).

If resources permit, most museum libraries collect auction, sale, and dealer catalogs. If a museum is actively collecting artworks, these constitute important resources with which curators keep abreast of what is happening in the market. Many libraries benefit from their curators' relationships with the auction houses and dealers, as the curators pass on the library catalogs that they have been given. However, to ensure a more comprehensive collection, libraries must subscribe to the catalogs of the houses they want to collect. Although most sale listings and catalogs are available online and presumably will continue to be accessible there, most libraries that collect this material are retaining the hard copies. These histories of sales are crucial for museum researchers, especially those working to establish provenance—an important element in determining both authenticity and establishing that an object has been acquired legally. Additionally, some illustrated catalogs offer the only published image of a given artwork, making them indispensable resources for researchers and conservators. In the past, museum libraries purchased yearly art auction indexes (still crucial because they have not been retrospectively digitized), and now most subscribe to at least one auction results database.

Because of art museum libraries' focus on object research, trade literature can also prove extremely useful. Resources such as art supply catalogs, paint sample books, and tool advertisements can all provide insight to conservators and other researchers studying the production of artworks. Collecting can be challenging because this material was ephemeral and thus few copies survive. Contemporary collecting can also quickly become overwhelming due to the large amount of material. Collection managers should not dismiss opportunities for acquiring trade literature out of hand but rather balance this against other collecting priorities.

Most museum libraries purchase from the same serial subscription lists as academic libraries, with an added emphasis on publications more specifically focused on art objects. Periodicals in museum studies, conservation science, and art-object research (such as *IFAR Journal*) all continue to be the bread and butter of museum libraries' subscription lists. Increasing numbers of visual arts subscriptions are completely available (with all images) in electronic form, and many libraries have moved solely to digital formats, when available. However, many journals are still only completely available in hard copy, requiring libraries to continue to manage (and claim) incoming issues. Open-access journals, although welcomed by libraries for costing nothing, present new challenges. For example, collection managers must put forth an effort to keep up to date with what is available and of sufficiently high quality to be added to the collection. Because open-access journals do not issue new publication or cessation of publication alerts, library staff must actively monitor for continued accessibility and other problems, such as URL changes. Advocacy, especially from libraries, have resulted in the push for more open-access scholarship. For example, the University of California adopted an Open Access Policy ensuring that future research articles authored by the University of California faculty will be made available to the public at no charge, and the Illinois Open Access to Research Articles Act requires open access for all scholarly articles produced at Illinois public universities. As open-access material becomes more readily available, museum libraries must find ways to make it available to its users.

DIGITAL COLLECTIONS AND COLLECTING

As has been noted, journals in electronic format are becoming increasingly more common, even as the field of the visual arts still lags behind most in transitioning. Access to runs of journals online has enabled many libraries to deaccession back issues or move them to remote storage. Vendors such as JSTOR and EBSCO also provide subscription packages with aggregated full text journal content with short embargos on current material. As a result, libraries need to decide whether maintaining an individual journal subscription for a year or two of current content is the best use of their budget.

Electronic books are also slow to supersede hard copy, and the inevitability of a complete transition to digital continues to be a question. Ever-shifting publisher licensing restrictions also continue to give museum libraries pause in committing to e-books. Although content in the visual arts continues to grow, the vast majority of published material is not available in electronic format. Nonetheless, many museum libraries are pursuing ways to provide access to digital books through vendor subscription packages and opportunities such as Books at JSTOR and Project Muse. Open-access books, such as the museum catalogs and publications generated through the Online Scholarly Catalogue Initiative, have yet to be embraced by the field despite the high-quality content and scholarship.

While also creating born-digital books, many museums and their libraries have engaged in retrospective digitization projects of catalogs, images, and archival materials. The Getty Research Portal aggregates and provides access to an extensive collection of digitized art history texts from a range of institutions worldwide. Participants must submit their bibliographic metadata to be included, and, while incomplete, the portal provides the largest collection of full text material dedicated to art history. Other projects such as the Digital Public Library of America and Gallica also provide important full-text digital material, including those in the visual arts.

Visual resources collections have been completely transformed by digitization: a chapter could be devoted to just this topic. Museum libraries typically rely on a combination of online resources, both paid and free. Whereas museum online collections play an important role and many now provide free, unrestricted use of their images, and search engines such as Google Images provide access to images of varying quality, most museums still purchase image databases, most typically Artstor. PHAROS, an international consortium of art historical photo archives, is also creating a digital research platform allowing for consolidated access to photo archive images and their associated scholarly documentation. As museum libraries have collected videos and DVDs as they have books, many are now also collecting streaming video through subscription services. Documentaries, performances, interviews, and video art are among the many opportunities for libraries to provide important content to their users. As art museums expand their exhibitions and collections of time-based media, their libraries will need to adjust to meet their users' evolving needs.

Art museum libraries have also been the primary collectors of artist, pamphlet, and ephemera files. They are now facing the challenge that much of the content they traditionally gathered is now available only on the internet. Artist, gallery, and art fair websites are just some examples of where valuable content is at risk of disappearing. Web archiving sites such as the Internet Archive's Wayback Machine help capture and save such sites, but archiving is incomplete and scattershot. Art museum libraries such as those participating in the New York Art Resources Consortium have begun to archive curated collections of websites in areas that correspond to the scope of the collections at each library. Projects such as the Advancing Art Libraries and Curated Web Archives in partnership with the Internet Archive is one initiative exploring and expanding web archiving among art and museum libraries and archives in order to assemble digital "ephemeral" collections.

ALTERNATE ACQUISITION METHODS

Philanthropy also plays a crucial role in developing collections. Personally fostering engaged individuals or more formally developing committee or friend groups may help provide necessary purchasing funds. Material donations can also play a valuable role in building the collections of libraries of all sizes. Libraries must have a written policy delineating to both staff and donors what will be accepted. For smaller libraries, gifts may heavily supplement the materials purchased outright; for larger libraries, donations often fill in holes or provide more obscure and rarer material that they may have overlooked. A whole chapter could be dedicated to the issues surrounding gifts because, despite their name, they are never free in regard to storage, searching, processing, and off-loading. In considering what donations to accept, libraries must carefully balance the actual value this material may bring to the collection against the cost of acquiring it.

Another method by which "free, but not free" material may come to the library is through exchange. In the past, most museum libraries participated in such programs, trading their institution's own publications with other museum libraries to both promote their own titles and receive materials to supplement their own collections. Often due to a strain in resources, exchange programs have waned, and many libraries have withdrawn from them. Today, some museums may still have formal exchange partners with whom they trade their latest catalogs. Other institutions have informal partnerships; for example, a library will make a request for a title and provide a list of materials that can be requested from them in return. Most libraries will try to accommodate exchange requests, if possible, even if no previous agreement has been made.

CONCLUSION

Adept collection managers can never just add and move on. For a collection to continue to live and thrive, the museum library must constantly adjust to make sure that research resources continue to be available to their users, whether these resources be on-site or online. Priorities may need to change over time and new material added while obsolete or superfluous items are weeded out. Regardless of collection size, the ace collection manager makes sure that all resources—including staff, budget, and space—are being used as effectively and efficiently as possible to provide the best foundation for the research conducted within its parent institution. A carefully cultivated collection will both serve the museum's needs today and facilitate the scholarship of generations to come.

NOTES

1. The longstanding standard text is Peggy Johnson, *Fundamentals of Collection Development and Management*, fourth edition (London: Facet, 2018). Another solid guide is Vicki L. Gregory, *Collection Development and Management for 21st Century Library Collections: An Introduction*, second edition (Chicago: ALA Neal-Schuman, 2019).

2. Joan M. Benedetti, editor, *Art Museum Libraries and Librarianship* (Lanham, MD: Scarecrow Press, 2007).

3. The largest group of examples is Ann Baird Whiteside, Pamela Born, and Adeane Alpert Bregman, *Collection Development Policies for Libraries and Visual Collections in the Arts* (Laguna Beach: Art Libraries Society of North America, 2000), 103–33.

3

Blood on the Walls, Blood on the Shelves

Decolonizing the Art Museum Library

Courtney Becks, University of Illinois at Urbana-Champaign

What you mean Her Majesty's London? / Where you think all her majesty
come from?

—Swet Shop Boys[1]

For truly interdisciplinary artists, scholars, or researchers, communicating about
their work can be a frustratingly uphill battle. They must explain themselves and
what they do, maddeningly, repeatedly, endlessly, for interlocutors of all sorts who
seem hard pressed to understand that a person *or* work may be or *do* more than one
thing (simultaneously).

This is because, this author posits, the very mental models that give twenty-
first-century Western society its shape and texture were formed in the crucible of
post-French Revolution capitalism, racism, and nationalism that gave the world
colonialism and its attendant enablers and alibis: social Darwinism and eugenics.

These mental models or conceptualizations insist upon—actually rely upon—the
organization of all modes and manners of knowledge, endeavor, and existence: vegeta-
ble, animal, and mineral. This nineteenth-century impetus or zeal for organizing the
unprecedented flow of knowledge or information (some yielded by various imperial
projects) resulted in conveniently reifying classifications, hierarchies, and disciplines
that fixed the "rightful" order of phenomena and occupations as well as *human beings*
in categories and rankings as trig and tidy as the compartments of a *Wunderkammer*.

M. Jacqui Alexander describes this undoing, forsaking, of human experience's
inherent wholeness, complexity, and interconnectedness:

> To this process of fragmentation we gave the name colonization, usually understood as a
> set of exploitative practices in political, ideological and aesthetic terms, but also linked in
> minute ways to dualistic and hierarchical thinking: divisions among mind, body, spirit;

between sacred and secular, male and female, heterosexual and homosexual; in class divisions; and in the divisions between the erotic and the Divine. We saw its operation, as well, in creating singular thinking: the mistaken notion that only one kind of justice work could lead to freedom.[2]

As Ania Loomba writes in *Colonialism/Postcolonialism*, "Colonialism and imperialism are often used interchangeably."[3] The European iteration differed from previous manifestations of colonization and empire, Loomba continues, because it "did more than extract tribute, goods, and wealth from the countries that it conquered—it restructured the economies of the latter, drawing them into a complex relationship with their own so that there was a flow of human and natural resources between colonised and colonial countries."[4] Put another way, not only were slaves and indentured laborers moving from their place of origin to a colonial margin, but also the materials produced by that unfree labor moved back to the imperial center—to be transformed into products that went out to the colonial margins' captive markets (often undermining the place's homegrown industry), creating unimaginable wealth for imperialists at each stage.[5]

It was this same 19th century that gave the United States the library and the art museum:

> Since the 19th century, the museum world has been characterized by simplistic oppositions in which everything is either one thing or another—a masterpiece or minor work, an original or a reproduction, a great artist or an apprentice, this species or that. Such shorthand, colored by the tasks of taxonomy, made the world manageable 100 years ago. But while in the 20th century many fields move from classification to analysis, museums remain dominated by 19th-century concepts of human nature.[6]

Indeed, nothing is more redolent of yesteryear's concepts of human nature than library classification systems. For example, within the Library of Congress Classification System, human sexuality is ensconced in "The Family. Marriage. Women" as the HQ Class. Esteemed African American Studies librarian Kathleen Bethel asks, "What would our libraries and information centers look like if the materials were arranged in a non-Western format?"[7] Founded as a public good, the American library shared in the imperial project's "civilizing" mission. As the populations of immigrants grew, it became clear that the library could render tremendous service as an instrument for vouchsafing middle-class manners, mores, and tastes to populations that had not yet begun their odyssey to whiteness in the United States. Wayne A. Wiegand writes:

> Since most of the reformers who pushed for the establishment of public libraries were from white Anglo-Saxon Protestant middle- and upper-class families, and since most of the people who staffed these libraries came from the same socioeconomic groups (i.e., possessed the same "character"), the collections they built and supported naturally reflected the cultural, literary, and intellectual canons they had found useful in constructing their own interpretations of reality, in making sense of their own worlds.[8]

In the introduction to *Art Museum Libraries and Librarianship*, Ann B. Abid writes that the justification for libraries in art museums can be thought to rest upon the documentation surrounding art objects,[9] which includes their patrimony and provenance. Though today the art museum (and the library) community is surely too sophisticated to subscribe to previously mentioned dualisms, more than a whiff of them nonetheless lingers. The hierarchy of creative expression is ever-present.[10] This is to say that fine art—that is, art for art's sake—is nobler than decorative arts, which generally serve some useful purpose, or even design. This is why plundered non-Western art objects were placed in "natural history" museums. "The art-historical emphasis on form is itself rooted in the history of the discipline," art historian Henry Drewal writes meta-analytically. "Its development during the age of imperialism means that objects were often torn from their cultural contexts."[11]

The natural history museum, obviously, is not the art museum. This is because the works in an art museum represent cultures of thinking: art for art's sake; the objects in the natural history museum, however, represent cultures without intellect: peoples who only know how to *be*. Even with the acknowledged influence African works of art had on artist Pablo Picasso, the great ur-patriarch of Western art and Modernism, those works are discussed in terms of emotions—not genius, artistic or otherwise. The non-Western cultural mode is being, not thinking. To make *art* is to think; to make an object with a ceremonial or practical function is to *be*. This, of course, flows into (extant!) discourses of "natural" or "instinctive" (rather than culturally learned or transmitted) behavior that buttress essentialist understandings of nonwhites, non-Westerners.

Considering the ground from which they sprang, it is unsurprising that museums and libraries, in general, are deeply colonized vectors committed to a white supremacist status quo. Less than a year ago, the Guggenheim got its first full-time Black American curator.[12] This hiring was preceded by another first in the museum's nearly one hundred years of existence: an exhibit curated by a Black person, Chaédria LaBouvier, who exposed the racialized professional violence she experienced working on the project.[13] Michelle Millar Fisher and Andrea Fraser address museums' other oppressive matrices in their article "Why Are Museums So Plutocratic, and What Can We Do About It?" They discuss the "pay to play" nature of major museums' governance and the fact that—because museums pay poorly—museum leadership roles have effectively become the province of the well off.[14] Libraries, whose workforce is over 85 percent white, are no less fraught as institutions, as the racist bullying of April Hathcock at the American Library Association's Midwinter in 2019 well illustrates.[15]

In the first quarter of the twenty-first century, nineteenth-century-born institutions like libraries and art museums find themselves in the dispiriting situation of needing to justify their existence. This, arguably, is the unsurprising evolution of the capitalist worldview that spawned them: that which does not yield ever-expanding profits and growth is imminently expendable. The public good is suspect in this *Weltanschauung*. Perhaps, though, libraries and art museums increase their chances of survival through relevance—that is, in finding a place in their audience's, in people's, lives.

In her article, "Reimagining the Museum," Eliza Williams interviews Maria Balshaw, then-director of the Whitworth Art Gallery at the University of Manchester. At the cost of fifteen million pounds, the Whitworth underwent a physical and apparently psychic transformation that "opened up" the institution. (Fortunately, for its pains, it was named Art Fund's Museum of the Year in 2015 and received a gold prize from Visit England the following year. Balshaw was appointed the Tate's first woman director in 2017.) Interestingly, the Whitworth is located in "a part of the city that has the most acute social and economic challenges."[16] The Williams's article also briefly discusses engagement work a staff member did with a community group that actually resulted in an exhibit. The article was useful and thought-provoking because of Balshaw's insistence on the museum's sociality. One of the last things she says is, "The cultural impact of museums is about bringing people and ideas and objects and artists together in a conversation about how we understand ourselves."[17]

Stony Island Arts Bank, located in the Chicago South Side neighborhood, Greater Grand Crossing, is a program site of the Rebuild Foundation, the non-profit founded by Theaster Gates that "leverage[s] the power and potential of communities, buildings, and objects that others have written off."[18] Elite media have variously styled Chicago native Gates an "opportunity artist" and "real estate artist."[19] The art world categorizes his work as public, social practice, or "socially engaged." With degrees in urban planning and ceramics, his forays into real estate have made him, as *ArtReview* famously put it, "the Mick Jagger of social practice."[20] That only carries one so far, though. Part of the Gates cachet is his professorship at the University of Chicago and his position as the executive director and founder of the Rebuild Foundation.

Namely, Gates has created something special in Greater Grand Crossing, which a *New York Times* article names as one of Chicago's most violent neighborhoods,[21] by purchasing and "reactivating" real estate and materials, respectively, society has long since written off. An impressive coup, Stony Island Arts Bank opened to high cultural acclaim during the first ever Chicago Architecture Biennial in October 2015. The Arts Bank, as staff and volunteers call it, is, for Gates, a work of art in itself. It houses the reactivated detritus of culture, both high and "low." The Arts Bank's special collections include the former editorial library of Johnson Publishing Company, the publishers of *Ebony* and *Jet*, lifestyle magazines beloved by millions of Black Americans, Instagram-ready as a (functional) stunning installation environment; the sixty-thousand-strong collection of de-accessioned University of Chicago Glass Lantern Slides; the Edward J. Williams Collection, which is comprised of about four thousand items which Gates refers to as "negrobilia," or cultural artifacts including consumer goods, crafts, objects, and so forth, that give testimony to the stereotypical, degraded images of Black Americans created and consumed in the United States and other parts of the world; and Frankie Knuckles' Record Collection, the patrimony of house music. (People and organizations seem to have a habit of entrusting Gates with extraordinary collections of art and cultural artifacts.)

A highly hybridized space, visitors find a "gallery, media archive, library and community center—and a home for Rebuild's archives and collections."[22] Stony Island Arts Bank is also a work in progress. It is not only Gates's own work of art, but also a space in flux, one that is intended to be in co-creation with the community, the neighborhood of which it is a part—calling to mind Balshaw's insistence on museums' sociality: "The cultural impact of museums is about bringing people and ideas and objects and artists together in a conversation about how we understand ourselves."[23]

The Arts Bank's programming and events center celebrate the Black American experience, history, and culture. Stony Island Arts Bank's past and present events include concerts, DJ sets, film screenings, exhibitions, artist residencies, and dialogues with figures like Thelma Golden. In summer 2016, Michelle Obama and her mother visited the Arts Bank while the author was there.

The Arts Bank's library is an attraction unto itself. Acquired by Gates during the downsizing of Johnson Publishing Company, the company's library served as a resource for writers. Founded during World War II, the Chicago-based company was more than a Black American success story. The company's publications and other business ventures, in a way, held Black America together, transmitting stories of triumph, aspiration, and the coming of better days.

Thus, for many, the Arts Bank is worthy of a pilgrimage. Books the authors inscribed with personal messages to the Johnson Publishing Company founder John H. Johnson make up a part of the collection. One may gaze upon the artfully arranged splendor, tens of thousands of books strong, knowing the central role it played in the stories that appeared in *Ebony* and *Jet*. The library's organization and cataloging were communal endeavors, with volunteers deciding upon an organization scheme that was meaningful and intelligible to them.

More than that, demographic changes of which everyone is aware hold the promise of a new way of working, of living, if one is able to exist in the space of hope and curiosity. In her essay, "The Real Multiculturalism," Amalia Mesa-Bains writes insightfully about nonwhites and museums and resources. "Consequently, all of the institutional and theoretical developments from which your institutions spring conflict with what we, as people of color, represent."[24] She goes on to discuss "resources, audience, and exhibitions."[25]

Without exaggeration, it's impossible to think of any aspect of life that colonial mental models and conceptualizations do not hinder in ways large and small—the least of which are not the art museum and its library. Complex organizations are "siloed" because the American mind has been shaped by the nineteenth-century urge to classify, separate, and apply labels. The impetus behind this urge is to know where to rank a work of art, scholarship, and so forth, in a well-internalized scoring system of status (and humanity) so clearly articulated in the previous discussions of colonialism.

In her article, "What Are Museums For?" Jo Marsh urges museum professionals to face the changing nature of museums head-on, discussing ways that different institutions have "invested in a culture of transformation project."[26] Marsh articulates a vision that could carry art museums, libraries, and other cultural heritage organizations into the future, to life as it is lived now:

> The 21st-century museum is not there just to care for and conserve collections. They're offering us, the "public," much more than the passive act of viewing. They provide us with a space—digital and physical—where we can redefine and immerse ourselves, co-create and co-curate, content we can activate and dynamic environments for shopping, eating and socializing. They also communicate their relevance by reflecting the world in which they exist.[27]

In the same way that the past isn't even past, the United States has never been what it used to be. Rather than cause for alarm, it is a beckoning to true freedom. Lies, illusions, and encumbrances that warp understanding of self and others can be shed to make way for the complexity of humanity and lived experience.

There are many ways forward to a future that embraces the humanity of all. The knowledge is there; perhaps one way would be art museums collaborating with organizations that are already serving communities of color. Any such collaborations or partnerships must be undertaken with humility, self-awareness, and willingness to take responsibility for institutional and personal actions that uphold oppression. Make no mistake: the future of museums depends upon authentic connection to the communities that have proven themselves endlessly vital and creative.

NOTES

1. Swet Shop Boys, "T5," *Cashmere*, September 29, 2016. https://www.youtube.com /watch?time_continue=1&v=q4Yb8AWXgLI&feature=emb_logo.

2. M. Jacqui Alexander, *Pedagogies of Crossing: Meditations on Feminism, Sexual Politics, Memory, and the Sacred* (Durham, NC: Duke University Press, 2005), 281.

3. Ania Loomba, *Colonialism/Postcolonialism* (London: Routledge, 2015), 19.

4. Loomba, 21.

5. Loomba, 21.

6. Lois H. Silverman and Mark O'Neill, "Change and Complexity in the 21st-Century Museum: The Real Relics of Our Museums May Be the Ways We Think and Work," in *Reinventing the Museum: The Evolving Conversation on the Paradigm Shift*, edited by Gail Anderson (Plymouth, UK: AltaMira Press, 2012), 193.

7. Kathleen Bethel, "Cataloging the Afrocentric Way," in *Culture Keepers: Enlightening and Empowering Our Communities*, Proceedings of the First National Conference of African American Librarians (September 4–6, 1992): 84.

8. Wayne A. Wiegand, "The Development of Librarianship in the United States," *Libraries and Culture* 24 (Winter 1989): 102.

9. Ann B. Abid, "Introduction," in *Art Museum Libraries and Librarianship*, edited by Joan M. Benedetti (Lanham, MD: Scarecrow Press, Inc. and Art Libraries Society of North America, 2007), xv.

10. Courtney Becks, "Amos Paul Kennedy, Jr., Letterpress, and Black American Print Culture," *Art Documentation* 38 (Spring 2019): 180.

11. Henry John Drewal, "Editor's Statement: Objects and Intellect: Interpretations of Meaning in African Art," *Art Journal* 47, no. 2 (Summer 1988): 71.

12. Alex Greenberger, "Ashley James Makes History as First Black Curator Hired by Guggenheim Museum," *ARTnews*, November 14, 2019. https://www.artnews.com/art-news/news/ashley-james-curator-guggenheim-museum-13581/.

13. Bad woman news (@badnewswoman, "It went down at the Guggenheim!" *Twitter*, November 5, 2019. https://twitter.com/badnewswomen/status/1191892273694461952.

14. Andrea Fraser and Michelle Millar Fisher, "Why Are Museums So Plutocratic, and What Can We Do About It?" *Frieze*, February 26, 2020. https://frieze.com/article/why-are-museums-so-plutocratic-and-what-can-we-do-about-it.

15. April Hathcock, "ALAMW: What Happened, and What Should Happen Next," *At the Intersection* (blog), January 30, 2019. Accessed October 1, 2019, https://aprilhathcock.wordpress.com/2019/01/30/alamw-what-happened-and-what-should-happen-next/.

16. Eliza Williams, "Reimagining the Museum: Maria Balshaw on Making Museums a Social Space," *Creative Review* 36, no. 7 (2016). https://www.creativereview.co.uk/maria-balshaw/.

17. Williams, "Reimagining the Museum."

18. "About Rebuild," Rebuild Foundation. Accessed October 1, 2019, https://rebuild-foundation.org/our-story.

19. In a December 20, 2013, article in *The New York Times Magazine* and in a January 20, 2014, *New Yorker* article, respectively.

20. "2013 Power 100," on ArtReview's website. Accessed August 8, 2016, https://artreview.com/power_100/2013 (site discontinued).

21. Ford Fessenden and Haeyoun Park, "Chicago's Murder Problem," *New York Times*, May 27, 2016. http://www.nytimes.com/interactive/2016/05/18/us/chicago-murder-problem.html?_r=0.

22. "Stony Island Arts Bank," Rebuild Foundation. Accessed October 1, 2019, https://rebuild-foundation.org/site/stony-island-arts-bank.

23. Williams, "Reimagining the Museum."

24. Amalia Mesa-Baines, "The Real Multiculturalism: A Struggle for Authority and Power," in *Reinventing the Museum: The Evolving Conversation on the Paradigm Shift*, edited by Gail Anderson (Plymouth, UK: AltaMira Press, 2012), 104.

25. Mesa-Baines, "The Real Multiculturalism," 107.

26. Jo Marsh, "What Are Museums For?" *Creative Review* 36, no. 7 (2016). https://www.creativereview.co.uk/what-are-museums-for.

27. Marsh, "What Are Museums For?"

4

Haptic Aesthetics

Artists' Books in Art Museum Libraries

Anne Evenhaugen, Smithsonian Museum, American Art Museum and National Portrait Gallery, and Tony White, The Metropolitan Museum of Art

WHAT IS AN ARTIST'S BOOK?

Artists' books were an important part of the avant-garde experimentation in the visual arts, origins that can be traced to the late 1950s and continued into the 1960s. This was a time of experimental ideas and actions, seeking to get art off the wall and into the hands of the viewer. Examples of such anti-establishment artistic activities included happenings, performance art, mail art, Fluxus, and conceptual art. By the early 1970s, curators began attempting to define and describe these publications. In 1973, Diane Vanderlip curated an exhibition at the Moore College of Art in Philadelphia entitled *Artists' Books*, and the phrase stuck. Following this exhibition, bookshops were founded to sell and distribute these unusual publications: Art Metropole (Toronto) in 1974, Other Books and So (Amsterdam) in 1975, and Printed Matter (New York City) in 1976, among many others.

Since Vanderlip's exhibition, many people have attempted to refine the definition of what constitutes an artist's book, and librarians have had to manage these varying interpretations. The simplest definition uses the Duchampian prompt: "it's an artist book if the artist says it is." In her essay "The Artist's Book Goes Public," Lucy Lippard described an artist's book as "neither an art book (collected reproductions of separate art works) nor a book on art (critical interpretations and/or artists' writings), the artist's book is a work of art on its own, conceived specifically for the book form and often published by the artist him/herself."[1] It is important to separate the artists' books published before Diane Vanderlip's exhibition from those that came after. Following her exhibition, artists began using the phrase *artists' books* to describe an intentional, self-conscious practice of publication and object production. Duncan Chapell's "Typologising Artists' Books" is an excellent, concise source for the definition of artists' books and related publications, such as zines, book objects

31

or sculptural books, Fluxus editions, pop-up books, fine printing, and illustrated books.² The term "artist's publication" can act as an umbrella term for published artworks of this genre.

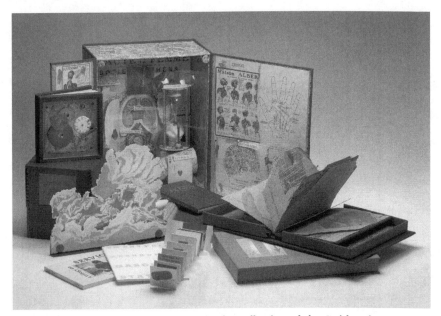

Figure 4.1.   Selection of artists' books in the collection of the Smithsonian Museum, American Art Museum and National Portrait Gallery. Photograph by Mark Gulezian, National Portrait Gallery.

Collecting artists' books can present challenges for some librarians working in an art museum context, especially if the museum's curators maintain a separate collection of artists' publications. For example, museums may treat artists' books as "works on paper" or as fine illustrated books, and these are most often handled as artworks, housed in art storage facilities, and tracked by the registrar. Libraries have a decidedly need-based definition; as organizers of information, librarians must be able to clearly identify something in order to classify it. To the librarian an artist's book is a *book*, first and foremost. This chapter aims to assist the art museum librarian in assessing an existing collection, in adding to or building a new collection, and in caring for artists' books.

EXISTING COLLECTION ASSESSMENT

Librarians that arrive in a new role have the opportunity to begin evaluating the collections under their management; this might include artists' books and related publications. Occasionally, that collection has not been curated, and one must decide if a publication or object is a book, and, as noted previously, the definition of an "artist's book" is still up for debate. Many artists' and photobooks of the 1970s (see figure 4.2) were stickered, stamped, and placed on the circulating shelves of libraries. At that time, as a contemporary phenomenon, some librarians didn't identify them as special collections materials, because these books looked much like other artfully produced publications. Regardless of the definition one adopts, determining the intent of the artist and the ultimate place in the library can be exciting.

Figure 4.2. Cynthia Marsh, *The Sporting Life* (Los Angeles, CA: Fat Heart Publications, 1975). Photograph by Tony White. Page detail. Thomas J. Watson Library, The Metropolitan Museum of Art.

In evaluating existing materials on the shelves, a simple method is to determine first if a publication is an artist's book or an exhibition catalog. If there is a checklist of art works, or an essay describing the exhibition or works on exhibit, it is an exhibition catalog and is likely not an artist's book.

Another method of collection assessment is to see what peer institutions have collected and identified as artists' books. This can mean comparing the collection to other institutional repositories or catalogs—which is also a useful way to become better acquainted with the genre on the whole. Major institutional repositories, such as The Museum of Modern Art Library or the Joan Flasch Artists' Books Collection at the School of the Art Institute of Chicago, have their collections fully described on OCLC or a stand-alone online database. However, be wary of publisher descriptions or materials in which OCLC records have received shelf-ready copy cataloging by an outside vendor. These may take a much looser definition of an artist's book than an artist, art librarian, or art historian would. As attention to artists' books has increased, so has scholarship on the genre, and using exhibition catalogs, dealer mail-order catalogs, and checklists may also bring examples or active artists to light.

COLLECTION DEVELOPMENT

Whether building a collection for the first time or adding to an existing collection of artists' books, defining what to collect (as well as what *not* to collect) is vitally important. Paramount for the art museum librarian is to hone the focus to their museum's current and prospective collecting scope. Artists' books can show dimension in an artist's oeuvre, include new or marginalized voices, highlight specific artistic practices in a new light, or tackle subject matter with a depth not possible in two-dimensional works, and therefore enhance the museum's ability to tell its story. But the library can only justify acquiring what dovetails with the overall institution's primary mission.

When building a collection of artists' publications, one can consider artist, format, binding, printing, structure, content, materials, and other unique or significant features (see figure 4.3). Other criteria may include geographic area, book format, related published works, book objects, multiples, unique works, and binding styles. Additional considerations might be whether to include fine bindings, letterpress-printed works, illustrated books with poetry or prose, *livres d'artiste, livres deluxe,* commercially printed books, and trade edition pop-up books. The collection development policy must address whether a library has the capacity to collect books/objects of unusual sizes or formats.

On the other hand, one may want to consider what to exclude on a case by case basis: books with food, animal carcasses, sticky or scented books, toxic materials, and damaged books (those that may have been subject to mildew or mold, stained, torn, crushed, or burned). If these are owned or purchased, it is important to know that it will require meeting additional preservation and handling criteria. Another option is to purchase two copies if the budget allows, so one can be handled and one left

Figure 4.3. Kevin Steele, *The Deep* (self-published, 2012). Photograph by Kevin Steele. Thomas J. Watson Library, The Metropolitan Museum of Art.

unopened and pristine. While preservation may not be the initial consideration in collection development, it is worth keeping in mind where and how the books will be stored when making acquisition decisions.

Other questions to consider are: Should the collection include books with out-of-date media, such as CD-ROMs, diskettes, cassettes, records, or magnetic media, and, if so, what are the playback options? What about Fluxus objects such as *Flux Deck* or *Smile in a Box*, sculptural book objects such as those by Barton Benes or Byron Clerx, or altered books such as those by Melissa Craig or Brian Dettmer? What is the library's tolerance for collecting ephemeral works? Even though a book is created by an artist, it still must meet the criteria set forth in the library's collection development policy, which should reflect the museum's needs, and ensure there is little to no duplication with curatorial collecting.

If a librarian working with an existing collection has determined its scope and how it should develop in the future, undertaking a gap-analysis of what titles may have been overlooked is another helpful step in managing artists' books. If the library has a strong existing collection of conceptual materials, but lacks publications by Sol Lewitt or Cynthia Marsh, the librarian can begin to build a desiderata list for future purchases and solicitations of donations.

Whether numbering a few hundred or a few thousand, an artists' books collection in an art museum library may be restrained due to budget, storage, staffing, and time limitations associated with specialized care, handling, cataloging, digitization, preservation, and teaching with the collections. However, there are many opportunities to ensure representation and activate even a smaller collection within these areas, depending on staff interest and expertise.

ACQUISITION STRATEGIES

The most common methods for acquiring artists' books include firm orders (online and in person), approval plans, book fairs, and direct orders from artists and publishers. Larger institutions may be able to afford to subscribe to every publication offered by a press or vendor, such as Granary Books or Printed Matter. Firm ordering —title by title—is time consuming but rewarding, and allows the librarian to learn more in-depth about the books they acquire. This can be done through book arts dealer websites, or in person when visiting bookshops or book fairs. If buying from a vendor or direct from an artist in the United States, the supplier may need to complete an IRS W-9 tax form for the initial transaction. Payments made through online payment portals such as Square or PayPal may allow payment without processing the IRS forms, but this should be confirmed with the museum's budget or procurement office.

A valuable source for acquisitions is the exhibitor listings for any of the international book fairs. For example, the MISS READ fair (Berlin) and the New York Art Book Fair list their exhibitors online. Almost all of the exhibitors include links to their websites. This sounds obvious, but some do not take the time to visit the websites of these publishers, artists, and distributors to purchase titles as part of collection development, and this review can prove valuable, especially as unique or popular titles may sell out quickly.

Buying in the field on behalf of an art museum library can be challenging. One may not have immediate access to the online catalog to check holdings. Not every vendor takes credit cards, and few are willing to send a copy of the book without receiving payment first. Occasionally a librarian may request to receive books first, then process payment, but individual artists or small publishers might not be acquainted with this practice. In addition, when buying for an institution, individual artists will also need to create an itemized invoice and provide an itemized receipt.

It may be best to ask the dealer or artist to place the book on hold for the museum to complete purchase through the normal workflow. It is preferable to request that the supplier ship the book to the library with tracking and insurance, rather than hand-carrying the item, to protect the investment in case of damage in transit. Books purchased online with a credit card may not require separate tax forms; the payment generates an electronic invoice and receipt, and the book is mailed directly to the library.

Many times book artists or dealers will contact the library about visiting in person to display books that they have for sale. This can be rewarding yet time-consuming when acquiring material, and it can be difficult to resist sales pressure in the presence of the artist. Those choosing to visit with an artist should take the opportunity to document how the artist handles the book and ask questions about materials, methods, and content. These notes will prove useful later when cataloging the work. Librarians may prefer to work with artists and dealers by visiting a website or having a paper prospectus sent to them. If a librarian is then interested in examining the book, he or she can ask to have it sent on approval. If the librarian decides to purchase the book, shipping charges can be added to the bill. Should the librarian decide not to purchase the book, the library pays for packing and return shipping.

Funding for the purchase of artists' books may compete directly with budgets supporting the acquisition of other books for the library collection, though some may have an endowment specifically for the acquisition of artists' books. Another source is acquisition through gift donations, and especially donations accompanied by funds intended to offset the costs of processing. Many potential donors ask the library to accept their books or archives without fully realizing that libraries incur significant costs to acquire, catalog, preserve, and make collections available to library patrons. The fact that libraries must consider storage costs for every volume they store, on-site or off-site, in perpetuity, often surprises donors. When preparing to accept a large donation of books, a library should consider requesting funds to offset costs to preserve and make the books accessible. If one chooses to accept a donation, the United States Tax Code may allow charitable deductions for donations from individuals. A collection should be appraised by a qualified appraiser before the donation is made, and donors may be able to take the appraised value of the books as a tax deduction against their annual taxes.

RECEIVING, PROCESSING, AND CATALOGING ARTISTS' BOOKS

The acquisition, receiving, and processing of artists' books is similar to that for other books; however, artists' books do present challenges to any library. The staff will need to determine the threshold for treating these publications as artworks as opposed to trade monographs. Will the library retain the wrapping material in which a book arrives, or any ephemera that comes with the book? Should these be housed with the book, in a special enclosure, or stored separately, perhaps with other documentation? If the latter, where should they be stored, cataloged, and arranged (see figure 4.4)?

The library should develop a procedure for photographing books as they arrive to record how a book was packaged, the covering material used, and the book's condition after opening. The library must decide if artists' books will be cataloged only, or if an image management program such as CONTENTdm should provide visual access to these unique materials. Libraries may also use their digital asset management system to add thumbnail images to the online catalog record, such as in an 856 MARC field. Bookplates should not be used unless on housing; instead, staff can select a location in which to write the call number in pencil. Barcodes should be placed only on the enclosures or on acid-free, lignin-free paper bookmarks—never on the books.

Cataloging for identification and description is the primary mechanism for art museum libraries to make collections accessible. As mentioned previously, artists' books don't always look special, and items that have been poorly cataloged by

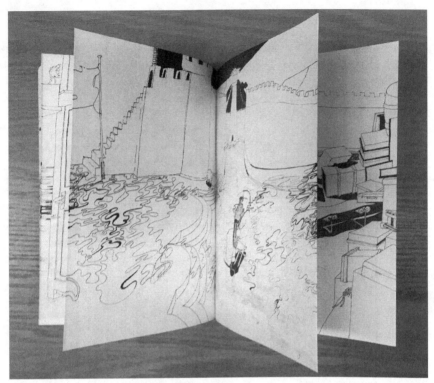

Figure 4.4.   Jan Voss, *Detour* (Amsterdam: Boekie Woekie, 1989). Photograph by Tony White. Page detail. Thomas J. Watson Library, The Metropolitan Museum of Art.

non-specialists may make for ineffective records. And artists' books may lack the basic bibliographic information a librarian requires, or they may have characteristics that are difficult to describe. A cataloger may rely on a colophon, the artist's website, or any documentation the collecting librarian has gathered. Rare book cataloging guidance can be especially useful, as it is suited to treating the book as an individual object and to describing materials, collation, binding, provenance, and so forth. The terms for artists' books' description and the rules for cataloging are still improving, and current standard texts to guide the cataloger can be found in the reference list of this chapter.

STORAGE AND PRESERVATION OPTIONS

Secure and protective storage is important for housing and accessing artists' books in the library. Artists' books do not generally conform to publishing standards. They may have loose elements, non-standard wrapping materials, bags, photographs, non-standard content or pages, toxic materials, food, and basically every imaginable material. Enclosing, preserving, and making them available for viewing is often a challenge. Does the library have proper storage areas for oversized objects? Is there access to staff who can make protective enclosures for storage and handling, or can a staff member be sent for training? For published books that are in the form of a standard codex, storage and access are simplified, but the library must consider these questions to best preserve and make these materials accessible for the long term.

Locked storage space with a dedicated heating, ventilation, and air condition-ing system is ideal, but most libraries must do the best with what they have. At a minimum, staff should store books on metal shelves in a light- and dust-free envi-ronment. Protective enclosures are most effective when custom-sized to each title to maximize structural support, especially for oversized or unusual formats, and exter-nal grants may be available for procuring. As an alternative, a library can store books that are ⅜-inch thick or less in call number order in acid-free, lignin-free hanging file folders in a metal filing cabinet, spine side down. The hanging file system has been implemented at numerous institutions.

HANDLING, USE, AND DISPLAY

Artists' books require handling procedures similar to those in special collections libraries to promote preservation and conservation, and should have similar circula-tion and tracking, handling, and use policies.

Extra care must be taken when providing access to individual users and groups. Policies should be shared in advance and include details such as requiring library visitors to wash their hands after arriving at the library, tie back long hair, use only pencils (libraries should provide these) for notes, and take photographs with phones. Food, beverages, and chewing gum should be strictly prohibited when using any spe-cial collections, and personal items such as coats or bags should be stowed away from the reading area. Entrance into special collections storage areas should be restricted to select library staff, and visitors should be asked to use the online catalog in advance to select materials to examine. Librarians should take care not to make exceptions to these policies, even for curators or donors.

More practically, presentations for group use is similar to recommendations for rare books. Arranging tables and chairs to avoid crowding, cleaning the surface of the tables, and using placemats (11" × 17" pieces of paper suffice) and foam cradles in front of each chair with an artist book on each mat. The librarian must remain in the room and be available to answer questions and to ensure the books are being handled correctly (or not handled at all). Books should stay on the table and not be pulled into a reader's lap to support and protect the structure of the book.

Opportunities for exhibition, guest lecture series, and social media exposure are all great advantages of building and sustaining a collection of artists' publications in the library. "Show and tell" sessions for visitors in the museum space or special donor viewings can bring in new artist's book lovers and open up a hidden collection. A museum librarian may also consider informing curatorial staff of new acquisitions to spark their interest, such as in a regular "new and notable" book list disseminated to all staff.

The primary challenge with artists' books is that they are a haptic medium, meant to be handled and touched, to be read and experienced. Presenting artists' books in exhibition cases is necessarily an exercise in frustration in that the books can only be viewed under glass. Yet displays are critical to promote the collection. Librarians are encouraged to spend time learning about exhibition best practices—do not overfill the cases, give the books room to breathe, and make sure to plan the layout of books and labels in advance. A basic knowledge of making or purchasing book supports and wedges and providing the appropriate lighting and length of light exposure is essential. If one has little or no knowledge of such practices, museum colleagues or a consultant can provide suggestions.

As with special collections, if the library is willing to lend artists' books, there should be a basic loan policy in place. Will loans be made only for the institution's exhibitions, or to other museums and libraries? Will the museum registrar's office offer support in working through a standard facility report or issues of insurance, shipping, and display? What if conservation is needed prior to lending? Who is responsible for damaged or lost books?

In addition to displays or exhibits of artists' books, the library can explore options for online exhibits or social media such as blogs, Instagram, or Tumblr. These provide several benefits, in preserving works while allowing visual access, increasing awareness of collections, and disseminating information about the works beyond the walls of the institution. There may be considerations with respect to copyright and fair use, but if the institution has a social media policy, there may be opportunities for promoting the artists' books collection using current and relevant applications.

FINAL THOUGHTS

Taking time and care to manage a collection of artists' books and publications, while more labor intensive than general library collections, is a satisfying opportunity for librarians. As with any special collection title or volume, artists' books have a special status in that they are publications that serve as research resources as well as art objects. Working with colleagues, donors, dealers, and book artists can enhance connections to the books and create further opportunities for engagement with visitors, scholars, artists, and visionaries interested in how artists are transforming books in new ways.

NOTES

1. Lucy Lippard, "The Artist's Book Goes Public," in *Artists' Books: A Critical Anthology and Sourcebook*, edited by Joan Lyons (Rochester, NY: Visual Studies Workshop Press, 1985), 45.

2. Duncan Chapell, "Typologising the Artist's Book," *Art Libraries Journal* 28, no. 4 (2003): 12–30.

REFERENCES

Art Metropole. www.artmetropole.com/about.

Art-rite, no. 14 (winter 1976/1977).

Campos, A. *Multiple, Limited, Unique* (New York: The Center for Book Arts, 2011).

Chappell, D. "Typologising Artist's Books," *Art Libraries Journal* 28, no. 4 (2003): 12–20.

CONTENTdm. www.oclc.org/en/contentdm.html.

Drucker, J. *Figuring the Word* (New York: Granary Books, 1998).

Indiana University Libraries Book Repair Manual, enclosure treatments. www.indiana.edu /~libpres/manual/index.html.

Klima, S. *Artists Books: A Critical Survey of the Literature* (New York: Granary Books, 1998).

Lippard, L. "The Artist's Book Goes Public," in Lyons, J. (ed), *Artists' Books: A Critical Anthology and Sourcebook*, edited by J. Lyons (New York: Visual Studies Workshop Press, 1985).

Moeglin-Delcroix, A., Maffei, G., Liliana Dematteis, L., and Rimmaudo, A. *Guardare, raccontare, pensare, conservare: quattro percorsi del libro d'artista dagli anni '60 ad oggi* (Casa del Mantegna, 2004).

Printed Matter. www.printedmatter.org/what-we-do.

Where to Buy Artists' Books

Artist's Book Fairs (Los Angeles, New York, Seoul, Tokyo, Mexico City, etc.); Codex International Book Art Fair; 8-Ball Zine Fair (Tokyo); I Never Read, Art Book Fair Basel; Libros Mutantes Madrid; MISS Read Artist Book Fair (Berlin); Offprint Art Book Fair Paris and London; Rencontres d'Arles.

Art Metropole (Toronto); Boekie Woekie (Amsterdam); Buchhandlung Walther König (Berlin); Dashwood Books (New York City); Flotsam Books (Tokyo); Motto Books (Berlin); Printed Matter (New York City); Ulises (Philadelphia), among many others.

Cataloging Resources

Art Libraries Society of North America. Artists' Books Thesaurus. http://allisonjai.com/abt /vocab/index.php.

Thurmann-Jajes, A., Boulanger, S., and Stepančic, L. *Manual for Artists' Publications (MAP): Cataloging Rules, Definitions, and Descriptions* (Research Centre for Artists' Publications at the Weserburg/Museum of Modern Art, 2010).

White, M., Perratt, P., and Lawes, L. *Artists' Books: A Cataloguer's Manual* (ARLIS/UK & Ireland, 2006).

Researching Artists' Books Online

Archive Artist Publications, Munich, Germany, www.artistbooks.de

Artexte, Montreal (Quebec) Canada, https://e-artexte.ca/

Book-Arts-L, https://www.philobiblon.com/book_arts-l.shtml
Centre for Artists' Publications, Bremen, www.weserburg.de
Library of the National Gallery of Canada, Ottawa, Canada: The Art Metropole Collection
    Database, http://bibcat.gallery.ca:81/screens/opacmenu.html
The Museum of Modern Art Library, DADABASE, http://arcade.nyarc.org/search~S8
The National Library's Collection of artists' books and multiples, http://bibcat.gallery.ca/
Study Center of Museu d'Art Contemporani de Barcelona, www.macba.cat
Victoria and Albert Museum, London, United Kingdom, V&A Artists' Books Database, www
    .vam.ac.uk/page/a/artists-books/

Selected Notable Collections with Artists' Books

Clark Art Institute
Cleveland Museum of Art, Ingalls
Jack Ginsberg Collection on Artists' Books, Johannesburg
Library Indiana University, Bloomington
Library of Congress
Metropolitan Museum of Art, Thomas J. Watson Library
Museum of Modern Art
National Gallery of Art
Otis College of Art and Design
Rhode Island School of Art and Design
San Francisco Museum of Modern Art
School of the Art Institute of Chicago, Joan Flasch Artists' Books Collection
Smithsonian Libraries
Stedlijk Art Museum Library
University of California, Los Angeles
University of Washington, Allen Library
Victoria and Albert Museum
Walker Art Center
Yale University, Robert B. Haas Family Arts Library

5

Ephemeral Survival

Managing Physical and Digital Artist File Collections

*Alexandra Reigle, Smithsonian Museum, American
Art Museum and National Portrait Gallery,
and Simon Underschultz, National Gallery of Australia*

Many art museum libraries have built distinctive special collections that include artist files—ephemeral materials collected over time that document an artist's life and practice. Also called vertical files, ephemera files, or personality files, they are vital to research on contemporary and lesser known artists, often providing critical information not available elsewhere that may verify a theory or completely change the trajectory of a research project.

PHYSICAL EPHEMERA

Types of Materials

Physical ephemera files are primarily secondary source published materials, mass-produced and not intended to last for a long time. Because of this, researchers are often surprised to find that ephemeral files often contain extremely rare items that may have high research and monetary value. It should be noted that some artist file collections include primary source materials such as museum correspondence or pieces of ephemera with marginalia. The scope of each library's collection depends on its collection development policy.

The most common items in artist files, as seen in figure 5.1, include a wide range of formats:

Announcements, architectural drawings, artist statements, artworks, auction catalogs, brochures, checklists, commercial gallery catalogs, clippings, cultural artifacts, diaries, digital files, exhibition catalogs, institutional publications, interviews, invitations, journals, mail art, manifestos, manuscripts, maps, memorabilia, microforms, negatives, oral

Figure 5.1. Colonial artist Mary Morton Allport's artist file, held in the National Gallery of Australia Research Library and Archives. Photograph by Simon Underschultz.

histories, pamphlets, photographs, postcards, posters, press releases, price lists, prints, private view cards, resumes, scripts, serials, slides, and transcripts.[1]

Collection Development

Many ephemera collections were formed organically from curator and researcher files that may have always been collected in the library or by donation from an internal or external source. Before the internet became a common way to disseminate information, these files allowed libraries to both store and organize small materials that, because of limiting staff resources, were not candidates for full cataloging. Moreover, the simple filing system could provide easy access to hard-to-find materials that curators and librarians had been collecting.

Like any library collection, artist files also benefit from having a collection development plan and policy, especially if the library hopes to keep the collection active and growing. This will help focus the collection and avoid retaining materials that are out of scope. Both the plan and policy should list detailed criteria; these documents become particularly helpful when the following factors are considered.

Content

The topic of the materials usually matches that of the library and the museum's collections. Examples are materials specific to a country (American), region (Texas), type of art (glass), or identity of the artist (gender, race, gender identity, culture). Recently, many libraries have chosen to narrow the topic of their collections through collaborative means. For instance, each library within a consortium or within a local region may choose to focus on separate, specific topics (for example, local textile artists) that best serve their users and reflect their museum's collections. Although an individual artist file collection might not have everything a patron needs, the librarian can suggest another collection for the patron to contact. This allows for more efficient use of collection space, the ability to devote more attention to a smaller scope of materials, and mutually beneficial collaborations between institutions.

Additional factors such as the local significance and research value of materials may also be considered by collection managers when determining what should be included in artist files. For instance, considering whether an item has clear publication information or if it has been self-published can be a determining feature when considering research value. Clippings from magazines that have no clear citation information may be declined. However, some institutions may choose to keep these materials regardless.

Format

Artist file collections can lose focus easily if there are no set criteria for what is acquired. Often the format or condition of the material is important. For instance, items that may harm the other materials in the files must be carefully considered and isolated if kept. Photos, photo negatives, slides, newspapers, and very acidic paper all need to be specially housed in archival polyester sleeves or non-acidic paper sleeves or envelopes.

Size

A common characteristic for determining what will be added to the files is number of pages or dimensions. Usually any item with no more than thirty to forty pages may be included; any larger item should be considered for cataloging. The physical dimensions of the item are also often considered. The average physical dimensions of an artist file are often determined by folder size, either letter or legal. Oversize items such as posters need special consideration and handling and should be stored in flat files or boxes to avoid damage.

Organization

Artist file collections usually have two main parts: one is devoted to specific individuals, sometimes referred to as "personalities," and the other to institutions. The individuals' files contain materials that pertain strictly to one person, such as solo exhibition pamphlets. Types of individuals that would have files include:

Administrators, architects, artists, authors, bookbinders, collectors, connoisseurs, critics, conservators, craftsmen, curators, dealers, designers, educators, filmmakers, historians, journalists, patrons, printers, publishers, scholars, etc.[2]

Institution or corporate files may contain materials about multiple artists, such as group exhibition catalogs that were produced by one organizing entity. Filing items by the institution assures that materials featuring several artists can be more easily discovered rather than filing a copy of the item in each individual artist's file. Many libraries include any institutional entity that might have an art exhibition or may be a location with significant art pieces, including:

> Academic institutions, architectural firms, archives, auction houses, commercial galleries, foundations, foundries, galleries, governmental bodies, historic sites, institutes, kunsthalles, libraries, monuments, museums, publishers, religious organizations, research centers, private collections, societies, etc.[3]

The form of name assigned for each artist is commonly based on the Library of Congress Name Authority File. Other relevant resources include the Program for Cooperative Cataloging "funnel" project for art-related names, the Art Name Authority Cooperative and the Getty Research Institute's Union List of Artist Names. Using standard forms of names assures consistency within the library and when sharing bibliographic information among other institutions. On a global scale, the Virtual International Authority File combines multiple international authority files from fifty-nine national libraries (including the Library of Congress, the Union List of Artist Names, and Wikidata) and subject thesauri into a single service hosted by OCLC. This resource links the headings from contributors to a unique numeric identifier, which can be added to metadata in linked open data applications.

In addition to folders devoted to individual artists, subject files are useful when there is no reasonable category established in the artist or institution files, such as art festivals and award documentation. These may be organized using terms from the Library of Congress Subject Headings or other standard terminologies such as the Getty Research Institute's Art and Architecture Thesaurus.

Collection Storage

Ephemera file materials are usually held in archival folders that are labeled with the name of the individual or institution. An individual or institution may have more than one folder depending on the amount of material. These folders are then stored in alphabetical order according to name within their respective category.

The traditional method for storing artist file folders is in file cabinets with four or five drawers that can hold legal size hanging folders, as seen in figure 5.2. Flat file cabinets or file boxes can be used to hold large format items without folding or damaging them. Collections should be stored in a cool, dry, temperature-controlled environment with minimal exposure to sunlight in order to ensure long-term preservation.

Figure 5.2. Cabinet drawer filled with artist files, located at the Smithsonian American Art and Portrait Gallery Library. Photograph by Alexandra Reigle.

Access

There are different options when determining the best way to provide access to artist files. The strategy used is determined by factors such as how the collection fits within the library collection and the availability of staff and time.

Most artist file collections are viewed on-site at the library in a way that library staff can surveil the patron. Often, artist files are not allowed to leave the library for fear that materials could easily go missing due to their small size and/or value and that they would be nearly impossible to replace. Because many artist files may contain unique resources, many libraries use access policies similar to those in use for special collections or archival materials. However, some libraries do allow their files to circulate to staff at their discretion.

Depending on the policies of the collection, library staff may provide patrons with low-quality on-demand scans of materials in the files. Digitization of artists' files would allow for these unique materials to be more widely discoverable; however, this monumental task requires significant funds and staff time, and an institution's commitment to negotiating copyright issues. Many items included in artist files are under copyright, either by the artist creator or a gallery, publisher, or photographer. In the 2013 article "Digitizing Ephemera Reloaded," author Kai Alexis Smith describes various approaches that libraries have taken to share these files within the copyright

restrictions. These include the Guggenheim Museum's use of "precautions that address copyright issues: a detailed rights and restricted use policy is displayed [on
their website], the images cannot be downloaded, and the images are not at a high
enough resolution for publication." Because of the complexity of copyright compliance, Smith recommends libraries restrict access to within the library.[4] Although
the lure of digitizing artists files is strong for many libraries that wish to share these
important research materials more widely, ensuring copyright compliance, as well as
the cost and staffing required to do the digitization work, keeps many libraries from
pursuing this strategy.

Artist file records that are searchable online and available to the public often
generate a lot of reference questions. In some cases, these records may be discoverable through a library's local catalog or through large library networks like Worldcat. However, many artist files are not cataloged and discoverable in these types of
systems. In these cases, access may be provided through spreadsheets, webpages, or
local databases. Many local databases are built using software like Microsoft Access or
FileMaker Pro and can allow for greater customization or even integration with other
institutional databases. Access to these local sources is often, however, available only
in the library or on a networked drive accessible only by museum staff.

MARC Records

Using MARC records for artist files is perhaps the most desired and helpful
method to provide access to artist file collections. At a basic level, artist file MARC
records will include the name of the artist, a generic description of what is in the
artist files, and perhaps a location name or code. This easily integrates artist files into
the library catalog and ultimately saves a step for researchers.

Developing a MARC template and cataloging standards for artist file collection
records is something that was developed somewhat recently and required the input
of many librarians with artist file collections of various sizes and scopes. The Art Libraries Society of North America's (ARLIS/NA) Artist Files Working Group released
Artist Files Revealed: Documentation and Access in 2010 after extensive research with
its members. This document provides many important recommendations, including
guidelines for minimal and expanded level MARC records, and sample records,[5] and
is a helpful document for managing many aspects of artist file collections. This document demonstrated how records could range from simple ones with basic information to those that were more robust with added details and extra fields. In 2019, Sam
Duncan, a coordinator of the ARLIS/NA Artist Files Working Group, published an
artist file MARC standard built on top of the recommendations provided in *Artist
Files Revealed*. The standard was created through further surveying and discussions
with OCLC catalogers and the ARLIS/NA Cataloging Advisory Committee.[6]

Promotion

Artist files, like other special collections in the art museum library, can be shared in many ways. Investing time and effort into promoting this collection can be beneficial for a library and its parent institution. Because many items within the files were designed as promotional tools, they often contain eye-catching graphics that can be used in social media posts. Posting images of material in an ephemera collection, particularly unusual items, can generate attention and interest. Artist files can also be used in programing events like Wiki Edit-a-Thons that support local artists and artists organizations.

Staying abreast of the exhibitions and projects curators are developing for the museum gives librarians an opportunity to search artist files for relevant content that could be included. This not only gives the collection more exposure—it also demonstrates that the library has special collections and that it is involved and supportive of what the museum does.

If the library has access to exhibition space, it is worth developing small exhibitions of art ephemera to increase exposure to wider audiences. It is also good practice to include artist file materials during tours or special events in the library. These opportunities can be tied to announcements of new donations of material or to showcase research utilizing the ephemera collection. A great example is the 2013 Museum of Modern Art Library exhibition, *Please Come to the Show*, curated by Museum of Modern Art Library bibliographer David Senior, which included specially selected materials from their artist file collection.

DIGITAL EPHEMERA

Ephemera files originally began as collections of printed materials distributed by mail or in person to announce an exhibition or event. Today, this information is more frequently issued to subscribers via email and posted to websites. Like their printed counterparts, digital ephemera may include biographical information, artist interviews, and other timely details that serve as the only records of an event—resources that curators and art researchers value even more because of the impermanence of websites and electronic mail. As a result, librarians have begun to develop new ways to capture, maintain, and preserve collections of ephemera in electronic form.

This section will explore practical methods for managing digital ephemera collections as well as ideas for making them accessible to researchers.

Collecting Guidelines

As with printed materials, art museum libraries depend on the library's collection development policy, financial resources, and staffing to determine the types of digital ephemera collected. Unlike printed materials, however, the sheer volume of digital resources (websites, electronic mail, social media) and the measures necessary to catalog and archive these resources often requires a more focused collection policy. For example, the National Gallery of Australia Research Library and Archives (NGARLA) collects born-digital ephemera from art organizations and artists based exclusively in Australia and New Zealand (see figure 5.3). Although printed material on international artists is still acquired, the narrower collecting guidelines for born-digital resources will remain focused on preserving Australian and New Zealand art history as a manageable goal—and one that is demonstrably tied to NGARLA's mission.

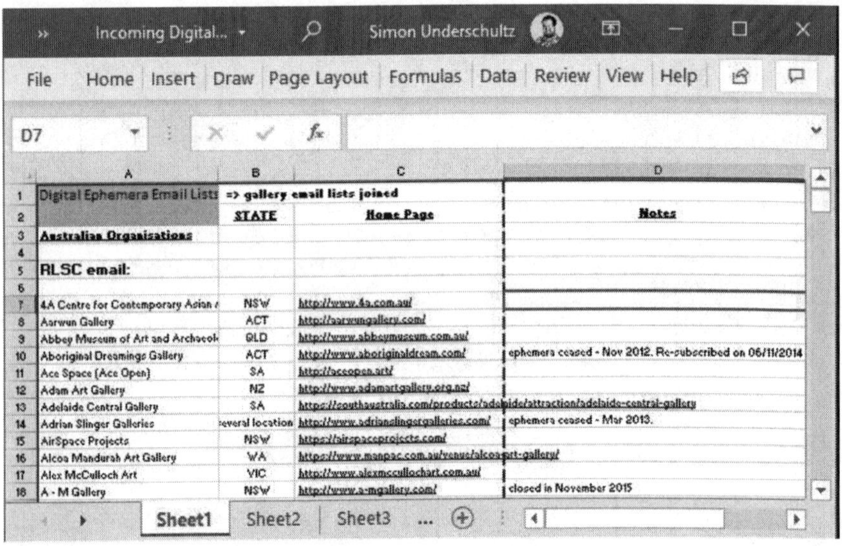

	A	B	C	D
1	Digital Ephemera Email Lists	=> gallery email lists joined		
2		STATE	Home Page	Notes
3	Australian Organisations			
4				
5	RLSC email:			
6				
7	4A Centre for Contemporary Asian A	NSW	http://www.4a.com.au/	
8	Aarwun Gallery	ACT	http://aarwungallery.com/	
9	Abbey Museum of Art and Archaeol	QLD	http://www.abbeymuseum.com.au/	
10	Aboriginal Dreamings Gallery	ACT	http://www.aboriginaldream.com/	ephemera ceased - Nov 2012. Re-subscribed on 06/11/2014
11	Ace Space (Ace Open)	SA	http://aceopen.art/	
12	Adam Art Gallery	NZ	http://www.adamartgallery.org.nz/	
13	Adelaide Central Gallery	SA	https://southaustralia.com/products/adelaide/attraction/adelaide-central-gallery	
14	Adrian Slinger Galleries	everal location	http://www.adrianslingergalleries.com/	ephemera ceased - Mar 2013.
15	AirSpace Projects	NSW	https://airspaceprojects.com/	
16	Alcoa Mandurah Art Gallery	WA	https://www.manpac.com.au/venue/alcoa-art-gallery/	
17	Alex McCulloch Art	VIC	http://www.alexmccullochart.com.au/	
18	A - M Gallery	NSW	http://www.a-mgallery.com/	closed in November 2015

Figure 5.3. List of email subscriptions to art organizations, actively maintained at the National Gallery of Australia Research Library and Archives.

Conversion and Storage

Born-digital ephemera usually comes to libraries in the form of emails, which are not ideal for storage, preservation, and access because their formats rely on in-house systems and email preservation software—options not all libraries will have or be able to acquire. A natural inclination is to print the emails and simply file them with printed ephemera, but this method is problematic for several reasons: in addition to the cost to the environment of printing and to the amount of physical storage space that will be necessary, printed emails lack contextual information such as links and metadata that are essential for discovering and understanding the documentary evidence they contain.

The currently preferred approach is to convert emails to an archival format and store them digitally. Interfaces such as extensible markup language (XML) and portable document format (PDF) have open standards and published codes that enable files to be reconstructed if lost. Among archival institutions that employ archival formats as part of their preservation strategies, XML is the most common.[7] The Tate, for example, prefers PDF (or PDF/A for archival purposes) formats because they are compatible with systems already used at the Tate and because PDF is common and easily readable by most computers.[8] Emails must be converted and saved one at a time, however; in addition to applying consistent and meaningful file names, it is a time-consuming process and can be a major factor in determining how much born-digital ephemera can be acquired.

If the institution does not have a digital asset management system (DAMS), some art museum libraries may choose to save the PDF files in folders on an internal networked library drive that is routinely backed up. This is a practical solution that will suffice until the files can be saved into a DAMS that would provide easier access and an improved workflow for adding descriptive metadata.

Discovery and Access

Discovery of and access to born-digital ephemera poses significant challenges to those outside of the holding institution. If the digital ephemera is stored on an internal networked drive, it remains invisible to the researcher without a means of retrieving and presenting relevant information in a meaningful way. Some libraries are, however, developing innovative methods to enhance discoverability of their digital ephemera collections. The E H McCormick Research Library at the Auckland Art Gallery Toi o Tāmaki in New Zealand, for example, has looked to established resources that could point to born-digital ephemera:

> The Find New Zealand Artists website has obvious potential given its current role as a central hub for artist names and artist file listings. It is however, a database of names that *points* to resources, not a database that contains the resources (such as the emails or PDFs). It would indicate to the user that an e-file exists but a visit to the Library would then be required, as with the physical files, unless an e-ephemera database—and here things could get complicated due to copyright issues—were developed for online public access.[9]

Australian national copyright policies permit the National Gallery of Australia to preserve copyrighted material (including born-digital ephemera) and provide on-site access to staff and public users for the purposes of research.[10] Users can access born-digital ephemera files through the reading room computer simply by searching the folder structure on the desktop. However, similar to the physical files, users often need to be directed to the born-digital collection by staff.

The NGARLA is currently implementing Ex Libris' DAMS, Alma Digital, which will allow the library to store born-digital ephemera files in the library catalog rather than on a publicly inaccessible internal drive. Users will be able to find digital ephemera when they search the online catalog for artist names (a MARC record exists for each Australian and New Zealand artist file in the physical ephemera collection). Copyright restrictions require that digital files are accessible only at the NGARLA through a designated range of IP addresses.

Art Websites

Gallery and artist websites are important sources of information for researchers and have also replaced paper-based documentation in many ways. Websites can be artistic expressions themselves—the graphic design, layout, and even the site navigation are sometimes used in creative and unique ways, and the biographical and exhibition information they present can be invaluable. But websites can be even more ephemeral than their paper counterparts and often disappear into the digital void without a trace. Using web archiving methods, numerous libraries have been able to preserve art websites and make them accessible for future research.

Web archiving basically entails harvesting and capturing "snapshots" of websites as they appear on the live web at a specific time—generally through the use of a web crawler—and storing the web captures in a standard file format for future preservation and access.[11] There are a plethora of articles[12] on web archiving, so this essay will not examine the detailed processes involved, but instead will explore how art libraries might incorporate web archiving into their digital ephemera capture strategies.

In 2010, the NGARLA established a partnership with the National Library of Australia to archive websites in PANDORA, Australia's web archive. Currently, ten partners contribute to PANDORA. Each has its own set of selection guidelines based on their area of responsibility—the National Gallery of Australia's focus being websites related to Australian visual arts. All partners utilize the PANDORA Digital Archiving System to contribute titles to the archive, which is located centrally at the National Library.[13] The PANDORA partnership and the New York Art Resources Consortium (NYARC) examples emphasize that entering a collaborative network is an effective method to begin a sustainable and successful web archiving program.

Art museum libraries can capture, preserve, and make accessible art websites by engaging in partnerships and leveraging web archiving tools already established. For example between 2013 and 2015, NYARC, which comprises the Brooklyn Museum, The Frick Collection, and The Museum of Modern Art, established a collaborative web archiving plan and subscribed to Archive-It. Since Archive-It's launch in 2006, over six hundred partner organizations have used its end-to-end hosted solution to create, store, and provide access to collections of web content.[14]

COMMON CHALLENGES

Printed and digital artist file collections, although extremely valuable, are not always a viable option for all art museum libraries. Many collections have been moved or stored where they cannot be easily accessed because libraries are not able to adequately maintain the collection.

Lack of Time and Resources

Artist files are extremely labor- and time-intensive. When there is a steady stream of materials coming from museum staff and art institutions, it is often difficult to keep up with filing and reformatting. While many libraries depend on volunteer work for this process, it may not be enough. Determining what items to keep and when new files should be made also requires high-level research work, which is usually the task of library staff.

Lack of Space and Proper Facilities

Many libraries do not have the facilities to house the collection in a proper way to provide access. Art museum libraries already have a difficult time with maintaining their footprint in museums and often this can mean that there is no physical space to store the files. This may force libraries to locate files in off-site storage that is difficult to access, expensive, and discourages use.

Even if there is space for artist files, they may not have the proper environmental storage conditions; archival folders, filing cabinets, and climate controls are costly. In the case of digital ephemera, some libraries do not have access to DAMS to store and manage their collections. In both cases, if the items cannot be stored safely, there is a greater chance that the materials will be damaged or lost.

Atypical Material Formats

Librarians encounter donated ephemera in the form of thumb drives, CD discs, and original artwork that cannot be easily cataloged but still have research value. There are ways to work around some of these atypical material formats, such as printing out items from the CD disc or providing special housing for original artwork. Tedious methods like these are dependent on how much staff, supplies, and time can be devoted to an artist file collection.

Overall, the collection manager is faced with determining whether an item has significant research value, if the item's placement in the artist file collection provides the best access and context, and if the item will be harmed or cause harm to other items in the collection. If the item has significant research value but does not belong in the library, it is best practice to determine a suitable home for the item in a different department within the institution or a different institution altogether. For instance, an original artwork could be offered to the museum collection or to the archives of another institution that holds the artist's papers. The desire to acquire an item, especially if it is particularly rare or interesting, should not take precedence over determining the best repository for an item.

Collection Bias

Museum collections have systematically ignored artists due to the color of their skin, their gender, or gender identity, a topic heavily covered and supported statistically in Maura Reilly's book, *Curatorial Activism: Towards an Ethics of Curating.* Artist files usually reflect the collecting of their institution, acquiring heavily on the artists within the museum's collection.[15] It can be argued that ephemera collection bias is primarily the result of passive acquisition that relies on legacy donations. However, as Lucy Lippard emphasizes in the foreword to *Curatorial Activism*, curators and collection managers should feel an ethical obligation to "intervene" when biases and voids are noticed.[16] To ignore these issues would be a form of curatorial laziness, "an unwillingness to think beyond the precedents, out of the box, around the block, out of the comfort zone that can result in involuntary misogyny, racism, homo/lesbophobia."[17] Librarians should devote time to analyzing gaps and researching proper names and terms will serve to strengthen collections and promote equal representation and access. If time cannot be dedicated to proper ethical methods that acknowledge and confront bias, the collection suffers.

CONCLUSION

The value of artist files is often extolled by art museum librarians and patrons alike. Their research value is undeniable, but librarians can look deeper and think about opportunities to promote their collections and advocate for the expense that comes with their growth and maintenance. Although born-digital ephemera collection management is still in its infancy and its true potential as an art research resource has not yet been realized, the way in which printed ephemera collections have connected individuals with art history through their value as cultural evidence amply demonstrates the remarkable success art museums have had with building and promoting these resources. It doesn't take much effort to imagine born-digital ephemera collections holding just as much value to art museum libraries in the near future.

NOTES

1. Artist Files Working Group ARLIS/NA, *Artist Files Revealed: Documentation and Access* (Art Libraries Society of North America, 2009, 2010), 4. http://www.arlisna.org/images /researchreports/artist_files_revealed.pdf.

2. Ibid., 5.

3. Ibid.

4. Kai Alexis Smith, "Digitizing Ephemera Reloaded: A Digitization Plan for an Art Museum Library," *Art Documentation: Journal of the Art Libraries Society of North America* 35, no. 2 (Fall 2016): 331–32.

5. Artist Files Working Group ARLIS/NA, 7.

6. Samuel Duncan, "Best Practices for Cataloging Artist Files Using MARC," ARLIS/NA Artist Files Special Interest Group (blog), last modified October 17, 2019. Accessed November 13, 2019, http://artistfiles.arlisna.org/best-practices-for-cataloging-artist-files-using-marc/.

7. Jackie Bettington, Kim Eberhard, Rowena Loo, and Clive Smith, editors, *Keeping Archives* (Canberra: Australian Society of Archivists, 2008), 502.

8. Holly Callaghan, "Electronic Ephemera: Collection, Storage and Access in Tate Library," *Art Libraries Journal* 38, no. 1 (2013): 27–31.

9. Catherine Hammond, "Escaping the Digital Black Hole: E-Ephemera at Two Auckland Art Libraries," *Art Libraries Journal* 41, no. 2 (April 2016): 107–14.

10. The Parliament of the Commonwealth of Australia, *Copyright Amendment (Disability Access and Other Measures) Act 2017*, no. 49, 2017. Accessed June 12, 2020, https://www.legislation.gov.au/Details/C2017A00049.

11. Sumitra Duncan and Karl-Rainer Blumenthal, "A Collaborative Model for Web Archiving Ephemeral Art Resources at the New York Art Resources Consortium (NYARC)," *Art Libraries Journal* 41, Special Issue no. 2 (April 2016): 116–26.

12. "Press and Publications," NYARC. Accessed August 25, 2020, http://nyarc.org/press.

13. "Pandora Partners," Pandora: Australia's Web Archive. Accessed April 8, 2020, http://pandora.nla.gov.au/partners.html.

14. "About Archive-it," Archive-It. Accessed April 7, 2020, https://www.archive-it.org/blog/learn-more.

15. Maura Reilly, *Curatorial Activism: Towards an Ethics of Curating* (New York: Thames & Hudson, 2018).

16. Lucy R. Lippard, "Foreword," in *Curatorial Activism: Towards an Ethics of Curating*, edited by Maura Reilly (New York: Thames & Hudson, 2018), 11.

17. Ibid., 10.

6

Building Web Archive Collections in Art Museum Libraries

Sumitra Duncan, The Frick Collection/New York Art Resources Consortium

Art museum librarians are seeing a shift to web-based publishing for creative and scholarly output from galleries, artists, arts organizations, and researchers. Many resources that have traditionally been collected in print format by art museum libraries and archives now pose new challenges to collection and preservation, especially given that born-digital publications are highly ephemeral, in that websites might only exist for a number of days before changing or disappearing. Web archiving, or the process of collecting web-based content with a web crawler and preserving the collections in an archival format, is a means of addressing the challenges associated with the born-digital publication shift that is currently underway. Web archiving is still very much an emerging practice in art museum libraries, with the 2017 National Digital Stewardship Alliance Web Archiving Survey results reporting that out of the 104 total responses, only 2.5 percent of respondents were affiliated with a museum.[1] This chapter examines the evolution of web archiving as a collection development practice in art museum libraries, the resource and technology constraints faced in engaging in web archiving, and the imperative for preserving art resources for future analysis in art history scholarship. This chapter also highlights the potential for scaling web archiving efforts via interinstitutional collaborations to archive born-digital art-rich materials.

WEB ARCHIVING AS A COLLECTION DEVELOPMENT ACTIVITY

Building collections of born-digital art ephemera anticipates the needs of the future art researcher. Art-rich materials are increasingly published only to the web, and there is a strong likelihood of significant gaps in the art historical record and resulting adverse implications on future scholarship should these resources disappear from the web before they are collected and preserved. The final report from the 2013 study, "Reframing Collections for a Digital Age: A Preparatory Study for Collecting and Preserving Web-Based Art Research Materials," undertaken by three consultants and the New York Art Resources Consortium (NYARC) director's group, identifies and discusses "the organizational, economic, and technological challenges posed by the rapidly increasing number of web-based or 'born-digital' resources that document art history and the art market."[2] This study cautions that websites produced by galleries, auction houses, and artists are potentially at higher risk of losing content or disappearing altogether. The study's consultants also warn that "the more an organization is focused on contemporary art, the more likely it will publish its materials electronically and without a surrogate."[3]

Web archiving is the process of capturing, or harvesting, web-based content with a web crawler and preserving the files in an archival format, called a WARC. "The WARC (Web ARChive) format specifies a method for combining multiple digital resources into an aggregate archival file together with related information."[4] Web archiving as a collection development activity offers art museum libraries and archives a means of addressing the publication shift from print to digital, a shift that is already well underway and will only accelerate. Additionally, archiving specific born-digital resources in order to create permanent links in citations of web-based material is a necessity for the future of scholarly publication. "Both link rot and content drift pose a threat to the long-term persistence and integrity of the new-era scholarly record."[5]

With a plethora of materials being produced and then at times rapidly disappearing from the web, crafting and approving a collection development and preservation policy specific to websites is imperative to building an active web archiving program within an art museum library. Policies will ideally outline responsibilities within the library or museum for decision-making as it pertains to resource selection and curation of web archive collections, as well as workflow and procedural decision-making for collection management, harvesting, quality assurance, description, and access, and long-term storage and preservation. The initial efforts of developing a collection development and preservation policy for born-digital resources could be undertaken in collaboration with museum staff outside of the library, but given the collection development expertise that already exists within the art museum library, it is logical to center web archiving activities within the library or archives.

Interdepartmental buy-in will remain crucial to the success of initiating a program of web archiving. As Emily Rafferty wrote in her article on developing a digital preservation policy at the Baltimore Museum of Art, "Meeting with staff and trustees to review the policy and incorporating their input resulted in increased awareness of the need for digital preservation, improving the likelihood of cross-departmental support as well as future funding for digital preservation projects."[6] Integrating the practice of web archiving into the art museum library's existing workflows for collection, description, and access are a clear means of incrementally shifting focus and tangible resources to born-digital collecting. The first step in this process requires a review of existing collection development policies to determine how they might be expanded, or if an entirely new policy should be drafted that encompasses these emergent, complex formats.

Globally, dozens of web archiving initiatives are well-established at national libraries and archives, universities, and research institutions, many of which fulfill legal deposit mandates to document national history and preserve national web domains. The most widely known web archive is the Internet Archive's Wayback Machine. The Internet Archive began to archive the freely available open web in 1996. Users of the Wayback Machine can input a URL or search via keyword to identify previous iterations of a website at specific dates in time, which can then be viewed and navigated as they existed on that date. With 391 billion webpages archived and freely accessible as of late 2019, the Wayback Machine serves as a monumental resource to both researchers and the general public. Many art museum libraries are additionally uploading their digitized materials to the Internet Archive in an effort to promote their discoverability to broader global audiences.[7] In 2006, the Internet Archive developed Archive-It, a subscription-based web archiving service, for use by organizations in building their own curated collections of web resources. As of this writing, Archive-It is working with nearly seven hundred partner organizations, spanning colleges and universities, state archives, state libraries and historical societies, federal institutions and non-governmental organizations, museums, and art libraries, and public libraries.[8]

As web archiving as a collecting practice has gained traction in research communities, additional open-source tools have been developed over the past few years to complement the web archiving capabilities of the Internet Archive and Archive-It. One such tool is the Webrecorder software, most recently in development as a project of the non-profit arts organization Rhizome, with the support of grant funding from The Andrew W. Mellon Foundation. Webrecorder is a freely available high-fidelity capture and replay tool that focuses on harvesting dynamic web content. This tool is available as a desktop application and also presently has a web interface which can be utilized by registered users to harvest, manage, and access the archived sites in collections (either publicly or privately) from the Webrecorder site.[9] Other freely available tools for harvesting WARCs or derivative data from social media sites include Social Feed Manager and twarc, which are used to collect from social platforms such as Twitter, Tumblr, and Flickr, and are extensible to other platforms.[10]

ART MUSEUM LIBRARY WEB ARCHIVING PRACTITIONERS

As stated previously, web archiving remains an emerging practice in art museum libraries, with the 2017 National Digital Stewardship Alliance Web Archiving Survey results reporting that out of the 104 total responses, only 2.5 percent of respondents affiliated with a "museum." In contrast, 61 percent of survey respondents identified "college or university" as their organization type.[11] In comparison with art museum libraries, colleges and universities have historically greater access to staff and financial resources to devote to the development and ongoing practice of web archiving. However, both organization types currently lack the impetus of a legal deposit mandate to collect all born-digital publications produced within specific national domains. A 2018 report, *Advancing Art Libraries and Curated Web Archives: A Community Survey*, states that 75 percent of those respondents from institutions engaged in web archiving activities indicated that their practice was primarily focused on their own institutional web presence.[12] Survey respondents noted that areas of interest for building future collections, perhaps collected collaboratively, would be thematic and include materials such as social media, news and current events, artist files, auction catalogs, and born-digital exhibitions.[13] Of current North American Archive-It subscribers, the following art museum libraries focus on archiving their own institutional web presence: Art Gallery of Ontario, Hillwood Estate Museum and Gardens, Museum of Contemporary Art Chicago, National Gallery of Canada, Nelson-Atkins Museum of Art, Royal Ontario Museum, Smithsonian Institution, the Corning Museum of Glass, The Getty, and the Whitney Museum of American Art.[14] Art museum libraries and archives such as the New Museum and Newfields at the Indianapolis Museum of Art are utilizing the Webrecorder tool to archive their own institutional websites.[15]

Several art museum libraries and consortia within North America are also actively engaged in building web archive collections that are subject-based and event-based in nature, a challenging practice given the decision-making that is required for selection and curation of born-digital resources. The Sterling and Francine Clark Art Institute Library began web archiving born-digital content directly related to the Venice Biennale in 2013. As Andrea Puccio, assistant collections management librarian at The Clark, wrote, "with more material being produced solely online with each successive Biennale, . . . it became clear that including the web content was critical to maintaining the depth and breadth of the collection."[16]

NYARC, which consists of the libraries and archives of the Brooklyn Museum, The Frick Collection, and The Museum of Modern Art, is actively building both subject-based and institutional web archive collections.[17] As of late 2019, NYARC had developed a robust collaborative web archive program with ten Archive-It collections and over six terabytes of WARC files, with content spanning the museum's own websites, ephemeral art resources, artists' websites, auction houses, catalogs raisonnés, New York City gallery websites, and sites devoted to scholarship for the restitution of lost and looted art.[18] Preserving one's own museum website is a natural first action in tackling web archiving and is an effort that is directly justifiable as a collection development and preservation priority to an organization's administration.

The National Museum of Women in the Arts conducted web archiving of websites of contemporary women artists on the web between 2011 and 2016 and has been archiving their own institutional website since 2011. Heather Slania, the former director of the Betty Boyd Dettre Library and Research Center, National Museum of Women in the Arts, wrote that for small institutions, "Having a strong reason to begin web archiving is imperative. In general, most institutions respond favorably to allocating money to preserve their own histories."[19]

The Art Libraries Society of North America (ARLIS/NA) Artist Files Special Interest Group conducted a pilot project with Archive-It from 2013 to 2015 to explore the capture of born-digital artist ephemera. The Special Interest Group's project resulted in the recommendation that "library budgets and collection development policies need to be rethought in order to expand collections from paper-based and digitized materials to include born-digital ephemera. In addition to building the collections, libraries need to link them so that they can be cross-referenced and cross-searched."[20]

ACCESS AND DISCOVERY

When engaged in building web archive collections for art museum libraries, it is advisable to consider mechanisms for access and discovery at the initial stage of program planning, and, ideally, to outline procedures for description and access alongside one's collection development policy for websites. Institutional approaches to descriptions vary, especially in that programs for web archiving are perhaps based alternately in the library or in the archives at museums (should the library and archives operate as discrete departments). Staff responsible for web archiving can utilize multiple methods to enhance user discovery: insertion of links to institutional web archive captures in existing finding aids, creation of new finding aids to represent their collections, creation of bibliographic records for specific websites that are archived as part of thematic or events-based collections in their collection purview, or relying more wholly on full-text search functionality of web archive collections via indexing completed at the time of WARC file harvest. Additionally, some web archives are described at the collection level only, versus cataloging for each website or for unique objects or documents embedded in websites that require item-level cataloging. The OCLC Research Library Partnership Web Archiving Metadata Working Group produced a report in 2018 that outlines the variance in descriptive practice across the broader web archiving community (art museum libraries are represented in those surveyed, but comprise a small subset). Given that web archives are largely unique, OCLC's report ultimately suggests taking a hybrid approach with archival and bibliographic metadata and descriptive elements, in that there might be "value of blending practices for web content, . . . with both bibliographic and archival practice, and may be described at the item level, collection level, or both. In some settings, this work may offer opportunities for collaboration across multiple organizational units."[21]

BEST PRACTICES AND RESOURCE CONSIDERATIONS

Tools for harvesting and replaying WARC files, though impressive, are still imperfect in their precision and capacity to keep pace with advances in web development. As a result, art museum libraries engaged in web archiving will find it crucial to conduct quality assurance reviews of their web captures. "Quality assurance is the manual process of reviewing and, when necessary, improving the completeness and accuracy of harvested websites. It begins with identifying missing content (web pages, images, downloadable documents, etc.) and/or functionality (navigation, responsive scripts and applets, etc.)."[22] Given the visual nature of many of the scholarly resources that are collected by art museum libraries, fully capturing and rendering the visual appearance, behavior/functionality, and all embedded data on websites is a necessity. Lack of automation inherent in many of the available web archiving tools and software results in a time-consuming process for those involved in quality review of archived sites. Additionally, certain types of content that are frequently deployed in web design can pose challenges to being adequately archived and rendered. With every website being unique and varying in size, depth, and embedded technologies, difficulties can arise in appropriately predicting how much time and effort will be required to fully archive specific resources in web archive collections.

Before art museum libraries can invest in establishing a practice of web collecting, it is imperative to first develop a policy specific to web archiving and preservation of web-based art resources. Given the push and pull of competing priorities within the art museum library, the lack of established policy might deter action in taking first steps for an inaugural collecting initiative, such as preservation of the library's own institutional web presence. As Archive-It notes, "Conflicting and evolving policy decisions from various stakeholders, as well as shifting organizational structures and job responsibilities, pose further obstacles to establishing best practices . . . stakeholders have not fully adopted the belief that web archiving is crucial to their digital preservation activities; as a result, funding remains limited or non-existent."[23] Gaining approval at art museum libraries for a new budget line for subscription-based web archiving software might be unfeasible at many institutions, but an approach of reallocating a portion of collection development funds for web archiving subscription services would be an intermediate step. This adjustment to collections budgets is a reflection of both the realities of constricted art museum library budgets in general, as well as the shift of publishing models from one of solely print to born-digital.

Perhaps of even greater concern to budgets of art museum libraries than the decisions and costs of subscriptions for collecting, storage, and preservation are those resource constraints such as insufficient staff time to devote to the practice of web archiving. According to the *Advancing Art Libraries* report, respondents rated "lack of staff" and "insufficient budget" as having the highest barrier to engaging in web archiving, versus lower barriers such as "lack of skills among existing staff" or "lack of discoverability tools for web archives."[24] Of the twenty-three institutions surveyed in the 2016 Harvard Library "Web Archiving Environmental Scan," it is notable that "more than half of participants report having no dedicated full-time staff for their web archive projects."[25]

Copyright considerations have been a barrier to some art museum libraries grappling with initiating a web archiving practice, but as Heather Slania wrote, "The literature has proven that web archiving is transformative and fits under fair use. Copyright issues should not stop art librarians and others from web archiving."[26] NYARC has thus far sought publisher permission to include websites in their ten collections, yet it is often the case that website owners fail to respond in a timely manner. The Clark Art Library seeks permission for many of the sites included in their Venice Biennale collections, especially those with a login requirement, such as Facebook or those blocked by robots.txt exclusion files. For openly available sites, such as artist websites, Instagram, and Twitter, they do not seek permission in advance, which works favorably for capturing event-based ephemeral content published in real-time. As stated by the Archive-It team, "Not all organizations ask for permission before capturing content; many organizations are clear that as an archive and/or a library, their organization has the right and the mandate to capture publicly available content on the live web. 'Fair use' is a phrase the Archive-It team hears from partners when deciding to capture publicly available web content."[27]

WEB ARCHIVES AND THE FUTURE

Determining the ideal means of promoting researcher use of these unique collections are dependent on understanding how current constituents and future users will interact with web archives and their embedded data. The myriad potential uses of web archive collections are not yet fully defined, but given the digital shift in publication methods, future art research will be largely dependent on digital records. We already know that having reliable, persistent links to ephemeral web-published materials (including those that have been archived and then vanished from the live web) is an imperative. Digital art history use cases such as large scale data analysis utilizing WARC files are presently emerging. These use cases in the discipline will seek to answer research questions related to collection metadata, longitudinal and graph analysis, presentation of named entities that exist across collections, or variances in publication trends over time. A great deal of opportunity exists in data extraction, text analysis, data visualization, and data mapping from WARC files harvested in support of art and art historical scholarship.

Committing to preserve web resources in the long-term can be a cost-prohibitive consideration for many small and medium-sized art museum libraries, especially if they define their objectives in a way that requires the need to scale web archiving practices dramatically into the future. Establishing collaborations and cost-sharing models for web archiving programs, such as the consortial model developed at NYARC, will serve to alleviate a portion of the burden posed by growing digital storage and preservation requirements for born-digital collections. The libraries and archives of the NYARC institutions share the financial responsibility of their subscriptions to DuraCloud for long-term storage; to Archive-It for web archive collection harvesting, access, and management; and to NYARC Discovery (the Ex Libris Primo product) as an additional access point to web archive bibliographic records and full-text search results from their consortial Archive-It collections.

The co-moderators of the ARLIS/NA Web Archiving Special Interest Group, founded in 2016, have led introductory workshops on web archiving at annual meetings of ARLIS/NA, which has helped to lower the perceived barrier to entry in web archiving within the art library community. Additionally, the 2018 to 2020 Institute of Museum and Library Services–supported project *Advancing Art Libraries and Curated Web Archives*, undertaken by the Internet Archive in partnership with NYARC, further advanced awareness of current use and intention of art museum libraries to engage in building specialist art and art historical collections of web archives, as well as their need for tools, program development, collaboration, and training. In the coming years, advances in web development will alter the experience, look and feel, and behavioral functionality of websites and the published scholarship included in them. In keeping with this pace of change, web archiving harvesting technologies and playback mechanisms will also continue to develop and make improvements in an effort to improve fidelity and enhance quality assurance capabilities. As a result of these technological enhancements, improved automation, and training opportunities, the art museum library community will be better positioned to engage in the practice of web archiving in preserving both their own institutional web presence and building thematic collections pertinent to the future art scholar.

NOTES

1. National Digital Stewardship Alliance, "Web Archiving in the United States—A 2017 Survey," October 4, 2018, 7.

2. Deborah Kempe, "Reframing Collections for a Digital Age: A Preparatory Study for Collecting and Preserving Web-Based Art Research Materials: Final Report," New York Art Resources Consortium (NYARC), April 12, 2013. https://wayback.archive-it.org/4432/20190808165540/http://www.nyarc.org/sites/default/files/reports/reframing_final_report2013.pdf.

3. Deborah Kempe, "Reframing Collections for a Digital Age: A Preparatory Study for Collecting and Preserving Web-Based Art Research Materials: Summary of Consultants' Recommendations." New York Art Resources Consortium (NYARC), January 2013. https://wayback.archive-it.org/4432/20190808165602/http://www.nyarc.org/sites/default/files/reports/reframing_recommendations.pdf.

4. "WARC, Web ARChive File Format." *Sustainability of Digital Formats: Planning for Library of Congress Collections*, July 18, 2018. https://www.loc.gov/preservation/digital/formats/fdd/fdd000236.shtml.

5. Martin Klein, Herbert Van de Sompel, Robert Sanderson, Harihar Shankar, Lyudmila Balakireva, Ke Zhou, and Richard Tobin, "Scholarly Context Not Found: One in Five Articles Suffers from Reference Rot." *PLOS ONE* 9, no. 12 (December 26, 2014): e115253.

6. Emily Rafferty and Becca Pad, "Better Together: A Holistic Approach to Creating a Digital Preservation Policy in an Art Museum," *Art Documentation: Journal of the Art Libraries Society of North America* 36, no. 1 (Spring 2017): 149–62.

7. "Internet Archive: About the Internet Archive," 2019. https://archive.org/about/.

8. "Archive-It—Web Archiving Services for Libraries and Archives," Archive-It, 2019. https://archive-it.org/.

9. "Webrecorder: About." Webrecorder.io, 2019. https://webrecorder.io/_faq.

10. Art Libraries Society of North America (ARLIS/NA) Web Archiving Special Interest Group, "Resources—ART|WARC," 2019. https://web.archive.org/web/20190918003709/https://sites.google.com/site/arliswarc/resources.

11. National Digital Stewardship Alliance, "Web Archiving in the United States—A 2017 Survey," October 4, 2018, 7.

12. Internet Archive and New York Art Resources Consortium (NYARC), "Advancing Art Libraries and Curated Web Archives: A Community Survey," November 14, 2018, 10.

13. Ibid., 14.

14. Archive-It: Collecting Organizations, "Archive-It: Museums and Art Libraries," 2019. https://archive-it.org/explore?fc=organizationType%3AmuseumsAndArtLibraries.

15. Indianapolis Museum of Art, "Archives: Newfields," 2019. https://discovernewfields.org/archives.

16. Andrea Puccio, "From Shuttered Mosques to Mini Golf: The Venice Biennale on the Web Collection at the Clark Art Institute," Archive-It Blog, June 12, 2017. https://archive-it.org/blog/post/from-shuttered-mosques-to-mini-golf-the-venice-biennale-on-the-web-collection-at-the-clark-art-institute/.

17. Sumitra Duncan and Karl-Rainer Blumenthal, "A Collaborative Model for Web Archiving Ephemeral Art Resources at the New York Art Resources Consortium (NYARC)," *Art Libraries Journal* 41, no. 2 (2016): 116–26.

18. "New York Art Resources Consortium (NYARC)—Archive-It," Archive-It, 2019. https://archive-it.org/organizations/484.

19. Heather Slania, "Online Art Ephemera: Web Archiving at the National Museum of Women in the Arts," *Art Documentation: Journal of the Art Libraries Society of North America* 32, no. 1 (Spring 2013): 124.

20. Samantha Deutch and Sally McKay, "The Future of Artist Files: Here Today, Gone Tomorrow," *Art Documentation: Journal of the Art Libraries Society of North America* 35, no. 1 (Spring 2016): 41–42.

21. Jackie Dooley and Kate Bowers, "Descriptive Metadata for Web Archiving: Recommendations of the OCLC Research Library Partnership Web Archiving Metadata Working Group," OCLC Research. Dublin, OH, February 2018, 8.

22. Sumitra Duncan and Karl-Rainer Blumenthal, "A Collaborative Model for Web Archiving Ephemeral Art Resources at the New York Art Resources Consortium (NYARC)," 122.

23. Molly Bragg and Kristine Hanna, "The Web Archiving Life Cycle Model," Archive-It. The Internet Archive, March 2013, 1. http://ait.blog.archive.org/files/2014/04/archiveit_life_cycle_model.pdf.

24. Internet Archive and New York Art Resources Consortium (NYARC), "Advancing Art Libraries and Curated Web Archives: A Community Survey," 15.

25. Gail Truman, "Web Archiving Environmental Scan," Harvard Library Report, January 2016, 9, figure 2. http://nrs.harvard.edu/urn-3:HUL.InstRepos:25658314.

26. Heather Slania, "Online Art Ephemera: Web Archiving at the National Museum of Women in the Arts,"126.

27. Molly Bragg and Kristine Hanna, "The Web Archiving Life Cycle Model," 19.

7

Preservation and Conservation for Art Museum Library Collections

Progressive Approaches and Evolving Concepts

Beth Morris, Independent Librarian, Preservation Specialist, Book Conservator, and Scholar

Art museum library[1] collections sit precariously between the traditionally siloed institutions of libraries and museums. Although both libraries and museums are cultural heritage institutions, the staffing, infrastructure, and treatment of collections vary greatly from institution to institution. Art museum library collections are distinctive and indispensable to support focused research within their museums, while also boasting exceptional and inimitable objects, materials, and resources. Because they encompass the wide range of materials essential to support the work undertaken to fulfill the museum's mission through exhibitions, programs, and education, the library's collections are indispensable components of the museum's operations. Resources range from obscure exhibition pamphlets, artists' files, books with newspaper clippings or annotated handwritten notes, countless pieces of ephemera, historic auction catalogs, photograph archives, artists' books, special collections, and digital collections composed of varied file formats across multiple systems. With this extensive and all-encompassing range of materials and media, art museum library collections require exceptional care. Therefore, for their continued existence and use, preservation and conservation are equally vital for safeguarding the present and the future of art museum library collections.

Art museum libraries provide essential resources required for interested users to interpret and understand the museum's objects. Curators and researchers utilize these focused resources to analyze and define museum objects more clearly by studying and interpreting not only the object's artistic qualities, but also the social, political, and historical context surrounding an object's creation and creator. Research done in the library results in published works, professional presentations, exhibitions, or new interpretations for the collection as a whole. The value of the art museum library's collections should not only be seen in the service of the objects and information they provide, but for the future potential and value that has yet to be fully recognized.

Library collections, just as the objects of the museum, require effort to be preserved for future research and scholarship, for their intellectual content, and as a museum collection in its own right. Because most libraries entered art museums in the twentieth century, preservation and conservation efforts have prioritized the art object collections of the museum. Unfortunately, this has led to overall neglect and the failure to realize the true value and preservation needs of library collections. Reasons for this are not completely understood, but factors such as the individual institutional histories, the role of education in the intuition, as well as the professional practice expectations within a museum could all elucidate potential issues. However, in the changing landscape of cultural heritage institutions, librarianship, and preservation, it is time to champion a new norm and look toward the present and future stewardship of art museum library collections.

REDEFINING VALUE FOR LIBRARY COLLECTIONS

Determining value for library collections is an integral step in the preservation process, particularly when determining conservation needs. There are many unique factors that may contribute to the scholarly value of library collections, including collecting provenance marked by bookplates, marginalia added by curatorial staff or previous museum directors that display a history of scholarship, newspaper clippings or photographs added over the years from librarians or staff members, and even the library's own identifiers and acquisition numbers. Each of these distinctive properties can add greater value and scholarly potential to the object and to the collection as a whole. Although the value of marginalia and provenance are generally understood, other areas of value in library collections may be overlooked or unknown.

The hierarchical structure traditionally used to determine value for library materials was based on age, scarcity, market value, associational value, and, more recently, "artifactual" value. This needs to be reconsidered. Exhibition value, aesthetic value, inherent value, cultural value, (unknown/potential) research value, and evidential value must all be considered. These values are no longer defined by "rare" or "unique" features, but rather by their present and future needs as a collection, as many objects containing evidentiary value were produced in the nineteenth and twentieth centuries. The artifacts composing art museum library collections contain contextual histories of importance and value to art historians, sociologists, book historians, literary scholars, economists, bibliographers, media specialists, illustrators and designers, and conservators.[2] In order to best understand the conservation needs of an art museum library collection, the collection must be considered both in terms of the needs of individual significant volumes, and preservation and conservation strategies that impact the collection broadly.

PRESERVATION AND CONSERVATION:
A UNIFIED EFFORT IN A CHANGING LANDSCAPE

The fields of preservation and conservation for libraries and archives emerged in the latter half of the twentieth century, with a growing emphasis by the 1960s. Inter-related and inextricably connected, preservation and conservation go hand in hand for the overall care of collections. Although preservation encompasses all factors and activities for the care and maintenance of collections, conservation is focused more directly on the specific actions undertaken by conservators to examine, treat, and care for individual objects. "While preservation is essential to any collecting insti-tution, the way it has been practiced varies not only from place to place but from profession to profession. The literature in each field reflects overlapping yet distinc-tive professional practices and philosophies."[3] Just as each art museum is unique in its mission and collections, acts of preservation are performed in a variety of ways in accordance with existing budgets, staffing, and spaces; however, this does not mean that preservation and conservation should continue to go forth in this manner. New roles, collaborative partnerships, and workflows should be investigated to achieve a shared goal: to preserve all collections of the museum, deliberately and equally.

The essential elements of preservation are environmental control, disaster plan-ning, security, storage and handling, reformatting, binding, in-house repair, conser-vation, and digital reformatting and preservation.[4] However, these elements continue to evolve with the field and are being refined to provide a comprehensive approach to preservation for all analog and digital materials, regardless of format. Other activities discussed less frequently, such as integrated pest management, mold remediation, and mass deacidification, are now being addressed more due to improved, chemically stable, ecologically safe, affordable alternatives, as well as educational opportuni-ties. Implementation of collections-based approaches focusing on the environment, storage, disaster planning, or collection-level treatments have proven to be the most effective and beneficial preservation strategies for long-term stability and care. These actions are often called preventative preservation or conservation and are discussed later in this chapter.

Several aspects of preservation fall under the purview of art librarians, whereas other areas require collaborative workflows, outreach, and building rapport with other departments, starting from the top down.[5] For example, security, environmen-tal control, and disaster planning are all essential to preservation but are often deter-mined by other departments within the museum. For these elements to be addressed successfully, art librarians need to engage and converse with these departments. Ideally, museums have committees for disaster planning or emergency preparedness that can foster these dialogues between personnel and departments; however, library stewards must be willing to reach out to staff across the museum. Surprisingly, this will often open a new channel of communication about shared goals, logistics, and planning, and for determining what is achievable and mutually beneficial to all invested. Building interdepartmental relationships takes time and clear communication but allows the library's needs to be understood by more museum colleagues and ultimately leads to greater overall collections care through united approaches.

Other preservation elements, such as storage, reformatting,[6] digital reformatting, and digital preservation also require institutional support through dedicated space, staffing, equipment, technical infrastructure, and funding; these elements also require long-range planning, multi-departmental collaborations, and potentially multiple institutions or vendors. Although library staff can accomplish portions of these activities successfully, achieving sustainable workflows requires collaboration both internally, with other museum departments and staff, and often with external institutions or specialized vendors that may be needed to conduct requisite outsourced work. Furthermore, there remains an ongoing need for additional funding to support suitable storage solutions for physical and digital objects, development of digital preservation policies and infrastructures, and reformatting and digitization of collections. To satisfy these increased digital demands, additional equipment, materials, space, staff, and time are inevitable needs. Dedicated funding to further these actions will ensure continued preservation of the collections for persistent access, use, and discovery of objects of enduring value.

Digital reformatting, more commonly known as digitization, and digital preservation are two aspects of preservation that have been reconsidered in the past decade. Digitization is commonly mistaken as an act of preservation; this has been traced to the distorted use of the phrase "preservation is access, and access is preservation" spoken and published by Patricia Battin.[7] Digitization and digital objects create increased access to collections. Through the process of digitization, new digital objects are born that require preservation to sustain access and integrity of new material. A common trend found across most libraries, digitization has prevailed as a tool for increasing discovery and access to collections for almost two decades. Although it has enabled greater support and opportunities for library initiatives, it has also detracted from the core mission of preservation for physical collections, as well as the digital counterparts created. As discussed in the ARLIS/NA 2016 white paper *State of Art Museum Libraries*, the increased demand for everything digital has placed greater demand on librarians, who must learn new technological skills, rely on added interns or volunteers, and adjust workflows to accomplish digitization projects. Consequently, libraries often have less time for conservation and stacks maintenance of the physical collections. The essential role of physical collections remains critical to supporting the museum's mission, despite a continued lack of sufficient space, stable environments, conservation resources, and overall funding and staffing.[8]

Digital preservation has been defined separately from preservation based on the contrasting requirements for its storage; rapidly changing formats; required hardware, software, and systems for access and use; intellectual property rights; and capture and metadata properties. It has been acknowledged that the present state of the field is unsure how to fully preserve digital and born-digital content, but many professionals are reframing approaches by following the main guiding principles of analog preservation. This innovative strategy will provide a unified methodology for developing global and sustainable programs and policies that aim to maintain the authenticity of the object, consider the user, and place responsibility for preservation on all, from creators to users.[9] While migration and emulation are current methods used in digital preservation, experts from many different disciplines are collaborating on the development of open source systems, stabilized media formats, and pioneering infrastructures. These initiatives offer potential solutions for sustainable preservation of digital assets with perpetual access.

PRESERVATION STARTS IN THE LIBRARY

The single greatest factor affecting the physical conditions of collections is the environment. Three essential components to monitor are temperature and relative humidity, light, and pollutants. Separately or combined, these three elements can cause deterioration to paper-based collections through chemical reactions that result in mechanical stresses to books; mold or fungi growth; oxidization and structural breakdown of paper fibers; fading or bleaching of cover material, text, or images; and increased levels of acidity overall. Maintaining a stable environment in these areas, as well as good housekeeping, such as routine dusting and cleaning, will prevent further deterioration caused by insects, pests, and other biological agents that prefer warm, damp, and dusty environments.[10] Although other departments in the museum commonly monitor temperature and relative humidity, it can be advantageous to invest in an individual unit[11] to monitor specific areas prone to vulnerabilities, resulting in data-driven evidence of the situation.

As paper-based print collections continue to be important and regularly used in the field, art museum librarians need to reabsorb routine preservation activities into core responsibilities. Nineteenth-century paper was produced from durable cotton rag and cloth, but by the end of the Industrial Revolution wood-pulp served as the primary source of commercial paper. Due to already shortened fibers and high lignin content, wood-pulp paper deteriorates rapidly as relative humidity and light chemically react, generating acidic and weak paper structures referred to as "brittle books." Many brittle books have been lost, and other issues remain with acid migration of poor materials and unacceptable storage and cleaning.

Preventative preservation and collection-level treatments, combined with regular dusting and protective enclosures, can provide solutions. Mass deacidification can be completed in groups of materials or for individual objects through specific vendors, which offer aqueous or nonaqueous treatments that infuse materials with an alkaline buffer that stabilizes pH levels.[12] Integrated pest management arose from the food and agricultural industries and has been readily applied to libraries, archives, and museums in recent years because of its nonchemical approach to proactively monitoring the overall environment for harmful insects, pests, and mold or fungi that pose risks to collections; it simultaneously provides safe, non-destructive methods for removing pests and mold from collections.[13] Often coinciding with environmental concerns, mold remediation is conducted in-house or through vendors based upon the scale of the problem. Many educational resources exist to provide basic training for librarians and staff on how to identify and deal with mold, with supporting resources and materials for proactive preservation methods in preventing future occurrences.[14] Preventative preservation actions such as mass deacidification and mold remediation should be researched and discussed thoroughly with preservation staff, library-based conservators, potential vendors, and senior administrators; however, more immediate actions can be made collaboratively with conservation, facilities and operations, curatorial, and other departments to develop unified preservation efforts in integrated pest management.

From simple to complex, preservation issues abound, and librarians allied with support staff, students, or volunteers can accomplish routine collections maintenance, handling and storage, binding, and in-house repairs. Education and instruction are instrumental to all of these, but particularly for in-house repairs and handling and storage, as this is often where the most damage can occur. Enclosures, boxes, folders, encapsulation, and containers offer a variety of protection for materials in less than ideal storage environments. In-house repairs can range from simple page mends, dry cleaning, and hinge tightening, to more advanced repairs such as spine repair, re-casing, or re-backing. The amount of skill, training, time, space, tools, materials, and staff available for in-house repairs varies greatly across the field; nevertheless, decades of literature consistently demonstrate in-house repairs are more cost efficient and provide stabilized materials with fewer losses than other standard practices. Binding is typically outsourced to a commercial bindery for serials and monographs, but attitudes have shifted toward reduced binding practices. Changes in binding practices by large research libraries over the past fifteen years cited in the *FY2015 Preservation Statistics Survey* continued to show a long-term decline in the practice.[15] Previously, libraries may have done "binding out of habit" rather than by purposefully determining binding needs based on a thoughtful preservation plan.[16] More economic and preservation-friendly alternatives include purchasing standard-size or custom enclosures, binding only when necessary, or binding in-house.

Several key principles have evolved from library and conservation programs. "First, when materials are treated, the treatments should, when possible, be reversible; second, whenever possible or appropriate, the originals should be preserved. Only materials that are untreatable should be reformatted; and third, library materials should be preserved for as long as possible."[17] These guiding treatment principles for preserving and conserving library collections reflect a genuine understanding of the nature and value of the materials and the collections themselves. The most difficult and complex repairs and conservation treatments are also the most needed in many libraries. Complex treatments require at least one of the following: a dedicated book conservator, collaborative work with museum conservators, highly skilled staff with dedicated time, outsourced work to private conservators, grant funding for specific treatments, specialized training, or a combination of these.

Preservation in tandem with conservation should be practiced in the same manner for library collections as the art collections, providing equal status and level of care to all the museum's collections. Answers to how this work is to be achieved have been posited for decades, yet some museums without dedicated book conservators have already found ways to fulfill this need. Cross-departmental training and professional development has enabled some librarians to devise solutions to item-level treatment with the assistance of paper conservators and their departments. Others have sought grant funding to support these needs, even if only on a temporary basis, whereas other museums have hired conservators with book conservation backgrounds to split time between two departments to enable equitable care of all collections. Ideally, museums should create a dedicated position best suited to address these needs:[18] an individual with a synthesis of education and skills in libraries, preservation, and conservation, capable of working across departments to accomplish preservation at varied levels for the library and the museum. With a broad preservation background, the museum would gain value from this individual's abilities, and library collections would benefit from full preservation services shared with other museum departments. A specialized emphasis on library collections would provide a complete range of treatments with rationale and purpose as well as a critical understanding of library collections, their uses, and potential needs.

PRESERVING FOR THE FUTURE

As collections sitting within the larger museum, it may seem at first that library collections are at a disadvantage. But it is important to remember that libraries are central to the museums' operations, and for that reason they hold the promise of the future. With one foot set in each world, art museum librarians are positioned to advance new modes of preservation and conservation for library collections both within librarianship and the museum. Preservation practices that have guided large research libraries have resulted in the significant loss of artifactual material simply due to general collection approaches to mass quantities of materials, understaffed units, and the inability to "deal" with materials of partial, potential, or unrecognized research and artifactual value.[19] More studies are being brought forth on the value and importance of nineteenth- and twentieth-century publisher's cloth bindings, the majority of which have been lost due to standard commercial binding practices done unnecessarily to make bindings more "durable" with buckram bindings, milled spines, and oversewn text.[20] This singular example in which present and potential value were not considered exemplifies how the loss of our cultural record continues to occur based on arbitrary classifications of "rare" and "general." In museums, libraries must redefine their own collections through their own preservation practices and the education of their colleagues and users. Librarians must advocate, converse, and demonstrate the significance of the library's collections: highlight the multiverse of the book as a three-dimensional object; the individuality and range of ephemera in typeface and illustration; and the diversity of paper quality, inks, and handwriting found within a collection of papers. Draw upon the similarities of libraries and museums to collect, inspire, create opportunities for learning and inquiry, and *preserve* those collections that create our cultural identities and record of humanity. The art museum library's mission is the same and deserves the same attention. Preservation is the only way to ensure these great efforts to preserve not only the information within, but rather the entirety of the object carrying it, will be "read"[21] in its original context by all potential fields of scholarly inquiry, now and in the future.

NOTES

1. Because library and archival collections vary greatly by institution and structure, they can operate together or independently, and range in purpose and scope. "Art museum library collections" and "library collections" are used to refer broadly to the collections of libraries and archives found within museums.

2. Stephen G. Nichols and Abby Smith, *The Evidence in Hand: Report of the Task Force on the Artifact in Library Collections* (Washington, DC: Council on Library and Information Resources, November 2001), 9–16.

3. Michèle Valerie Cloonan, "Preservation in Context: Libraries, Archives, Museums, and the Built Environment," in *Preserving Our Heritage: Perspectives from Antiquity to the Digital Age*, edited by Michèle Valerie Cloonan (Chicago: American Library Association, 2015), 59.

4. As defined in 2015, Northeast Document Conservation Center (NEDCC), *Preservation 101* [online textbook] (Andover, MA: Northeast Document Conservation Center, 2015), https://www.nedcc.org/preservation101/session-1/1what-is-preservation#Preservation.

5. Author describes the process of creating and implementing a preservation program at an art museum library in Beth Morris, "Optimizing Collections Care: Configuring Preservation Strategies for Unique Art Library Collections," *Art Documentation: Journal of the Art Libraries Society of North America* 34, no. 2 (2015): 301–20.

6. Reformatting is any activity where original material is migrated to a more stable format with the intent to preserve the original, and includes preservation photocopies, facsimiles, microfilming, photographing, duplication, digital imaging, and audiovisual and media migration, dependent on media type.

7. Patricia Battin, "From Preservation to Access: Paradigm for the Nineties," *IFLA Journal* 19, no. 4 (1993): 367–73.

8. Anne Evenhaugen, Shaina Buckles Harkness, Alison Huftalen, Nicole Lovenjak, Mary Wassermann, and Roger Lawson, editors, *State of Art Museum Libraries 2016: ARLIS/NA Museum Division White Paper* (Art Libraries Society of North America, 2016): 6–9. https://www.arlisna.org/images/researchreports/State_of_Art_Museum_Libraries_2016.pdf.

9. See figure 2.1 in Ross Harvey and Martha R. Mahard, *The Preservation Management Handbook: A 21st-Century Guide for Libraries, Archives, and Museums* (New York: Rowman & Littlefield, 2014). Preliminary elements critical to forming this were investigated and identified in Jeannette A. Bastian, Michèle V. Cloonan, and Ross Harvey, "From Teacher to Learner to User: Developing a Digital Stewardship Pedagogy," *Library Trends* 59, no. 4 (Spring 2011): 607–13.

10. Harvey and Mahard, *Preservation Management Handbook*, 72.

11. Temperature and humidity chart recorders are economic. The author has discovered, through personal research over the years, that many electronic data loggers are the more expensive option for monitoring temperature and relative humidity. She used a Dickson pen chart for years and found it to be very reliable, and Extech is another brand that she's come across that offers one of the most affordable digital "data loggers" available (data are imported directly to computer and is read in same manner as other pen chart recorders). At the time of this writing, any of these models can be purchased at reasonable cost.

12. Denice Rovira Hazlett, "Book Cleaning: Specialized Vacuums and Deacidification Products Help Libraries Preserve Books and Other Materials," *Library Journal* 41, no. 19 (November 15, 2016): 48–49.

13. Johanna G. Wellheiser, *Nonchemical Treatment Processes for Disinfestation of Insects and Fungi in Library Collections* (Berlin/Boston: De Gruyter, Inc., 2013), 1–8, 19–38, 83–87.

14. Maria Grandinette, Jacqueline Wagner, Brenna Campbell, and Lindsey Hobbs, Mold and Pest Training Presentation on "Preservation Programs and Services," Princeton University Library, 2018. http://library.princeton.edu/preservation/programs-and-services#mold-and-pest -remediation; Tara Kennedy, "Mold!" Connecting to Collections Care Online Community. Webinar series. February 11, 2013, https://www.connectingtocollections.org/moldrecording/; Michelle Brown, "Mold Prevention and Remediation," Association for Library Collections and Technical Services, Webcast. April 27, 2010, http://www.ala.org/alcts/confevents/upcoming /webinar/pres/051310mold.

15. Annie Peterson, Holly Robertson, and Nick Szydlowski, *Preservation Statistics Survey Report: FY2015* (Washington, DC: Preservation and Reformatting Section, Association of Library Collections and Technical Services, American Library Association, December 2016), 15. http://www.ala.org/alcts/sites/ala.org.alcts/files/content/resources/preserv/presstats/FY2015 /FY2015PreservationStatistics.pdf.

16. Brian J. Baird, "21st-Century Preservation Basics," *American Libraries* 48, no. 3/4 (March/April 2017): 56.

17. Michèle Valerie Cloonan, "The Preservation of Knowledge," in *Preserving Our Heritage: Perspectives from Antiquity to the Digital Age*, edited by Michèle Valerie Cloonan (Chicago: American Library Association, 2015), 86. (Originally in *Library Trends* 41, no. 4 [March 1993]: 594–605.)

18. Author's observation from current state and past experience. See Paul Banks, "A Library Is Not a Museum," in *Preserving Our Heritage: Perspectives from Antiquity to the Digital Age*, edited by Michèle Valerie Cloonan (Chicago: American Library Association, 2015), 68–69. (Originally in *Training in Conservation: A Symposium on the Occasion of the Dedication of Stephan Chan House, Institute of Fine Arts, New York University*, edited by Norbert S. Baer, 1989: 57–65); Don Etherington, "Historical Background of Book Conservation: The Past Forty Years," *Collection Management* 31, no. 1–2 (2007): 21–29; Roberta Pilette, "Book Conservation within Library Preservation," *Collection Management* 31, no. 1–2 (2007): 213–25.

19. Banks, "A Library is Not a Museum," 68.

20. Randy Silverman, "Can't Judge a Book without Its Binding," *Libraries and the Cultural Record* 42, no. 3 (2007): 301–3.

21. G. Thomas Tanselle, "Libraries, Museums, and Reading," *Raritan* 12, no. 1 (Summer 1992): 83.

II

ACCESS, OUTREACH, AND COLLABORATION

8

Prioritizing Special Collections in the Art Museum Library

Lee Ceperich, Virginia Museum of Fine Arts

Special collections departments are becoming increasingly vital to the success of the art museum library. This increase in prominence directly corresponds to the growing value that society in general, and museum audiences in particular, attach to authentic objects and experiences. Demographic shifts and technological advancements have generated new expectations for audience engagement that has reshaped curatorial practice. These circumstances provide an unprecedented opportunity for art museum librarians to collaborate across the institution and capitalize on their assets to increase engagement and enhance the visitor experience for the benefit of the museum. Art museum libraries that leverage their special and archival collections are well positioned to support progressive institutional missions and to flourish in the rapidly and continually evolving information landscape.

Specifically, the assets to accentuate are the unique holdings found in special collections and the singular combination of expertise and skill that librarians possess in information management in the service of discovery, accessibility, and engagement. The prospects for growing and leveraging assets to promote teaching, learning, research, and understanding are numerous. Although challenges presented by increasing the role of special collections within the museum must be mitigated, creative strategic planning to alleviate budgetary constraints and storage concerns is possible in art museum libraries of all sizes. The following insights are intended to inspire art museum librarians to increase the visibility of their collections—and promote their expertise—to leverage core skills in greater service to communities.

TYPES OF SPECIAL COLLECTIONS

Special collections in the context of this chapter include archives. Libraries, archives, and museums share fundamental objectives focused on research, access, and preservation, and are often viewed collectively in the literature as cultural heritage institutions.[1] In addition to institutional archives and manuscript holdings, the materials typically found in an art museum library's special collections are acquired to contextualize the art collections and document the history of the institution. They may include sketchbooks, scrapbooks, artist and subject files, rare books, artifacts, auction catalogs, ephemera, audiovisual material, photographic resources, antiquated equipment, digital resources, and focused assemblages of published materials. Individually and collectively, these resources document the history of the museum and of its art objects as well as the research and collection development activities of current and previous curators, donors, and librarians.

CHALLENGES FACING ART MUSEUM LIBRARIES

Primary source material has become increasingly important to the art museum library due to ongoing challenges faced by art museum libraries of all sizes. The myriad challenges have been thoroughly discussed in the professional literature for the past several decades and include shrinking budgets and staff. This situation arises from a lack of appreciation for the role that museum libraries play in contributing and supporting research and scholarship combined with changes in expectations and increased job responsibilities of librarians. Members of the Museum Library Division of the Art Libraries Society of North America conducted a survey in 2015 to identify some of the internal institutional pressures facing art museum libraries. They noted in the *State of Art Museum Libraries 2016 White Paper* that art museum library directors had been asked to provide value propositions to museum administrators to justify the cost of space, staff, and budget for the library.[2] Quantitative data for use and value of special collections have been problematic to obtain as no standard measurement tool exists and collections and practices vary considerably among libraries. The return on investment for the art museum library has defied definition, and attempts at quantification have not been adopted consistently as the value is, by its nature, intangible and subjective. The Canadian knowledge management company Lucidea examined the issues in a six-part blog in 2017 in an effort to promote their own assessment tools. They confirmed what those in the field already knew, namely that "the library is labeled as just an operational cost center; it's not associated with cost savings or revenue generation, and as a result it is underfunded."[3] Therefore, strategic *and* bottom line contributions to organizational success are being overlooked. They also state that clients have expressed that in their institutions "the library is low priority; its services and deliverables are not tied to organizational strategy; staff and content are underutilized, and it is ultimately supplanted by other departments or other initiatives."[4]

As a result, art museum libraries have seen a reduction in staff and budgets as roles have expanded to include digital outreach responsibilities while collection growth has increased. This predicament has resulted in backlogs of uncataloged and unprocessed material, reductions in public service hours, and an increasingly overwhelmed workforce. These challenging circumstances can be seen as an impetus to reinvigorate art museum libraries and change perceptions of value. One way to do this is by focusing on special collections departments and promoting collections for research and exhibition purposes while simultaneously highlighting staff expertise in information management.

Space Planning

Due to the increasing availability of online resources, curators, museum staff, and outside researchers are more often conducting research virtually rather than in museum library spaces. As a result, museum administrators may scrutinize reading rooms when use declines; these spaces often occupy prime real estate within the museum, and an empty reading room soon catches the gaze of administrators who begin envisioning the space for other uses. To increase use of the reading room, library staff can explore hosting more classes, programs, and events. If, however, the reading room is underutilized, not conducive to use of special collections materials, or staff and budgets are cut to the point that public hours are not sustainable, then the reading room should be repurposed. A perceptive library director might consider prioritizing special collections acquisitions and use over core collections and reconfiguring existing spaces accordingly. Another strategy that can further activate the library's collection is the idea of relocating the art museum library under the collections department to form a research center. The center might include special collections along with a print study room adjacent to collections of works on paper, conservation spaces, and image resources, and could feature a central shared space for public services and research.

As use of the traditional analog research collection declines and as materials are moved off-site, consolidated, or absorbed by nearby academic institutions, the importance of unique holdings in special collections increases, and the ability of staff to provide access to information online and to make meaningful connections between content and users becomes essential.

The demand to view rare books, archives, and artifacts, however, will likely rise as digitization and online availability of unique material continues to grow. Digital surrogates serve discoverability, which in turn increases demand for consulting the originals on-site. Dedicated research areas are also needed for researchers to use resources such as location-restricted or proprietary electronic resources that are only available on-site. However, as open access increases and the need to access purchased content in the physical library diminishes, physical use of the space for this purpose will also likely decrease.

Library professionals concerned about declining on-site use should be reassured by the fact that although space configurations may require changes, places on the art museum campus dedicated to research, teaching, and storage of physical collections will always be needed.

Special Collections Storage

Storage space within museums is always in high demand for art objects as well as for library resources, and there never seems to be enough space. Archives, in particular, require ample storage space for a wide variety of formats. To complicate matters further, all museum collections require climate-controlled environments; some photographic collections need cold storage facilities. Off-site storage rental, purpose-built storage spaces within the museum, and cross-departmental and cross-institutional storage arrangements are options. All require expenditure of funds and careful long-range strategic planning. Museum administrators should be regularly apprised of projected growth estimates and corresponding storage needs as part of the museum's strategic planning process.

Budget Considerations and Funding Sources

Many art museum libraries may not have a budget specifically designated for archival or special collections acquisitions. There are several options to consider when assessing financial resources available to fund collection development. The easiest course of action is to reallocate annual book acquisition budget resources for core collections by adopting a purchase-on-demand model. Another strategy might be to reallocate funds for licensed online content, serial subscriptions, and bindery services. One also might consider appealing to other departmental budget managers for funding from exhibition and curatorial budgets. Acquisitions needed for exhibition purposes might be tied into the exhibition budget or to endowments that specify expenditures for archives, special collections, and book purchases. Librarians should also consider working with the development office to identify donors or friends' groups that are amenable to offering support to special collections, and working with administrators to find opportunities for library and archival collection donations that could be negotiated along with the purchase of artwork.

Government Grants

Grant funding can be crucial in supporting the special collections department's mandate to offer access to primary source materials to a wider audience. Although library resources have traditionally supported the museum's internal research and educational needs, broad public access to special collections has been limited. Aside from scholars, the general public has been largely unaware of the existence of these specialized resources. As more collections are digitized and made available on the internet, awareness and use have increased. The positive impact on scholarship in the arts and related fields has meant that digitization projects have been increasingly funded by grants.

Federal agencies such as the Institute of Museum and Library Services and the National Endowment for the Humanities, as well as privately funded organizations such as the Samuel H. Kress Foundation and the Council on Library and Information Resources, have prioritized support for projects to process and catalog unique materials in order to expose hidden collections and underused resources; this represents a move toward democratizing the scholarly landscape and encouraging initiatives that they see as catalysts for social change.[5] The Institute of Museum and Library Services is the primary source of federal support for the nation's libraries and museums, and their stated mission is to create a nation in which museums and libraries work together to transform the lives of individuals and communities.[6] Between 2008 and 2014, the Council on Library and Information Resources, with support from the Andrew W. Mellon Foundation, funded the Cataloging Hidden Special Collections and Archives competition that awarded $27.4 million in funding for academic, cultural heritage, and other collecting institutions for the purpose of revealing previously hidden materials.[7] As staffing shortages are an ongoing concern, grant proposals were able to include costs for temporary staff. Library directors should try to turn these limited-term grant funded positions into permanent positions when the grant term ends.

COLLECTION DEVELOPMENT

Art museum libraries can benefit greatly by having a collection development policy that outlines the main subject areas collected, indicates coverage levels from minimal to exhaustive, and highlights areas of specialization that distinguish the library. By establishing the library as an essential destination for access to particular subjects or by virtue of distinctive holdings, the library becomes a research destination. Librarians must be creative. The library could be the go-to resource for nineteenth-century bookplates by an obscure artist or the only library in North America to hold complete unbound runs of a certain trade publication. If the collection holds important unique material, any scholar working in the field would be compelled to consult the library's holdings. At the same time, ensure the collection development policy provides for baseline coverage of all applicable areas related to the museum's collection so that the library has the broadest appeal to the widest audience. Furthermore, library staff must be prepared to capitalize on unexpected acquisition opportunities that could be indispensable to the museum's mission.

Diversification

In order to remain socially relevant, museums and libraries should endeavor to diversify collections, programming, outreach, and staffing. Dr. Johnnetta Betsch Cole, director of the National Museum of African Art, Smithsonian Institution, Washington, DC, delivered the keynote address at the American Alliance of Museums meeting in Atlanta in 2015. She stressed that diversification in the museum space is the most critical issue that will impact the future of museums and that diversity is inextricably linked with the social value of museums.[8] Cole pointed out that, as illustrated by U.S. Census data, the demographics of the United States are changing rapidly and that in the next thirty years, the United States will become a majority-minority country.[9]

As art museums strive to meet this mandate of change, special collections can and must support the effort through prioritizing acquisition and access to new content associated with diverse audiences and seek opportunities to acquire material that will meet the interests and needs of underserved audiences. The benefit of diversification and reexamination of traditional cultural perceptions that inform collection and exhibition practices will allow museums to remain relevant to society. As Olga Viso asserted in her opinion piece for the *New York Times* in 2018, "If museums want to continue to have a place, . . . [t]hey must position themselves as learning communities, not impenetrable centers of self-validating authority."[10]

ACCESSIBILITY

As information professionals, library staff are uniquely qualified to take the lead in making physical and online content discoverable and accessible. To this end, technical services librarians, archivists, and catalogers possess the expertise in metadata creation and can ensure that descriptive metadata avoids intentional or unintentional cultural biases that limit resource discovery. There is a lot of information available to assist librarians and administrators to ensure that physical spaces in the museum follow Americans with Disabilities Act standards.[11] Because art museum libraries have an obligation to ensure that their collection spaces and intellectual content are equally accessible to all, librarians have an opportunity to ensure that accessibility standards are a matter of institutional policy. By sharing this expertise, museum administrators will recognize that librarians and archivists possess the skills needed to lead cross-departmental efforts to ensure that accessibility for all becomes a reality in art museums.

EXHIBITIONS

Exhibitions of special collections materials within the library, online, and in the galleries should be a priority for the art museum library. Exhibition exposure coupled with online documentation of associated content is the best way to ensure that resources are seen by as many people as possible. The trend toward the inclusion of bibliographic content in museum exhibitions has been a boon to special collections departments. First, the philosophical shift provides a broader context in the humanities and underscores the importance of the material to the narrative of the exhibition. When juxtaposed with art objects in exhibitions, the objects from special collections serve to make connections between audience and object in a meaningful way; the materiality of primary sources serves to foster human connections by illustrating the universal human experience across time and cultures. An example of an exhibition that relied heavily on special collections materials to convey the personal life of an artist was *Van Gogh and the Colors of the Night* shown at the Museum of Modern Art in New York from 2008 to 2009.[12] The selection of books and letters exhibited along with the artwork gave viewers vivid insight into the artist's creative journey that is essential to understanding Van Gogh's work. In addition to telling the story of an artist's inner thoughts, documentation found in special collections may be thoughtfully utilized to reveal truths and unknown histories by illuminating stories that have been hidden or ignored. Showing an issue of the *Black Panther Newspaper* alongside Emory Douglas's graphic art can give great insight into the political climate of the 1960s, for example. Highlighting narratives of underrepresented communities supports institutional priorities of promoting diversity, inclusion, and accessibility.

Secondly, participation in permanent or temporary exhibitions connects the library department with all aspects of exhibition development, from initiating conservation and digitization efforts to installation, marketing, publications, and programming. The involvement perpetuates awareness and generates continued interest in library resources. Following this collaborative model, for the past ten years the Virginia Museum of Fine Arts (VMFA) has consistently shown special collections resources in the permanent galleries and frequently included special collections materials in traveling exhibitions. Past examples include *Gordon Parks: Back to Fort Scott* in 2016 and *Edward Hopper and the American Hotel* in 2019. In 2021, the VMFA exhibitions *Virginia Arcadia* and *Man Ray: The Paris Years* will feature a wide selection of rare books and period documentation that are integral to the shows.

By attending exhibition planning meetings, the art museum librarian will be well prepared to identify internal and external resources that will enhance the content of the exhibition. All new acquisitions and incoming exhibitions present new objects that may either tie in with existing material in special collections or prompt acquisitions to fill in gaps. Once resources have been identified, the librarian can work with curatorial and exhibition planning staff to acquire items from outside sources that may be borrowed from other libraries or purchased. Curators often discover rare books and materials from outside sources during the course of their research but neglect to check their own institution's library holdings. To counteract this phenomenon, librarians should stay abreast of exhibition checklists and communicate regularly with curators and curatorial staff regarding exhibition plans. Colleagues are invariably delighted to learn that the resource sought is readily available on-site, thereby avoiding an unnecessary purchase or contract for an outside loan. Even if the desired item is not held by the institution, the librarian may be able to arrange a loan or purchase the material for the library's collection. If art museum librarians invest time to build relationships and trust with other departments in their own organizations, their colleagues will become attuned to consulting librarians and considering library resources for exhibition as a matter of course.

It is imperative that library professionals take the initiative to foster collaboration between the library and other departments in the museum. Library staff should be encouraged to network with colleagues at every possible opportunity, including meetings and social events, and to take an active role in a broad range of museum activities. Collaboration with curatorial colleagues is vital because they are responsible for object acquisitions and exhibition development. Curators are often overworked and under stress to meet deadlines and therefore will likely be receptive to offers of assistance. Offer your expertise by identifying special collections materials that will relate to objects in their checklists. Showing library materials in the permanent galleries and in temporary exhibitions is an unparalleled opportunity for museum libraries to increase the visibility of their holdings and to demonstrate how relevant they are to the work of the institution. An example of a successful curatorial collaboration at VMFA centered on the acquisition of material for VMFA archives that ultimately resulted in the critically acclaimed *Working Together: Louis Draper and the Kamoinge Workshop*,[13] a photography exhibition that included manuscript material, books, video, serials, and even camera equipment. The library would not have been able to acquire these objects without the gift purchase arrangement made by leadership at the VMFA. The exhibition and catalog would not have been possible without the dedicated efforts of the curator, archivist, and other museum staff supported by a major National Endowment for the Humanities grant. The result of this collaboration was the establishment of an online research portal that supports ongoing scholarship and discovery.

Other departments present opportunities for collaboration, too. The education department is another core constituent of library content and services. Collaborate regularly with adult and childhood educational staff to learn of resource needs for teachers for standards of learning and K–12 education. Partner with the educational staff to present special collections materials in classes, symposia, and workshops. Let the director's office and development teams know that staff from the library are available to make presentations highlighting library resources for trustee orientations and VIP tours. Host your professional organization's meetings at your library and offer tours of special collections. If your institution has a travel program for members, express your interest in hosting a tour and giving lectures to highlight relevant museum and special collections resources associated with art and sites visited on the trip. Increase your exposure to donors by attending member events and high-level fundraising affairs.

If a museum has an active paper conservation program, the library may work with museum conservation professionals already on the museum payroll to eliminate the need for permanent or contract conservators on the library staff. Librarians can benefit from offering library materials as projects for graduate internships in conservation, a scenario that is equally beneficial to the library and the student.

As societies and museums evolve simultaneously, the function of the art museum library is changing. By creatively embracing new ways of working and sharing collections, the art museum library will remain vital to the success of the museum. Prioritizing unique resources and supporting a museum's mission to effect meaningful social change, the museum art library will continue to thrive into the next century.

NOTES

1. Sidney E. Berger, *Rare Books and Special Collections* (Chicago: Neal-Schuman, 2014), 421.

2. Anne Evenhaugen, Shaina Buckles Harkness, Alison Huftalen, Nicole Loveniak, Mary Wassermann, and Roger Lawson, editors, *State of Art Museum Libraries 2016: ARLIS/NA Museum Division White Paper* (Art Libraries Society of North America, 2016), 6–9. https://www .arlisna.org/images/researchreports/State_of_Art_Museum_Libraries_2016.pdf.

3. "Part Two—Overcoming 6 Challenges to Special Library Sustainability" *Lucidea* (blog), February 24, 2017. Accessed August 14, 2020, https://lucidea.com/blog/overcoming-6 -challenges-to-special-library-sustainability-part-two/.

4. "Part One—Overcoming 6 Challenges to Special Library Sustainability" *Lucidea* (blog), February 24, 2017. Accessed August 14, 2020, https://lucidea.com/blog/overcoming-6 -challenges-to-special-library-sustainability-part-one/.

5. A. Freeman, S. Adams Becker, M. Cummins, E, McKelroy, C. Giesinger, and B. Yuhnke, *NMC Horizon Report: 2016 Museum Edition* (Austin, Texas: The New Media Consortium, 2016), 10.

6. Elizabeth Holton, "IMLS Announces National Study on Museums, Libraries, and Social Wellbeing: New Research Will Measure Institutions' Critical Role in Their Communities," press release, August 29, 2018. Accessed August 14, 2020, https://www.imls.gov/news /imls-announces-national-study-museums-libraries-and-social-wellbeing.

7. Joy Banks, *The Foundations of Discovery: A Report on the Assessment of the Impacts of the Cataloging Hidden Collections Program, 2008–2019* (Council on Library and Information Resources: September 2019).

8. Johnnetta Betsch Cole, Keynote Address, "Museums, Diversity, and Social Value," American Alliance of Museums Annual Meeting, April 27, 2015. https://aamd.org/our-members /from-the-field/johnnetta-cole-museums-diversity-social-value.

9. Ibid.

10. Olga Viso, "Decolonizing the Art Museum: The Next Wave," *New York Times*, May 1, 2018. https://www.nytimes.com/2018/05/01/opinion/decolonizing-art-museums.html.

11. Since the ratification of the Americans with Disabilities Act in 1991, the U.S. Department of Justice has compiled a comprehensive body of literature on implementing accessibility standards. See U.S. Department of Justice, Civil Rights Division, "Information and Technical Assistance on the Americans with Disabilities Act," accessed August 19, 2020, https://www .ada.gov/2010_regs.htm.

12. Museum of Modern Art Department of Communications, press release, September 16, 2008. Accessed May 14, 2020, https://assets.moma.org/documents/moma_press-release _387158.pdf.

13. Virginia Museum of Fine Arts, "Exhibitions: Working Together: Louis Draper and the Kamoinge Workshop: February 1, 2020–October 18, 2020." Accessed May 14, 2020, https:// www.vmfa.museum/exhibitions/exhibitions/working-together-kamoinge/.

9

The Life of the (Third-) Party (System)

Integrated Library Systems and Discovery Layers

Dan Lipcan, Peabody Essex Museum

As expected, the landscape of bibliographic control and discovery has shifted significantly since the 2007 publication of *Art Museum Libraries and Librarianship*.[1] Libraries are often conservative when making changes or migrating systems, as these processes can be time-consuming, expensive, and fraught with the possibility of losing important data. Much consolidation has occurred in the field, as vendors that were once start-ups decide to sell, more venture capital money has entered the equation, and libraries have decided to migrate to better-performing systems.[2] In this vein, one development that will have major implications on the library systems universe occurred as of the writing of this chapter—yet it remains to be seen how libraries will be affected by this in the longer term:[3] Innovative Interfaces announced its acquisition by Ex Libris.[4] To this point vendors have, in general, expressed a commitment to maintaining legacy and acquired products, but the realistic expectation should be that eventually they will become burdensome to support and develop. Libraries that remain on outdated systems must recognize that migration will be necessary—if only to offer new and essential functionality and interoperability—and should prepare accordingly.[5]

A SAMPLING OF THE CURRENT STATE OF ART MUSEUM LIBRARY SYSTEMS

An informal and limited survey of art library museum systems was conducted in order to construct a general impression of the state of the field.[6] A list of librarians self-identifying as "Museum Librarian" was downloaded from the Art Libraries Society of North America member directory.[7] Names were discarded, institutions were de-duplicated, and all but art museum libraries were removed. The resulting total of sixty-three art museum libraries' catalogs were consulted online and, based on direct observation of the results, statistics were compiled. Library catalogs were counted as either (a) unavailable to the public, (b) a "traditional" integrated library system, or (c) a library services platform. Discovery layers were tallied as either present or not present. Consortial relationships, such as several libraries sharing a single catalog, or a library's appearance as a "branch" of a larger external system's catalog, were noted.

As shown in figures 9.1 and 9.2, over half the surveyed libraries continue to use a "traditional" integrated library system, and the adoption of discovery layers remains low at 36.5 percent. Several factors might be attributed to this delay: a lack of financial or staff resources; a lack of confidence that these systems are mature, or that they will be accepted by the user base; a desire to let other/larger institutions figure it out; and an unwillingness to face major changes.[8] The danger in these attitudes is multi-dimensional: beyond abdicating opportunities to help shape the future of library systems and interfaces, the risk of further marginalization, resource cuts, and closings arise if the library is not engaging users where—and in how—they are doing their research.

THE INTEGRATED LIBRARY SYSTEM
AND LIBRARY SERVICES PLATFORM

"Traditional" integrated library systems (ILSs), based on a client-server architecture, remain in wide use in art museum libraries. Some examples are Millennium by Innovative Interfaces,[9] Aleph and Voyager from ExLibris,[10] and Horizon by SirsiDynix.[11] Typically, these systems are managed and hosted by an external vendor responsible for development in response to customer feedback and technological and conceptual changes. The ILS consists of modules for each facet of library activity: circulation, cataloging, acquisitions, and more; some systems require additional licenses with each concurrently open module, which can result in rejected connections if too many staff are using too many modules simultaneously. MARC remains the foundation of the cataloging schema.

The traditional client-server architecture, in which library software is installed on specific workstations, is proving increasingly difficult to support in a more mobile working environment. A long-overdue move toward web-based staff interfaces is therefore very welcome and will prove essential to future work patterns. The associated conveniences in access and administration should not be underestimated. However, this change has come very gradually and often at the expense of innovation while vendors figure out how to implement and license this approach.[12]

The desire to move libraries into a semantic web environment has driven the library community to develop new models, cataloging codes, and ontologies that continue to evolve, often more rapidly than supporting technologies can mature. Now, some library systems' data structures—those of Library Service Platforms (LSPs), that is—are more open and can be operated by using application programming interfaces and other machine-based tactics. These systems offer full CRUD

Library System Categories in a Sample of Art Museum Libraries

● Integrated Library System   ● Library Services Platform   ● None/Private/Unavailable

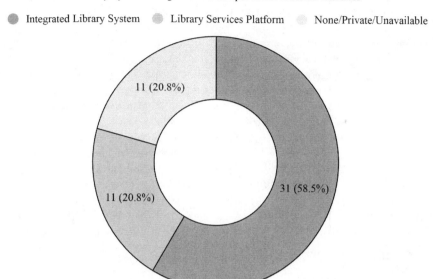

11 (20.8%)

11 (20.8%)

31 (58.5%)

Figure 9.1. Library system categories in a sample of art museum libraries. Created by the author.

Discovery Layers in a Sample of Art Museum Libraries

● Present   ● Absent

Figure 9.2. Discovery layers in a sample of art museum libraries. Created by the author.

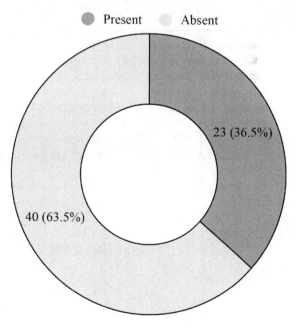

23 (36.5%)

40 (63.5%)

(create-read-update-delete) application programming interfaces for batch and machine harvesting and editing. Other significant benefits of LSPs are their ability to translate library data into Linked Open Data and, perhaps crucially for libraries operating within museum contexts, the opportunity to integrate the library catalog with the parent organization's other systems.

A significant concern for museum libraries, particularly those that are short on staff or technical skill and expertise, will be how to manage and execute a migration of library data and implement a new system or platform that has expanded functionality. Leveraging that increased functionality requires a rethinking of what is essential to library operations, a willingness to consider jettisoning long-established practices—or even traditional structures—and investing in building staff skill sets.

Many of the larger or more well-funded art museum libraries have migrated to systems more commonly categorized as LSPs, following the lead of large academic libraries. LSPs like Alma from ExLibris[13] or WorldShare Management Services from OCLC[14] are designed to handle a universe with a different proportion of electronic and digital collections to traditional print. Web-based interfaces are standard, workflows are integrated into the platform, and there is support for a wide variety of cataloging and data standards.

The increasing expense of ILS and LSP licensing and implementation has created a market for the adoption of open-source systems like Koha.[15] A library is unable to avoid some cost, because an open source system needs to be customized to a library's specific and immediate needs. Some libraries rely on consultative relationships for developing the open-source ILS, much like the traditional arrangements between libraries and ILS vendors. However, these arrangements are expected to be more flexible than the typical ILS contract[16] and development work that is sponsored by a library is shared back with the community so others can reuse the code.[17] The cautionary tale here is that an open-source system, although "free," still requires investments in maintenance and development, and may require an increased reliance on the museum's information technology structure. To date, several art museum libraries have implemented open-source systems, notably the Rijksmuseum Research Library,[18] The Betty Boyd Dettre Library and Research Center at the National Museum of Women in the Arts[19]—both on Koha—and the Art Reference Library of the North Carolina Museum of Art,[20] an Evergreen system[21] administered by the State Library of North Carolina.

Consortial approaches to the programming and development needs of these systems have also risen as an alternative to the outsourcing of this work to traditional library system vendors. Several museum libraries' catalogs and discovery systems are tied to another institution's catalog, as if they are a branch library. Organizational efficiencies can be realized, and partners can be relied upon to provide staff with the necessary technological skill sets, but some degree of independence and control must be compromised. For example, as with the North Carolina Museum of Art, the Royal Ontario Museum is affiliated with a larger institution—in this case, the enormous University of Toronto Libraries.[22] The Royal Ontario Museum offers access to their library collections in exchange for the use of the university's library systems,[23] a relationship that benefits both partners—and frees the museum to devote precious resources elsewhere.

DISCOVERY LAYERS AND MUSEUM INTEGRATIONS

Discovery products—with the aim of providing access to a broader swath of library collections, primarily electronic resources and articles accessible through subscribed collections of e-journals—began to appear in the late 2000s.[24] The idea that a library user could, through a single search box replicating the Google experience, retrieve more than holdings in the print collection was undeniably attractive from a service perspective.[25] Returning to the informal survey of art museum library catalogs and user interfaces referred to earlier, 36.5 percent of libraries use a discovery layer separate from, or built on top of, the library catalog. The concept is simple, logical, and service-oriented: How can we enable our users to search simultaneously across all of our collections?

Yet, while the interface was familiar to and intuitive for users, questions arose. The most crucial of these is the misleading impression given to users that a discovery layer search returns results from among the entire spectrum of the library's collection. In practice, there are always databases and resources not profiled or accessible through a discovery layer; the question is how to communicate that succinctly to library users. The Getty Research Institute's instance of Primo, for example, provides one method of addressing this issue: clearly listing what is and is not being searched on its landing page.[26]

Another consideration is the complexity in setting up these systems and profiling them to connect to the appropriate databases and repositories. Recalling the change factors mentioned previously, significant time and resources—and new sets of staff skills—may be required to do so, and may engender changes in the library staffing structure itself.[27] Library systems vendors have built and support discovery products, such as Primo from ExLibris and Encore from Innovative Interfaces, that are intended to be implemented seamlessly with their systems, and already enjoy relatively broad adoption—yet they present their own set of issues. Vendor conflicts preventing indexing on a library's entire collection—for example, EBSCO preventing their resources from being made available to Primo customers[28]—may be mitigated by "agnostic" systems and discovery layers like OCLC's WorldCat Discovery[29] and open-source solutions like Blacklight,[30] but should not be a deciding factor.

One recent product release of note is Innovative's Inspire, a discovery service run by "a context engine built on BIBFRAME and linked data concepts"[31] and using a visually oriented interface for navigating and discovering resources.[32] It remains to be seen how Innovative's recent acquisition by Ex Libris affects the promotion, development, and adoption of the product over the longer term.

For museum libraries, the most encouraging development must be the effort to integrate library holdings with museum collections in a unified search. The work that has been done to present users with this flavor of federated search holds great promise to satisfy a long-held museum library desire to connect works of art with related research materials.

Some examples include the Rijksmuseum documentation entries in museum object records[33] that provide direct links to library catalog records for works referencing the object. The Philadelphia Museum of Art Library and Archives federated search platform[34] provides search functionality across museum objects, the set of library and archive records, several databases, and selected repositories of digitized materials. The Getty Search Gateway[35] from the J. Paul Getty Trust is another institutional search model: across the library catalog, digital collections, finding aids, and museum objects. Notably, it does not include article databases or external digital repositories; these may be searched either in the library's discovery layer, Primo, or entirely separately. The Georgia O'Keeffe Museum's "Collections Online"[36] (currently in beta testing) facilitates searching across multiple collection areas, including art, artist materials, archives, and O'Keeffe's books and possessions—a very promising model.

For these kinds of outcomes to succeed, the "parent" institution must be invested in integrating the library into collection search platforms, and librarians must be willing to advocate for inclusion. Otherwise there is little motivation for a museum's collection managers, curatorial staff, and web developers to consider the interests and needs of the library.

Art museum libraries today face a complex universe of options for library systems and discovery platforms. Due to the variety in museum libraries themselves—in collection size, budgetary power, collecting areas, staffing, and other attributes—it is impossible to prescribe one solution that will work for all. However, because (as has been said) "it's not about the catalogue anymore, it's about the data,"[37] we can rely on the decades invested in creating standardized resource descriptions to form the backbone of whatever comes next. In libraries, the catalog—the data about our collections—is the planet around which our other services orbit. It is therefore essential that we continue to think carefully about how we want our systems to work for us and for our users, and devote time and resources to building the skills and capacities to get us there.

NOTES

1. Joan M. Benedetti, editor, *Art Museum Libraries and Librarianship* (Lanham, MD: The Scarecrow Press, Inc., 2007).

2. Marshall Breeding, "Library Systems Report 2017," *American Libraries*, May 1, 2017. https://americanlibrariesmagazine.org/2017/05/01/library-systems-report-2017. Each spring, Breeding publishes a report on the state of library systems, several of which are cited here. These annual articles provide a convenient summary for librarians monitoring systems trends and developments. His website, https://librarytechnology.org/, includes an archive of these reports and is a comprehensive source of related documents and information.

3. Roger C. Schonfeld, "What Are the Larger Implications of Ex Libris Buying Innovative?" *Ithaka S+R Blog*, December 5, 2019. https://sr.ithaka.org/blog/what-are-the-larger-implications-of-ex-libris-buying-innovative.

4. Innovative Interfaces, "Ex Libris Signs Definitive Agreement to Acquire Innovative," *Innovative in the News*, December 5, 2019. https://www.iii.com/media/ex-libris-signs-definitive-agreement-to-acquire-innovative.

5. The author would like to add here that any mention of vendors, products, and systems in this chapter is not to be construed as an endorsement or recommendation.

6. This environmental scan was designed and executed by the author in September and October 2019.

7. "ARLIS/NA Membership Directory," Art Libraries Society of North America. Accessed October 4, 2019, https://www.arlisna.org/membership/directory.

8. Marshall Breeding, "Library Systems Report 2019," *American Libraries*, May 1, 2019. https://americanlibrariesmagazine.org/2019/05/01/library-systems-report-2019/.

9. "Library Software Products and Services," Innovative Interfaces. Accessed October 16, 2019, https://www.iii.com/products/. Millennium is not listed here, though it remains a supported product.

10. "Cloud-based Solutions for Higher Education," Ex Libris Ltd. Accessed October 16, 2019, https://www.exlibrisgroup.com/.

11. "Products," Sirsi Corporation. Accessed October 16, 2019, https://www.sirsidynix.com/products/.

12. Breeding, "Library Systems Report 2019."

13. "Alma Cloud-Based Library Services Platform," Ex Libris Ltd. Accessed October 16, 2019, https://www.exlibrisgroup.com/products/alma-library-services-platform/.

14. "WorldShare Management Services," OCLC. Accessed October 16, 2019, https://www.oclc.org/en/worldshare-management-services.html.

15. "Official Website of Koha Library Software," Koha Library Software Community. Accessed October 16, 2019, https://koha-community.org/.

16. "About," Koha Library Software Community. Accessed October 16, 2019, https://koha-community.org/about/.

17. "Custom Development," ByWater Solutions. Accessed October 16, 2019, https://bywatersolutions.com/services/custom-development.

18. "Rijksmuseum Research Library Catalog," The Rijksmuseum. Accessed October 16, 2019, https://library.rijksmuseum.nl/.

19. "Library and Archives," National Museum of Women in the Arts. Accessed October 16, 2019, https://nmwa.org/learn/library-archives.

20. "Library—NCMA," North Carolina Museum of Art. Accessed October 16, 2019, https://ncartmuseum.org/art/library/.

21. "Home—NC Museum of Art Library," State Library of North Carolina. Accessed October 16, 2019, https://art.nccardinal.org/eg/opac/home.

22. "About," University of Toronto Libraries. Accessed October 16, 2019, https://onesearch.library.utoronto.ca/about.

23. "Management Practice: Access and Circulation," Royal Ontario Museum Library and Archives, last revised March 2017. https://www.rom.on.ca/sites/default/files/imce/access_and_circulation_-_management_practice_-_december_2016_0.pdf.

24. Marshall Breeding, "Automation Marketplace 2010: New Models, Core Systems," *Library Journal* 134, no. 6 (April 1, 2010). https://librarytechnology.org/repository/item.pl?id=14672.

25. Marshall Breeding, "Plotting a New Course for Metasearch," *Computers in Libraries* 25, no. 2 (February 2005): 27–30. https://librarytechnology.org/document/11341.

26. "Library catalog," Getty Research Institute. Accessed October 19, 2019, https://primo.getty.edu/primo-explore/search?vid=GRI.

27. Dee Baldwin, Michael Kucsak, and Alice Eng, "Don't Touch that String! There Went the Databases," *Library Faculty Presentations and Publications*, University of North Florida 7 (2012). https://digitalcommons.unf.edu/library_facpub/7.

28. Breeding, Marshall, "The Future of Library Resource Discovery: A White Paper Commissioned by the NISO Discovery to Delivery (D2D) Topic Committee," 2015. http://www.niso.org/apps/group_public/download.php/14487/future_library_resource_discovery.pdf.

29. "WorldCat Discovery: Single Search of All Library Collections," OCLC. Accessed October 19, 2019, https://www.oclc.org/en/worldcat-discovery.html.

30. "Home," Project Blacklight. Accessed October 19, 2019, https://projectblacklight.org/.

31. "Innovative Inspire Discovery," Innovative Interfaces. Accessed October 19, 2019, https://www.iii.com/products/inspire-discovery/.

32. Innovative Interfaces, "Innovative Launches Inspire™ Discovery for Academic Libraries," April 10, 2019. https://www.iii.com/inspire-launch-april-2019/.

33. For an example, see "Documentation" under the "Object data" section of "Woman Reading a Letter, Johannes Vermeer, c. 1663," The Rijksmuseum, accessed November 2, 2019, https://www.rijksmuseum.nl/en/rijksstudio/artists/johannes-vermeer/objects#/SK-C-251,1.

34. "Philadelphia Museum of Art Library and Archives Search," Philadelphia Museum of Art. Accessed November 2, 2019, http://pmalibrary.deepwebaccess.com/pmalibrary/desktop/en/search.html.

35. "Getty Search Gateway Home," The J. Paul Getty Trust. Accessed November 2, 2019, http://search.getty.edu/gateway/landing.

36. "Collections Online," Georgia O'Keeffe Museum. Accessed April 24, 2020, https://collections.okeeffemuseum.org/.

37. Emmanuelle Bermès, "Enabling Your Catalogue for the Semantic Web," in *Catalogue 2.0: The Future of the Library Catalogue*, edited by Sally Chambers (Chicago: Neal-Schuman, 2013), 117.

10

Reconsidering the Reference Collection

Using Print Art Reference Materials as Training Tools

*Gwen Mayhew, Canadian Centre for Architecture,
and Annalise Welte, Getty Research Institute*

As the availability of digital research tools increases, it is becoming a common practice for libraries of all sizes and disciplines to reduce their print reference collection by deaccessioning these items or sending them off-site.[1] Although less prevalent in the arts than in other disciplines such as social sciences,[2] online resources are now replacing much of the print collection. Financial considerations, as well as a lack of space, make it especially appealing to favor online resources over print.[3] As onsite collections are reduced, this is a prime opportunity for librarians to reexamine print art reference materials with the goal of helping their staff, and by extension, their researchers, better utilize these resources that fill the gap that digital resources may not cover. In addition to space planning and budgetary decisions, coming together to analyze print resources also creates an opportunity for staff development and growth.

The twenty-first-century librarian or researcher may instinctually begin their research online.[4] After reviewing their library's print reference collection, Johnson et al. (2015) wrote that "librarian use of print reference in the age of Google was waning,"[5] and although the article focused on a large academic library, the same can be said for many museum libraries as well. There is a clear gap in the literature when it comes to the use (or lack of use) of print reference books in art museum libraries. However, there are many articles written on this topic that focus specifically on academic libraries, and many of the same principles can apply. Library catalogs, databases, and even some catalogues raisonnés may now be easily searched online and accessed from home or a local library. When looking for information, one may even begin with Google, by asking Siri or Alexa, or chatting virtually with a librarian. As today's college and graduate students begin careers in the museum world, it seems clear that they will expect important resources to be available online.

Meanwhile, recent graduates are coming out of library schools where they focused on electronic resources and how to use them most effectively—students are still being taught how to conduct a reference interview, but they are less likely to be taught how to use print reference materials effectively.[6] Gone are the days of librarians and researchers sifting through periodical indexes to find article citations, or browsing through multi-volume encyclopedia sets for that elusive entry on a specific topic. Although there are many obvious advantages to accessing digital information—including the ability to get it any time of day, translate materials instantly through Google Translate, or share the information via email with colleagues—print resources should not be overlooked as valuable research tools. As we move toward an increasingly digital future, it is essential that art museum librarians are still familiar with the print resources that may never be available online.

FIRST IMPRESSIONS

The reference collection is often the first thing a researcher sees when entering the library—rows upon rows of encyclopedias, indexes, dictionaries, and more. Although some libraries have already removed large swaths (if not all) of these materials,[7] most have not. The reference collection can reflect the depth and breadth of a museum's collection, and often includes resources like foreign language dictionaries and materials focusing on artists of a specific nationality, gender, or time period (or all of the above). Although the location of reference books hasn't necessarily changed in the last few decades, our reliance on them certainly has.

For libraries with closed stacks, the print reference collection may provide the only resources available to researchers quickly and without requiring staff to page the materials. The reference collection can be especially useful to the casual or accidental researcher who wanders into the library during a visit to the museum. Reference books provide researchers who may just be curious to learn more about an object or artist in the museum's collection with direct access to the answers they need, ideally promoting appreciation for the art library in the process.

That said, how many art museum librarians would say that they have "a bloated reference collection focused on the needs of patrons from 20 years ago offer[ing] little service to current patrons"?[8] What can librarians do to better serve the researcher in 2020 and beyond? Questions like this led the authors to investigate underutilized print reference collections with a number of queries in mind. Most importantly, are print reference books still useful? If so, why aren't they being used? Is it because librarians don't know what's in them? Or if they are truly not useful anymore—if one can really get all of the answers to "ready reference" questions online—why is so much importance placed upon them by presenting them to researchers as the first thing they see when they walk in the door? And if print reference collections are reduced, what should replace them?

When thinking about the print reference collection, art museum librarians can start by assessing the needs of their users and making sure that collections align with and support their research requirements. Collection development, periodic review, and weeding can all play an important role in keeping the reference collection useful and relevant. That said, it is important to consider what else could be placed in the prime space often allocated to the reference collection, if not traditional reference books. The answer will vary from library to library but can include catalogues raisonnés, materials related to exhibitions, or even space for display cases highlighting rare books from the library's collection.

GETTING TO KNOW THE PRINT REFERENCE COLLECTION

It is essential that any library considering how to approach its print reference collection first understand exactly what it has. A close review of the reference collection allows librarians to uncover surprising holdings such as the *Dictionary of Marine Artists* by Dorothy Brewington, a resource available only in print that provides biographical information on over three thousand maritime artists from all over the world. The Guide to Imagery series, published by the J. Paul Getty Museum and not available online, can help librarians assisting researchers with questions on a wide variety of subjects, including food, gardens, music, and Old Testament figures. Librarians can also have the opportunity to say hello to old friends, like all thirty-four volumes of the *Grove Dictionary of Art*. Classic volumes like *Guide to the Literature of Art History 1* and *2* and *Guide to Reference Books* can provide a broad overview of the strengths and gaps in reference collections.

Librarians should conduct a physical review to assess the print reference collection. Libraries that keep statistics on use have a clear advantage in making informed decisions related to collection development.[9] Tracking can include browse counting in the library's integrated library system, making notations in a statistics tracking tool like Gimlet, or by using other resources to gather reference statistics. Libraries with smaller budgets may consider using an Excel spreadsheet or Google Forms to compile and track reference interactions.

Libraries without a formal method of tracking use of reference materials should consider other ways of determining what in their collection is most consulted. This is a prime opportunity to reach out to curators, editors, educators, other staff, and volunteers in your museum to find out what they are using in the reference collection. What is already part of their "research toolkit," and what do they wish they had? Are there specific resources that they wish that the library, and more specifically, the reference collection, included? As these conversations progress, this is an important opportunity to bring up print resources related to their research topics of which they may not be aware.

Another consideration when thinking about the reference collection is being aware of the needs of users. In academic libraries, student research behaviors define a strong need for e-resources, but museum library users may have different require-ments.[10] Creating a formal survey to examine users' research needs is worth doing for any museum library reevaluating its print reference collection. Topics to consider include:

- What are my library's hours? Because reference materials don't circulate, are we open enough to allow our researchers to use our print reference collection?
- Who is using my library? Is it mostly full-time staff? Are there volunteers or contractual employees who would be better served by electronic subscription resources that they can access from home via a proxy server? Or would our users prefer to conduct their research using print resources in the library?
- Are there other libraries we can partner with to meet the needs of our research-ers? Obviously, art museums are more likely to have art-specific resources, but more standard or generic reference sources, both print and online, may be avail-able at nearby colleges and universities.

While these statistics are informative for acquiring additional materials, they can also be beneficial for the purposes of weeding and space planning. If space con-straints cause the reference collection to be evaluated for deaccessioning or weeding, use data can assist with making data-driven decisions. If there are duplicate copies or a digital version, one may feel more confident in considering those items for weed-ing. Digital versions can be linked to physical holdings in a library's catalog, allowing users to easily discover and access the online resource—or come in to view the print resource if preferred.

However, it is important to fully analyze any digital versions as they may not be a complete replica of the print version. For example, copyright restrictions may pre-vent images from appearing in a full-text entry, making an argument for prioritizing the print version. A moving wall can prevent current issues of a journal from being accessed online, creating a case for a possible compromise of sending issues off-site only after they become fully available online from a reliable resource. Digital ver-sions of classic resources such as the *Grove Dictionary of Art* and *Benezit* are available through a subscription to *Oxford Art Online*, but if a library is experiencing financial difficulties and needs to cancel its subscription, it will be important to retain these key research tools.

USING THE PRINT REFERENCE COLLECTION
AS A TRAINING TOOL

It is worth critically rethinking the way librarians think about print resources, from considering them as outdated tomes taking up precious storage space to appreciating them as valuable tools with demonstrated merit for research purposes. Evaluating these resources is helpful for determining use statistics, but it also aids staff in becoming more familiar with their own collection. In building this familiarity with print art reference books, they can be introduced more often in reference interactions with researchers. It is important to not only think of these print resources differently, but also to ensure that all library staff members will be equipped with the tools they need to understand and utilize these resources for themselves and the researchers they assist.

It is through this shift in thinking that the print art reference collection becomes the basis of training and development for all library personnel. Creating a training program highlighting print reference materials can take many forms. In developing training, librarians need to consider the frequency of meetings and, ideally, make them available to all library employees. It is essential that not just reader services staff are invited, but also those in all library departments and at all levels—acquisitions personnel may utilize bibliographies to find titles to add, whereas library administrators may think of these materials differently with regard to space planning. Incorporating a wide range of library employees can assist in showing staff that the sessions are valuable and worth their support. Seasoned librarians can reacquaint themselves with materials they may not have used for some time while new employees may be introduced to these materials for the first time. The more staff that become knowledgeable about these resources, the better users can be served.

To approach the print reference collection as a training tool for staff, begin by developing general themes that are within the scope of the collection. Pull print reference materials relevant to the chosen topic. Formulate practice reference questions based on the institution's collection or use real-life examples culled from email or anecdotal evidence. For example, a librarian could select an object from the museum's collection and search the print reference materials for relevant titles. Staff members may be asked to come up with one or two print titles that might assist in a reference question for a particular subject. Examples of themes include foreign language art term dictionaries, art encyclopedias, and iconography. A resource chosen for its relevance to art museum libraries for a training session on foreign language art term dictionaries could be *Courierspeak: A Phrase Book for Couriers of Museum Objects* by Cordelia Rose (1993). This multi-lingual guide delivers helpful terms on caring for and protecting art objects on loan, illustrated by comedic frogs. This book is not readily available as an e-book or in a digital format, which is the case for many older, out-of-print reference books. Commonly used online translation tools may be less effective for translating this type of specialized language. Digital resources can also work well in tandem with print sources. Conducting a search for Brazilian painter Regina Pujol yields no results in *Oxford Art Online* and Getty Union List of Artist Names. However, a search of *Allgemeines Künstlerlexikon*, a resource that is now available online, gave a citation for a print resource: *Diccionario de Pintores y Escultores Españoles del Siglo XX*. If this dictionary, which is not available digitally, had been weeded, it would have been difficult to find additional information on this obscure artist.

In order to add some levity to an otherwise potentially dry subject, the authors chose to call the training program they created PARM (Print Art Reference Materials) and took advantage of the acronym by incorporating cheese puns into their monthly presentations. One training session focused on a painting of a wheel of brie found in a museum collection (figure 10.1) and the print reference materials that could aid in researching it.

Adding more meetings to the calendar can be difficult; staff are often pressed for time and optional meetings can see low attendance. Integrating lighthearted elements (like clip art cheese figures) can engage the audience. Creating an informal meeting environment helps create interest and excitement. Including an absurd amount of cheese puns can turn a good meeting into a *grate* one. Bringing snacks for everyone who attends provides an added incentive to attend these trainings—cheese and crackers, chocolate chip cheesecake brownies, and other cheese-inspired snacks were especially successful.

Gauging the effectiveness of such a program can help argue for its longevity or highlight other areas in need of development. In some cases, the focus may be on weeding the print collection and expanding database subscriptions. In others, you

Figure 10.1. Antoine Vollon, *Still Life with Cheese,* The Metropolitan Museum of Art, New York, Bequest of William Hall Walker, 1917 (18.22.1).

may receive feedback from staff as they begin integrating more print resources into reference interactions or other aspects of library work. Recording simple statistics, including meeting attendance, will be helpful for planning future sessions.

THE VALUE OF THE PRINT REFERENCE COLLECTION

Print art reference materials are necessary to retain due to the significant gap in online art historical information. They may provide researchers with key materials that are difficult to digitize due to copyright, size, or condition. Paying close attention to these materials specifically, in a discussion-based review, can assist when making space determinations and thoughtfully weeding a collection. Simultaneously, active familiarity with the print reference collection develops a richer understanding of the collection, thereby helping staff better assist researchers. All staff may benefit—from interns learning reference skills to experienced managers rediscovering old favorites. Focused attention on the print reference collection can also encourage gathering statistics on use of databases and circulation records as well as promoting staff participation and teamwork.

Whether these materials are retained on-site in areas that are easy for researchers and staff to access, moved to storage off-site, or deaccessioned, they are worthy of close analysis. Thoughtfully delving into these resources becomes an educational exercise. As librarians create space for learning new trends in technology and digital resources, they must not leave all traditional resources behind. The print reference collection remains an important source of information for librarians and researchers alike.[11]

NOTES

1. Robert Detmering and Claudene Sproles, "Reference in Transition: A Case Study in Reference Collection Development," *Collection Building* 31 (2012): 19–22.

2. D. Vanessa Kam, "The Tenacious Book, Part 1: The Curious State of Art and Architecture Libraries in a Digital Era," *Art Documentation* 33, no. 1 (2014): 2–17.

3. Pamela Arbeeny and Lloyd Chittenden, "An Ugly Weed: Innovative Deselection to Address a Shelf Space Crisis," *Journal of Library Innovation* 5, no. 1 (2014): 78–90; Jim Martin, Hitoshi Kamada, and Mary Feeney, "A Systematic Plan for Managing Physical Collections at the University of Arizona Libraries," *Collection Management* 38, no. 3 (2013): 226–42.

4. John W. East, "'The Rolls Royce of the Library Reference Collection': The Subject Encyclopedia in the Age of Wikipedia," *Reference and User Services Quarterly* 50, no. 2 (2010): 162–69.

5. Anna Marie Johnson, Susan Finley, and Claudene Sproles, "Dismantling the Reference Collection," *The Reference Librarian* 56, no. 3 (2015): 161–73.

6. Denice Adkins and Sanda Erdelez, "An Exploratory Survey of Reference Source Instruction in LIS Courses," *Reference and User Services Quarterly* 46, no. 2 (2006): 50–60.

7. Detmering and Sproles, "Reference in Transition," 19–22; Jane Kessler, "Use It or Lose It! Results of a Use Study of the Print Sources in an Academic Library Reference Collection," *Reference Librarian* 54, no. 1 (2013): 61–72.

8. Mary Francis, "Weeding the Reference Collection: A Case Study of Collection Management," *The Reference Librarian* 53, no. 2 (2013): 220.

9. Johnson, Finley and Sproles, "Dismantling the Reference Collection," 61–73.

10. Leila June Rod-Welch, Barbara E. Weeg, Jerry V. Caswell, and Thomas L. Kessler, "Relative Preferences for Paper and for Electronic Books: Implications for Reference Services, Library Instruction, and Collection Management," *Internet Reference Services Quarterly* 18, no. 3-4 (2013): 281–303.

11. The authors wish to thank their families, colleagues, and the Art Libraries Society of North America community for their support of this project. Additional thanks to Grace Abanavas, Audrey Christiansen-Tsai, Jenny Davis, Martien de Vletter, Robyn Fleming, Dan Lipcan, Seth Persons, Jessica Ranne, Linda Seckelson, Sarah Sherman Clark, Daniel Starr, and William Welte.

11

The State and Vision of Exhibitions in Art Museum Libraries

Carol Ng-He, San José State University

A HISTORICAL AND LITERATURE OVERVIEW OF LIBRARY EXHIBITIONS

Sharing important library materials with visitors has long been an integral part of the work of librarians: library displays were documented in European libraries in the seventeenth century.[1] In the United States, the earliest writing that explicitly describes exhibitions in a library environment appeared in the 1980s and recognizes the pedagogical values of libraries and their exhibitions.[2] In the late 1980s, related discussions on exhibiting artists' books from art museum library collections in the galleries also appeared in print.[3]

Publications on exhibitions in art libraries have appeared in art library-focused periodicals, including the *Art Libraries Journal* and *Art Documentation: Journal of Art Libraries Society of North America*.[4] Nonetheless, published scholarship focused on exhibitions in art museum libraries specifically, has appeared less frequently than similar scholarship focused on exhibitions in public and academic libraries and special collections institutions.[5] Few references have been found about librarians who curate exhibitions, such as the late Rosemary Furtak, who was known for creating exhibitions with the Walker Art Museum's collection.[6] Other books like *The Twenty-First Century Art Librarian* (2003) and *Art Museum Libraries and Librarianship* (2007) address a wide range of topics concerning art museum libraries, but exhibitions and displays are only mentioned briefly, rather than being the focus of chapters.[7]

Exhibits in Archives and Special Collections Libraries (2013) covers archival exhibitions extensively. Author Jessica Lacher-Feldman points out that exhibitions create a narrative or platform that can be built upon in different ways, such as with public outreach and advocacy. Digital exhibits are acknowledged for their value in preserving cultural heritage. Additionally, the author offers a step-by-step process of creating exhibitions in-house.[8] Lacher-Feldman's insight about the foundational role that exhibitions play in public programming is applicable for art museum library exhibitions as well.

In searching databases that cover museums and art-related topics,[9] the number of English-language scholarly and peer-reviewed publications on exhibitions and art museum libraries published between 2016 and 2019 is low: only sixteen results for "art museum libraries" and "exhibitions" show up. A targeted search for exhibitions in popular art museum libraries, listed in appendix A, results in the discovery of sixty results, forty of which are from the search relating to Getty Research Institute alone. The low visibility and availability could be due to the fact that art museum libraries often adopt the terms "display" and "selectors" instead of "exhibition" and "curator" to avoid confusion with their parent institutions' object exhibitions and curatorial staff. Searches for exhibitions in other types of libraries reveal a different picture: 173 for academic libraries, 220 for public libraries, and 1,506 for archives and special collections combined.

The Institute of Museum and Library Services Museum Data Files for the Fiscal Year 2018 shows there are approximately 2,620 art museums in the United States.[10] According to the *State of Art Museum Libraries 2016 White Paper*, there are approximately two hundred staffed libraries embedded in art museums and galleries.[11] No statistics on exhibitions hosted or organized by art museum libraries have been identified.

Searching the websites of art museum libraries can provide a better sense of exhibition occurrences. Among the fourteen popular art museums in appendix A, four have a dedicated webpage for exhibitions, which account for less than a third of the total sampling.[12] Perhaps the earliest documented and virtually searchable exhibition organized by art librarians is *Raphael in the Library* at the National Gallery of Art Library in 1981. The exhibition presented "some of the more unusual material from the collection concerning Raphael" to complement another display of the reproduction of Raphael's work in the East Building Study Center[13] (figure 11.1). Because exhibitions and displays are integral to the work of art museum libraries and librarians who are expected to promote the library and its collections "through *exhibitions* [emphasis added], publications, reports, lectures, and other activities" as part of their jobs,[14] exhibitions are rarely given special attention in the literature. Many art libraries have dedicated display space so they can regularly share a rotating collection of materials that are curated around any number of themes but often relate to special collections, featured exhibitions in the galleries, or events.

METHODOLOGIES

To get an idea of the current state of exhibitions and exhibition spaces in art museum libraries, a survey was created via SurveyMonkey that was sent in June 2019 to the Art Libraries Society of North America's (ARLIS/NA) general listserv that

Figure 11.1. Installation view of the exhibition *Raphael in the Library* (April 23–July 2, 1981). *Credit*: National Gallery of Art, Washington.

reached over three thousand contacts, the ARLIS/NA Exhibitions Special Interest Group listserv that reached over two hundred contacts, and the Chicago Area Archivists listserv that reached over two hundred contacts (see appendix B). Thirteen people responded to the survey, and eight individuals participated in interviews conducted via phone and email to elicit deeper insights into institutional practices.

WHAT IS AN EXHIBITION?

In art museum libraries, an exhibition refers to a *curated* display, physical and/or digital, of materials that may include books, manuscripts, maps, letters, journals, catalogs, rare printed works, artist files, photographs, posters, ephemera, original correspondence, museum archival materials, and special collections items with narrative and interpretation embedded.[15]

Why Exhibit?

Exhibitions Support the Museum's Mission to Educate and Inspire.

As gleaned from the results of the industry-wide survey and a series of interviews,[16] exhibitions support the museum's mission in three ways:

1. They highlight, showcase, and promote collections and resources that might otherwise be hidden or known only by limited audiences.
2. They raise visitors' awareness and interest in the library.
3. Like *Raphael in the Library* at the National Gallery of Art Library, exhibitions enrich visitors' learning experience by connecting them with the museum's exhibitions and permanent collections.

All of these outcomes impact the educational charge of the museum's mission. They inspire curiosity, introduce new points of view, provide contexts, and most importantly, engage visitors to "contemplate, question, and interpret information from artfully exhibited materials."[17]

Exhibitions Enhance the Library's Atmosphere through Storytelling.

Exhibitions generate visual excitement while telling stories about select objects. Jonathan Lill, head of metadata and systems for the archives, library, and research collections at The Museum of Modern Art (MoMA), articulated eloquently: "Exhibitions tell stories with [the archives and library] materials, or stories that the materials allow them to tell."[18] The presence of rare materials also creates an aesthetically pleasing environment.[19]

Exhibitions Develop Staff Professional Skills.

Through developing exhibitions, library staff can hone their skills and expand capacity in areas like collection knowledge, teaching, and project management. Storytelling in exhibitions helps improve written communication skills that are transferable to other types of writing, such as grant proposals and finding aids. Personal skills such as balancing diverse viewpoints, increasing the ability to deal with complex topics, being resourceful, and increasing problem-solving abilities can be cultivated.[20] Not only do these competencies lead to better patron services, but they also enhance job satisfaction, which can lead to higher morale.

EXHIBITION COLLABORATIONS
BETWEEN ART MUSEUMS AND LIBRARIES

Often, library materials are frequently on display along with other art and artifacts in the museum's galleries. For example, The Margaret R. and Robert M. Freeman Library at the Virginia Museum of Fine Arts has book displays in the library as well as in the museum galleries. Figure 11.2 shows a book display in an exhibition that gives the history of the museum campus. The library also has a kiosk that allows visitors to flip through select books in their digital collection in the museum for learning enhancement.[21]

Librarians may act as co-curators for exhibitions in art museums and online. Unlike some academic or public libraries where art curators are not part of the institution, there is some tension around librarians describing their work as "curation," especially in art museums where curators exists.[22] As they intimately know their collections, librarians can share a wealth of knowledge with museum curators in developing the message of exhibitions. For example, the McCormick Library of Special Collections' curator was on the curatorial team for the *William Blake and the Age of Aquarius* exhibition in 2018 at the Block Museum of Art at Northwestern University, and gave public tours to the exhibition alongside the museum curator.[23] The New York Art Resources Consortium, consisting of the libraries of The Frick Collection, Brooklyn Museum, and MoMA, presented a digital exhibition entitled *This Kiss to the Whole World: Klimt and the Vienna Secession* (Union of Austrian Artists) to correspond with the city-wide program organized by Carnegie Hall in 2014. The exhibition remains online to date.[24]

TYPES OF EXHIBITION SPACES

Art museum libraries utilize different resources to exhibit their collections. The five most common spaces shown in this author's research are listed subsequently in order of usage frequency.

Display Cases

Display cases are the most frequently used exhibition spaces among art museum libraries. Libraries have one to four cases with a three-by-five feet footprint each on average (figures 11.2 and 11.3). They are built-in or freestanding and are located inside the library, near or outside the library entrance. Occasionally, additional stand-alone objects are included.

Having exhibitions outside the library entrance or in the hallways heightens visibility and public access. An example is a display at the Oriental Institute's Research

Figure 11.2. A display case at the Virginia Museum of Fine Art's Margaret R. and Robert M. Freeman Library. Photograph by Lee Ceperich.

Figure 11.3. An exhibit at the Hirsch Library of The Museum of Fine Arts, Houston. Photograph by Sarah Stanhope.

Archives of a folio volume (reprint) of engravings after paintings by nineteenth-century Scottish painter David Roberts made on visits to the Middle East. Because the Oriental Institute is a private library that requires identification card access to enter, this display "act[s] as a welcoming environment to library visitors and offer[s] an item of interest to anyone from the general public who visits the second floor hallway," states Foy Scalf, the head of Research Archives[25] (figure 11.4). Similarly, the MoMA library exhibition *The Dealer as Co-Conspirator: Selections from the Richard Bellamy Papers in The Museum of Modern Art Archives* was located on the lower level of its Lewis B. and Dorothy Cullman Education and Research Building.[26]

Web-Based Platforms

There is a wide spectrum of digital exhibitions with different levels of depth and a variety of materials presented in online exhibition content across art museum libraries. Some are counterparts to a physical exhibition, whereas others exist only online. Some blend elements of both with physical exhibitions that feature an online component from the library's respective museums and galleries.

The location of online exhibitions varies. They are typically embedded on the library's home websites and generally developed and maintained by departments

Figure 11.4.   A display of a folio volume (reprint) of images from the paintings of David Roberts outside the Oriental Institute's Research Archives. Photograph by Carol Ng-He.

outside of the library such as digital media or information technology. Social media such as Instagram, Tumblr, and Facebook, and other external web-based publishing platforms such as Omeka or Google Art and Culture have also been used by librarians because they provide more control and flexibility to incorporate multimedia components[27] (figure 11.5). Free from physical limitations, these digital platforms offer greater exhibition capacity and allow digital surrogates of materials to be on display for longer than their physical counterparts could be displayed.

Figure 11.5.   A screenshot of *This Kiss to the Whole World: Klimt and the Vienna Secession* online exhibition housed in Omeka, accessed on August 10, 2019, http://secession .nyarc.org/.

Pop-Up or Off-Site Spaces

Pop-up or off-site exhibitions include loans to outside organizations for a short period of time. Innovative mobile displays—such as the Virginia Museum of Fine Arts's Artmobile, a climate-controlled fifty-three-foot Volvo trailer that has Wi-Fi to connect visitors with the museum's educators—offer art museum libraries another way to share their materials. Interactive opportunities like this are designed to meet the expectations of twenty-first-century museumgoers.[28]

Museum Galleries

Rare books or other items are often included in the museum's permanent galleries to complement the exhibition. For example, *A BIT OF MATTER: The MoMA PS1 Archives, 1976–2000* was a special collaboration between curatorial staff and the archivist at MoMA in 2017. The exhibition showcased a selection of archival materials documenting the artists who worked and exhibited in the museum's building in its first twenty-five years (figure 11.6).

Figure 11.6. Installation view of the exhibition *A Bit of Matter: The MoMA PS1 Archives*, April 9, 2017–September 10, 2017, MoMA PS1, Long Island City, New York. Photograph by Pablo Enriquez. © 2017 The Museum of Modern Art.

THE MAKING OF ART MUSEUM LIBRARY EXHIBITIONS

An exhibition theme often starts with the objective to complement a museum exhibition, highlight a recent acquisition or significant collection item, or address current events or special occasions. The curatorial process can range from three months to two years depending on staff size, budget, and space. Generally, library staff act as the subject specialist or curator, and often work alone when doing research, writing content, or creating installations. Based on the survey responses previously mentioned, approximately 69 percent of exhibitions run for three to six months, and over 61 percent of these libraries have three to four exhibitions in a year. Exhibitions in gallery spaces can be on view longer.

Beyond the typical policy for loan requests, policies and procedures written specifically for in-house exhibitions are less common among art museum libraries, but some examples exist. The Museum of Fine Arts, Houston, has had an explicit library exhibition policy since 2015.[29] The Smithsonian Institution art libraries have calls for proposals that detail submission guidelines and the exhibitions' criteria for prospective curators.[30]

In contrast to the museum sector broadly, art museum libraries are less concerned with assessment, keeping the practice of library exhibition evaluation in an infancy stage. For example, Google Stats could provide some insights of the webpage traffic to digital exhibitions, but it is difficult to parcel out the number of individual exhibitions. Based on survey responses, it seems the desire to expose visitors to the collections' highlights outweighs the need for evaluation or justification.

AUDIENCE ENGAGEMENT

Art museum library exhibitions are generally intended for adults, including scholars, researchers, and university students. They also are occasionally intended for families and youth. To promote exhibitions, libraries may host lectures and talks, tours of the library and the exhibitions, book clubs, and even performance art events related to exhibitions. Teens also take part in programs such as the teen docent program through the Smithsonian's National Museum of American History.[31] Libraries can leverage their resources with a museum's education department for greater public engagement by collaborating on focused programming initiatives for teachers and students. In addition, libraries harness the power of social media by featuring exhibitions materials and highlighting their significance through posts on library or museum channels as well as Facebook live-type events, blogs, and occasional publications.

PROFESSIONAL DEVELOPMENT

Most staff in the study report they are self-taught in curating and organizing exhibitions. In some cases, library staff members have backgrounds and degrees specializing in art or art history and can easily apply those aesthetics to curating.[32] To support learning about exhibitions, professional associations like the Society of American Archivists Exhibits and Events Committee offer exhibition-related resources. The Society of American Archivists aims "to create a community of practice for those engaged in the exhibit and event spheres by . . . promoting adoption of best practices in curation, design, execution, and assessment of exhibits and events."[33] New special interest groups are formed and growing steadily in recent years. The ARLIS/ NA Exhibitions Special Interest Group was founded in 2017, and the Chicago Area Archivists Curating and Exhibitions Interest Group was established in 2019.

CHALLENGES

A lack of staff or staff time presents a challenge to almost all libraries, as exhibitions are not always part of the librarians' regular duties. In libraries with more employees, the availability of a dedicated staff person to mount the exhibitions may be limited because of competing project priorities at the museum. Additional learning about curatorial techniques, interpretation, and public programming requires dedicated time to develop.

Art museum libraries generally do not have an allocated budget line specifically for exhibit expenses, although new acquisitions that are exhibited are budgeted. About 77 percent of the libraries surveyed state that there is no designated exhibition staff person, and over 92 percent of the respondents have no budget for exhibitions. Fundraising may be necessary to obtain the support for the exhibition production.

Other physical challenges libraries face are space limitations, the number of display cases, and an exhibition location removed from public access. Some display cases are not in compliance with the Americans with Disabilities Act or conservation standards due to their old age (and again, the lack of budget to replace them). In some libraries, collaboration with other departments is often necessary for producing and printing labels and creating a website for a digital exhibition, while in other libraries this work is all completed by library staff members.

Digital exhibitions can eliminate the restriction of physical space, but without dedicated funding, the launching, maintaining, and updating of the exhibition website could be delayed because it relies on other departments' availability. Free web publishing platforms may not offer the style or layout needed. To create a fully realized digital exhibition, technical expertise in web design, managing a database, and even project management is required.

For art museum libraries to cope with the stated challenges and limitations, institutional support is necessary. More specifically defined job description guidelines, strategies, training, and a budget would affirm the paramount role of exhibitions in the library.

TOWARD CURATORIAL PEDAGOGY IN ART MUSEUM LIBRARIES

The ARLIS/NA 2016 white paper, *State of Art Museum Libraries* remarks:

> Internal collaborations are essential to the art museum library's existence. It should start from the top. . . . Librarians need to find a seat at the curatorial table, as a part of meetings on exhibition and acquisition planning. . . . Planning complementary exhibitions, developing online exhibitions, coordinating marketing efforts, and hosting exhibition-related programs and events are some of the ways that art museum libraries can further enhance the exhibition program of their institution.[34]

Although internal collaboration is key, so is external collaboration. If art museum libraries engage outside groups such as university students or local community groups in (co-)curating exhibitions, their associated spaces could be used as sites for object-based learning and as creativity incubators.[35] Having students act as curators for library exhibitions as part of a course is not a new concept; cross-disciplinary collaborations strengthen and broaden students' skills just as they do for library staff. Continuing this approach will create new synergies between the art museum library audience and collections, and truly advance the library's mission.

If curating became integral to the librarian's job, library schools would need to invest in helping students develop correlating competencies. Currently, less than 10 percent of about sixty master's degree programs in library and information science in the United States offer courses on exhibition-related topics tailored to library environments. Incorporating courses on curating and creating exhibitions in graduate programs would strengthen professional skills in this area. Internships and fellowships specifically focused on exhibitions in art museum libraries could offer an important training ground for the emerging librarian-curator. Further integrating exhibition practice into the education of future libraries would also inspire librarians to think about how appropriate an item would be for a particular exhibition and the voice it represents in the exhibition narrative.[36] The interconnection of exhibitions with other aspects of the library's operations deserves further study. To think more broadly when addressing the lack of formal training, partnerships with accredited museum studies and curatorial programs could share a curriculum, encourage creative learning, elevate the technical standards, and raise the public profile of library exhibitions. By providing these opportunities, future librarians would be better equipped with the foundational knowledge of curatorial practice and expertise in creating engaging and visitor-centered exhibitions.

APPENDIX A

- Art Institute of Chicago Ryerson and Burnham Libraries
- Cleveland Museum of Art Ingalls Library
- Detroit Institute of Arts Research Library and Archives
- Hirshhorn Museum and Sculpture Garden Library
- J. Paul Getty Museum—Getty Research Institute
- Los Angeles County Museum of Art Balch Art Research Library
- Philadelphia Museum of Art Library
- Metropolitan Museum of Art Thomas J. Watson Library
- Museum of Fine Arts Boston William Morris Hunt Memorial Library
- Museum of Modern Art Library
- National Gallery of Art Library
- Smithsonian American Art and Portrait Gallery Library
- Solomon R. Guggenheim Museum Library
- Whitney Museum of American Art Frances Mulhall Achilles Library

APPENDIX B

Survey questions:

1. What are the roles or purposes of exhibitions in your library?
2. What are the spaces in which your exhibitions are hosted? (Check all that apply.)
   a. Gallery
   b. Display cases
   c. Walls or hallways
   d. Pop-up/off-site (outside of library spaces)
   e. Online or designated website
   f. Social media (Instagram, Facebook page, etc.)
   g. Other
3. What are your target audiences? (Check all that apply.)
   a. University students
   b. Faculty/scholars/researchers
   c. General adults
   d. Families
   e. Youth
4. What do you exhibit typically? (For example, rare books, artists' books, etc.)
5. How big typically are your exhibitions? (For example, one display case, or 120 linear feet, etc.)
6. How long do your exhibitions run typically?
   a. Less than three months
   b. Three to six months
   c. Six to nine months
   d. Nine months to one year
   e. Over one year
   f. Other
7. How frequently do you usually have your exhibitions in a year?
   a. Once
   b. Twice
   c. Three or four times
   d. More than four times
8. Do you have a budget for exhibitions at your library?
   a. Yes
   b. No
9. Do you have designated staff to curate and/or coordinate exhibitions at your library?
   a. Yes
   b. No

10. Do you conduct evaluations on your exhibitions?
    a. Yes
    b. No
11. If you conduct evaluations, please describe your methodologies.
12. Do you offer programs or other outreach initiatives with the exhibitions?
    a. Yes
    b. No
13. If you offer programs or outreach initiatives with your exhibitions, please share some examples.
14. What are the challenges, limitations, and opportunities you are facing in hosting and developing exhibitions at your library?
15. What resources do you have or would you like to have to overcome the challenges and/or limitations?
16. What is the name of your art museum library? (Optional.)
17. What is your name and professional title? (Optional.)
18. Please provide your email address if you want a follow up.

NOTES

1. Dorothy Fouracre, "Making an Exhibition of Ourselves? Academic Libraries and Exhibitions Today," *The Journal of Academic Librarianship* 41 (2015): 377–85.

2. Amy Chen, Sarah Pickle, and Heather L. Waldroup, "Changing and Expanding Libraries: Exhibitions, Institutional Repositories, and the Future of Academia," CLIR. Accessed July 21, 2019, https://perma.cc/R3MZ-3HGU.

3. Hikmet Dogu, "Exhibiting Library Books in an Art Gallery," ACRL College and Research Libraries News. Accessed on January 3, 2020, https://perma.cc/HS6L-WRNB.

4. Karen Hinson, "Exhibitions in Libraries: A Practical Guide," *Art Documentation: Journal of the Art Libraries Society of North America* 4, no. 1 (1985): 6–7; Eumie Imm, "On the Wall, off the Wall: The Librarian as Exhibition Curator," *Art Documentation: Bulletin of the Art Libraries Society of North America* 9 (1990): 71–72; Ida Kolganova, "Creative Co-Operation between Librarian and Artists in the Russian State Arts Library," *Art Libraries Journal* 20, no. 2 (1995): 25–27; D. Vanessa Kam, "On Collecting and Exhibiting Art Objects in Libraries, Archives, and Research Institutes," *Art Documentation: Journal of the Art Libraries Society of North America* 20, no. 2 (2001): 10–15; Stacy Brinkman and Sara Young, "Information Literacy through Site-Specific Installation: The Library Project," *Art Documentation: Journal of the Art Libraries Society of North America* 29, no. 1 (2010): 61–66.

5. Fouracre, "Making an Exhibition," 2015.

6. "Remembering Rosemary Furtak, Champion of Artists' Books," Walker. Accessed January 3, 2020, https://perma.cc/QX7Y-HSSJ.

7. Terrie Wilson, ed., *The Twenty-First Century Art Librarian* (New York: Routledge, 2003), 62, 66–67; Joan M. Benedetti, ed., *Art Museum Libraries and Librarianship* (Lanham, MD: The Scarecrow Press, 2007), 141, 190, 205.

8. Jessica Lacher-Feldman, *Exhibits in Archives and Special Collections Libraries* (Chicago: Society of American Archivists, 2013).

9. Databases included the following: Art and Architecture Source, Bibliography of the History of Art, International Bibliography of Art, Design and Applied Art Index, Emerald Insight, Library and Information Science Collection, Library and Information Science Source, JSTOR, ScienceDirect, and Web of Science.

10. The Institute of Museum and Library Services, *Museum Data Files*, 2018.

11. Anne Evenhaugen, Shaina Buckles Harkness, Alison Huftalen, Nicole Lovenjak, Mary Wassermann, and Roger Lawson, editors, *State of Art Museum Libraries 2016: ARLIS/NA Museum Division White Paper* (Tucson, AZ: Art Libraries Society of North America, 2016): 4.

12. Forbes, "Top 10 Museums in America," September 19, 2016. https://perma.cc/5ZQR-7QS7; TimeOut United States, "The 29 Best Art Museums in America," February 21, 2017. https://perma.cc/MZM7-4YP7.

13. "Raphael in the Library: April 23–July 2, 1981," National Gallery of Art. Accessed on August 20, 2019, https://perma.cc/V2CK-TWCQ.

14. "Staffing Standards for Art Libraries and Visual Resources Collections (short version)," Art Libraries Society of North America. Accessed on January 4, 2020, https://perma.cc/5NCB-B2MZ.

15. B. Erin Cole, "I Am a Historian I Make Exhibits," *Contingent Magazine*, March 20, 2019. https://perma.cc/ZNZ3-GL7D; Smithsonian Campaign, "Discovering the Libraries Through Exhibitions." Accessed July 31, 2019, https://perma.cc/BS5S-A5PP.

16. A survey was sent to the ARLIS/NA and its Exhibitions Special Interest Group listservs on June 18, 2019, with thirteen people responding. A series of individual interviews was conducted with eleven respondents, all of whom have worked in museum libraries.

17. Lesley J. Brown, "Acquiring Literacy: A Library Exhibit," *RBM: A Journal of Rare Books, Manuscripts, and Cultural Heritage* 14, no. 2 (2013), 90.

18. Jonathan Lill, phone interview with author, July 26, 2019.

19. Foy Scalf, email interview with author, August 12, 2019.

20. Michael L. Taylor, "Special Collections Exhibitions: How They Pay Dividends for Your Library," *RBM: A Journal of Rare Books, Manuscripts, and Cultural Heritage* 19, no. 2 (Fall 2018): 121–32; Jessica Cochran, "The Skillful Curator: A Case Study in Curatorial Pedagogy and Collective Exhibition-Making," *Art History Teaching Resources*, March 3, 2017. https://perma.cc/Q3W7-RTJ6.

21. Lee Ceperich, phone interview with author, June 12, 2019.

22. Amelia Nelson, editorial review comment, 2020.

23. Scott Krafft, phone interview with author, August 6, 2019.

24. "This Kiss to the Whole World: Klimt and the Vienna Secession," New York Art Resources Consortium. Accessed on August 10, 2019, http://secession.nyarc.org/.

25. Scalf, 2019.

26. Lill, 2019.

27. Deborah Kempe, phone interview with author, June 13, 2019.

28. "VMFA on the Road: An Artmobile for the 21st Century," Virginia Museum of Fine Arts. Accessed on August 10, 2019, https://perma.cc/7ZYU-L6ES.

29. The Museum of Fine Arts, Houston, *Library Exhibition Policy*, Hirsch Library. The Museum of Fine Arts, Houston, 2015–2018.

30. Anne Evenhaugen, email interview by author, July 26, 2019; Lill, 2019.

31. "New Teen Docent Program in 'Cultivating America's Gardens,'" Smithsonian Libraries. Accessed October 2, 2019, https://perma.cc/3SYW-4WEY.

32. Sarah Stanhope, email interview by author, September 4, 2019; Ceperich, 2019; Kempe, 2019; Evenhaugen, 2019.

33. "Exhibits and Events Standing Committee," The Society of American Archivists. Accessed July 30, 2019, https://perma.cc/6Y8L-9CQD.

34. Evenhaugen, Harkness, Huftalen, Lovenjak, Wassermann, and Lawson, *State of Art Museum Libraries 2016*, 14.

35. Laurel Bradley, Margaret Pezalla-Granlund, Aisling Quigley, and Heather Tompkins, "Cultivating a Curatorial Culture through the College Library," in *A Handbook for Academic Museums: Exhibitions and Education*, edited by Stefanie S. Jandl and Mark S. Gold (Cambridge: Museumsetc), 432–61; Alexa Sand, Becky Thoms, Erin Davis, Darcy Pumphrey, and Joyce Kinkead, "Curating Exhibitions as Undergraduate Research," *CUR Quarterly* 37, no. 4 (2017): 12–17.

36. Traci E. Timmons, email correspondence with author, August 14, 2019; Alison L. Huftalen, email correspondence with author, August 15, 2019; Ian McDermott, email correspondence with author, August 19, 2019.

12

Evolution and Revolution

New Approaches to Art Museum Library Programming

Janice Lea Lurie, Minneapolis Institute of Art

The once well-defined functional boundaries that siloed libraries in museums are now less rigid as institutions examine their role and desired impact in their community and beyond. Most art museum libraries are now deeply rooted in the broader institutional mission and vision. For art museum libraries, and perhaps for all libraries, supporting institutional missions means that collaboration is no longer confined to specific operational functions such as interlibrary loan or cataloging but is now embedded as a core value that impacts most of the library's workflows. Art museum libraries are no longer just well-organized scholarly repositories that primarily exist to build and preserve collections and engage researchers, but instead focus on making their collections meaningful in new ways to all departmental functions within the museum. In this way the library is able to meet the needs of the institution's strategic plan and its strategic vision, while also serving the greater community.

Collaboration, outreach, creativity, and an understanding of the broader cultural environment are primary components of the librarian's toolkit in developing meaning and engaging library programs in art museums. This chapter discusses programming examples from several art museum libraries.

CHANGING CULTURE

To begin, libraries and museums must acknowledge and respond to changes in their audiences' perception and desire for cultural activities—those activities traditionally linked to the fine and performing arts. *Culture Track* is a survey produced by the design and marketing firm LaPlaca Cohen in partnership with Kelton Global that tracks the shifting patterns of "culture" and audience behavior for U.S. cultural consumers. *Culture Track '17* presents data and analysis that illustrates how the definition of culture is changing. The report focuses on a variety of cultural organizations, including museums, and it offers tremendous insights that have relevance for libraries, especially those embedded in art museums. The survey's findings revealed that consumers have ever-multiplying ways to spend leisure time and this, combined with new forms of communication and technological advances,[1] have redefined what "culture" now means.[2] That is to say that museums are in competition for visitors' limited free time in an environment where there are many ways to engage with "culture." "Audiences do not place priority on whether an activity is 'culture' or not. Now, culture can be anything from Caravaggio to Coachella, *Tannhäuser* to taco trucks."[3] Consequently, for cultural organizations to stay fresh and vital, they need to reassess the types of experiences and services they offer to their constituents.[4]

Culture Track '17 data also define what motivates audiences to choose a cultural experience to participate in:

- Will the experience provide fun?
- Does participation satisfy a need for self-improvement?
- Will the event broaden a person's understanding of the world?
- Can the audience find personal relevance?
- Is diversity well represented?
- Is there something there for everyone?
- Will attending an event provide a way to relieve stress?
- Will the participant learn something new or experience something new (digital and/or analog)?[5]

Activities that include social, interactive, and hands-on elements are seen as desirable by audiences. Ultimately, "Culture connects us to reality, and lets us escape it."[6] "Importantly, audiences value not only how cultural organizations treat them, but also how these organizations impact the rest of the world."[7]

Museums are actively involved in analyzing the impact of changes in audience behavior to ensure long-term relevancy. Museum strategic plans are often grounded in an understanding of the world's shifting social dynamics, from local to global, and frequently include a variety of theme-focused action plans or ideas that will guide the work of the institution moving forward. The library can be a vital partner in a museum's strategic planning process, offering expertise and insight as the institution implements programming that supports new interpretations of culture for the institution as a whole.

The art museum library can also serve as an important partner in supporting the art museum's work on social justice through programming developed around themes of creativity, empathy, equity, diversity, and inclusion. Art museum libraries can actively create "engagement" opportunities that serve as bridges between the museum and the community. To realize this objective, libraries must collaborate across departments within the museum, as well as with external partners.

STRATEGIES FOR IMPACTFUL PROGRAMMING

Outreach is a primary impetus for librarians to find many ways to interpret and promote their collections. This includes:

- Consulting with curators when selecting library material for the collection
- Having library materials included in both museum and library exhibitions
- Providing research services for the museum staff who are developing exhibitions and publications
- Marketing the library and archive collections through social media and the web
- Digitizing collections for online access
- Developing research guides for the website
- Working with faculty from area institutions in providing information literacy instruction for students
- Providing tours of the library and its collections for community organizations

In addition to the traditional modes of engagement mentioned here, outreach programming in today's libraries needs to be closely paired with collaboration and a creative rethinking of the boundaries that define the work of an art museum library with the organization. This involves library staff becoming very familiar with the institution's mission and strategic plan, as well as the broader culture of the overall museum field. Librarians must be aware of, and consider the value of, studies like those generated by *Culture Track*, the American Alliance of Museum's *Trendswatch* publication, and the work of its Center for the Future of Museums, as well as the New Media Consortium's *Horizon Report*.[8] Being open to experimentation and establishing a friendly, collegial, and creative rapport with all museum staff is part of this process.

As an example, library programs at the Minneapolis Institute of Art are part of the museum's larger Curatorial Affinity Program. Through this initiative the Minneapolis Institute of Art library has emerged as a creative partner in co-engineering new ideas for library programming with staff from other museum departments, especially from the area of Lectures and Academic Programs.[9] After implementing successful programs, the library is seen as a place where new approaches for institutional programming are being realized. Program examples include staging an Edible Book Festival, holding Wikipedia Edit-a-Thons, and hosting a mini read-a-thon entitled "Artists in Their Own Words" in celebration of International World Book Day. The elements that make library programs unique are those that are adapted to the museum's current initiatives and customized in a way that always highlights the art collection. Creating a local program for the museum around a nationally or internationally known library or book event gives the program engagement traction as well as a chance to connect with an audience that may be new to the museum.

Wikipedia Edit-a-Thons offer libraries the opportunity to add art-related content to this free online encyclopedia. As art museums have strong international collections spanning the history of art, raising awareness of the diverse artists represented in these collections has become a focus. Ensuring that underrepresented artists are documented in Wikipedia is important work that supports broader initiatives to democratize information and support social justice and equity. The process of learning how to edit in Wikipedia empowers people to effect positive change and is something that a library visitor can continue after the museum visit. Consequently, their visit is not a passive moment, but rather an active experience where human understanding is promoted through a museum's art and library collections.

People are at their best when they create, whether writing an article in Wikipedia, painting a "masterpiece," or working at a potter's wheel. These experiences address the new understanding of culture and the expectations that cultural consumers have for learning something new, making the world a better place, enjoying a social experience, and finding a place to have fun. In terms of strategic planning for museums, when institutions ask themselves how they can communicate the importance of their collection in meaningful ways to their audiences, Wikipedia editing is one of the answers. The powerful psychological bond formed between the act of creating or editing Wikipedia entries and learning something new about art helps to solidify the experience about the museum acutely in the consumer's mind.

The library is an essential bridge in connecting people of all backgrounds to creative experiences while also promoting knowledge, learning, understanding, self-expression, self-respect, hope, and the admiration of others.

COLLABORATIVE ART MUSEUM LIBRARY PROGRAMS: SURVEY RESULT EXAMPLES

In an effort to understand programming initiatives at art museum libraries across the nation, a programming survey was conducted with several art museum libraries about their outreach programs and collaborative initiatives. Responses illustrated several themes common to creation and implementation of library programs, including collaboration, creativity, and innovative connections to their collections.

In 2014, the Hirsch Library at The Museum of Fine Arts, Houston, became a site for an artistic intervention entitled, *Adding a Beat! Hirsch Library Project*. Hanna Yoo, a Critical Studies Fellow from the Museum's Core Residency Program of the Glassell School of Art, coordinated a series of site-specific performance pieces throughout the Hirsch Library's reading room and conference space. The event featured three performances and one sound installation produced by eight local artists and musicians who reinterpreted the library's collection and space through the lens of contemporary art practice. After the opening performance, one of the motion-activated sound installations remained on view in the library for several weeks. Ultimately, the collaborative program brought increased visibility to the library because the group of artists shared their vision of it as a vibrant place for creative inquiry and experimentation.[10]

The Ryerson and Burnham Libraries held a drop-in art making event as part of the Art Institute of Chicago's second annual Block Party in July 2019. Throughout the day, the library hosted hourly workshops for making pop-up cards based on designs from both the museum's and library's collections; a display of library pop-up books complemented the event. This participatory occasion reached a wide cross-generational audience of 317 attendees, many of whom had never visited the library. This was a wonderful opportunity for the librarians to talk about the library and its function in supporting research about the museum's collections. Although we don't normally think of people making art in scholarly research libraries, inviting the public in to use glue sticks, scissors, and other art-making supplies was actually an important outreach event for the library in building new audiences. This one-day program created a memorable social experience for its visitors that could lead to further engagement with both the museum and its library.[11]

As part of The Metropolitan Museum of Art's "MetFridays" series, the museum held an "Artist's Choice" program featuring several collaborating artists. Tauba Auerbach, one of the participating artists, worked with the Thomas J. Watson Library in a book-making project that involved numerous visits to the library over a period of several weeks. Inspired and informed by works in the Watson Library's collection, she created a book entitled *A Partial Taxonomy of Linear Ornament—Both Established and Original—Arranged by Shape, Symmetry, Dimension, Iteration and Projection: Containing Extrude the Extrusion and Ornament as Entheogen.* The project culminated in a "MetFridays" event with Tauba curating a selection of titles from the Watson Library and giving a talk about these books and her book-making project. Visitors were also shown a working copy for one of the taxonomy books she created from her experiences in the Watson Library. The artist's large following on social media gave tremendous visibility to the library and helped to solidify new connections with the community and build new audiences for both the museum and its library.[12]

New York City was the host of a city-wide festival organized by Carnegie Hall in 2017. For *La Serenissima: Music and Arts from the Venetian Republic,* staff of The Frick Art Reference Library collaborated with their Frick colleagues as festival partners. One result was a Tumblr blog, "The Frick and La Serenissima: Arts from the Venetian Republic," which documented Venetian history as seen through the collections of the Frick's library and photo archives. Many benefits resulted from this collaborative initiative. A key outcome was the Frick's staff learning about the range of professional expertise throughout their organization. When collaboration is combined with outreach, it not only creates community success, but also strengthens the institution. And with this project, the library played a central role in making this happen.[13]

The four hundredth anniversary of Shakespeare's death in 2016 was the impetus for an international event that included an exhibition entitled, *First Folio! The Book that Gave Us Shakespeare.* The exhibition was offered through the American Library Association in collaboration with the Folger Shakespeare Library and the Cincinnati Museum Center. In association with Wayne State University and the Detroit Public Library, the Detroit Institute of Arts became a host site for exhibiting one of the eighteen traveling folios. A variety of programs were held at each of the three collaborating institutions. The exhibition drew exceptional museum attendance, with over eighteen thousand people visiting during its four-week run; it brought many visitors to the museum that would likely not have normally attended.

The Detroit Institute of Arts Research Library and Archives worked together with many of its museum departments in ensuring the success of this exhibition. Understanding the immortal appeal of Shakespeare and the lure of seeing such an important book was key for providing the visiting public with an enjoyable experience that was both rare and memorable. This exhibition also highlighted the visibility and importance of the museum's library. It exalted the idea of books and the beauty of words in shaping artistic vision. The museum's library, as the keeper of words, was instrumental in envisioning this exhibition for the Detroit Institute of Arts.[14]

The Mary R. Schiff Library and Archives at the Cincinnati Art Museum has hosted for the past seven years a program in the library called "Dialogues with Artists." Working in conjunction with other museum departments and members of the artist community, library staff invite two local artists three to four times a year to the library, where those artists share their creative insights and motivations for making art with the public. Each artist also brings an artwork to the event. Attendees can engage in conversation with the artist while also enjoying some wine and cheese. This event is directly related to the museum's strategic plan in connecting and inspiring the community through the power of art.[15]

Family day events are generally free museum-wide programs geared for family audiences and held as an ongoing series. The Margaret R. and Robert M. Freeman Library at the Virginia Museum of Fine Arts began collaborating in 2019 with its education department and outside organizations to hold Family Day events in the library. One of these themed events, "ChinaFest: Year of the Earth Pig," featured students from the University of Richmond who presented a storytelling session in the library along with a language workshop. A selection of children's books and art books were also displayed. Another Family Day event was "Celebrate African and African American Art: Mali." The library collaborated with the Virginia Friends of Mali, who presented oral storytelling traditions. Important examples of Malian mud cloth, known as bògòlanfini, were displayed during a presentation about the art of creating these unique textiles. The library's participation in family events has expanded its audience base while also fulfilling elements of the museum's strategic plan for engaging and delighting both diverse populations and families.[16]

Art book clubs are also vibrant conduits for collaboration in museum libraries. The Saint Louis Art Museum's Richardson Memorial Library offers a reading program entitled "SLAM Members Book Club," which is actually a membership department program. Membership handles the mechanics of the program, such as contacting speakers and catering; the library facilitators select the books, help plan the program, and lead the book discussions. The titles selected must relate to the museum's collection or exhibitions. Quite often this is done in conjunction with a museum docent from the Learning and Engagement Department. The book club meets four or five times a year and includes an informal talk by a guest speaker who gives a slide presentation on a topic related to the book discussed. This event, which attracts about fifty to eighty museum members per meeting, provides a wonderful social experience that is participatory, fun, and educational. Through cross-department collaboration, the library is addressing a need that was revealed in members' survey responses: providing interactive and intimate experiences at the museum.[17]

All of these programs highlight the creative approaches that art museum libraries are taking to create engaging opportunities for their audiences. These programs expand traditional programming offerings while creatively integrating the attributes that define our evolving understanding of how modern visitors engage with culture. Developing these programs necessarily involves the art museum library, working in partnership with other museum departments, with the shared goal of fulfilling the institution's strategic plan, mission, and vision.

WHAT IS THE NEW ART MUSEUM LIBRARY?

Discussions about the role of the art museum library frequently involve questions about where it should be placed within the organizational structure. Because a library is comprised of so many different elements—cataloging, online access, archives, preservation, programming, collection development, research, public services, visitor experience, learning, donor relations, advancement, and so on—where it resides organizationally will differ from institution to institution.

The library *is* a collection, but it is *about* a multiplicity of functions. Both elements must be brought together to break down the traditional silos of an organization's culture. The new art museum library must be flexible and imaginative. It can flourish in situations that involve the dynamic of collaborative ideation and be comfortable with sharing group ownership for an idea, concept, or program. As both cross-department collaboration and engagement become key to the library's purpose in fulfilling the museum's strategic plan, the boundaries established by organizational charts may no longer be as important as they once were.

Libraries must continue to embrace their heritage of collecting, preserving, and making their collections accessible for research while simultaneously considering how they are unique and what that means for the museum. By animating words, whether written, read, or spoken, through collaborative programs, art museum libraries have tremendous potential to become an "engagement" bridge between their parent institutions and their communities.

NOTES

1. La Placa Cohen Advertising Inc. and Kelton Global, *Culture Track '17*, 13. Accessed November 3, 2019, https://www.culturetrack.com/research/reports/.

2. Ibid., 14.

3. Ibid., 20.

4. Ibid., 111.

5. Ibid., 26, 31, 36, 38, 40, 46, 55, and 113.

6. Ibid., 59.

7. Ibid., 84. See also the recent controversy over the definition of "museum" put forth by the International Council of Museums in Vincent Noce, "What Exactly Is a Museum? ICOM Comes to Blows Over New Definition," *The Art Newspaper*, August 19, 2019. https://www.theartnewspaper.com/news/what-exactly-is-a-museum-icom-comes-to-blows-over-new-definition.

8. See Center for the Future of Museums, "Trends Watch 2020: The Future of Financial Sustainability," American Alliance of Museums. Accessed August 6, 2020, https://www.aam-us.org/programs/center-for-the-future-of-museums/trendswatch/ and https://www.aam-us.org/programs/center-for-the-future-of-museums/trendswatch-2020/; New Media Consortium (NMC), "Horizon Report: Museum Edition, 2010–2016," Educause. Accessed August 6, 2020, https://library.educause.edu/resources/2016/1/horizon-report-museum-edition-2010-2016.

9. Thank you to Susan Jacobsen, Minneapolis Institute of Art's manager of Lectures and Academic Programs for collaborating with Minneapolis Institute of Art's library staff in creating new programs for the museum through its library. And a special thank you to Minneapolis Institute of Art's librarian Meg Black for helping to cocreate exceptional library programs with library team members Kay Beaudrie, Renee Gresham, and myself.

10. Jon Evans, Museum of Fine Arts, Houston, the Hirsch Library, email to author in response to a survey, 2019.

11. Stephanie B. Fletcher, Art Institute of Chicago, Ryerson and Burnham Libraries, email to author in response to a survey, 2019.

12. Jared Ash, The Metropolitan Museum of Art, the Thomas J. Watson Library, email to author in response to a survey, 2019.

13. Deborah Kempe, The Frick Collection, The Frick Art Reference Library, email to author in response to a survey, 2019.

14. Maria Ketchum, Detroit Institute of Arts, Research Library and Archives, email to author in response to a survey, 2019.

15. Galina Lewandowicz, Cincinnati Art Museum, the Mary R. Schiff Library and Archives, email to author in response to a survey, 2019.

16. Kristin Alexander, Virginia Museum of Fine Arts, The Margaret R. and Robert M. Freeman Library, email to author in response to a survey, 2019.

17. Clare Vasquez, Saint Louis Art Museum, Richardson Memorial Library, email to author in response to a survey, 2019.

13

Local Consortia and Museum Libraries

Partnering for the Future

Alba Fernandez-Keys, Indianapolis Museum of Art at Newfields

Collaboration is an essential part of twenty-first-century librarianship. Whether public or private, small or large, collaboration streamlines processes and cuts expenses. For small libraries, joining a consortium may provide a professional network and support discovery services; for larger institutions, consortium membership may enhance holdings in specific subject areas and increase purchasing power. Whichever the motivations for partnership, in this era of shrinking library staff and budgets, "[f]ormal programs of collaboration have become a matter of broader and more urgent interest among libraries of all types and sizes as means of controlling erosion in the quality of collections and services."[1] In this chapter, the author will discuss consortial partnerships in the context of the art museum library.

A consortium is a formal community made up of more than two libraries that agree to collaborate in certain aspects of their work. It may exist to provide more resources—materials, technology, services, or subject expertise. Consortia may exist at the city, state, regional, national, or international level, and individual libraries often belong to multiple groups that address separate issues. In a thorough chapter titled "The Consortial Landscape," Greg Pronevitz[2] outlines the most common services established through consortial agreements: training, shared electronic content, cooperative purchasing, and delivery of materials; followed by consulting, shared integrated library system (ILS) cooperative collection development, and shared digital repository, among other benefits. In addition to these services, consortia may provide cataloging or digitization services or support, collective institutional repositories, or even publishing services. Simply put, consortium members participate in order to take advantage of economies of scale. In this author's opinion, another important benefit of local collaboration and partnerships is to increase visibility and awareness with the immediate public and donor community.

Historically, art libraries have collaborated with one another by producing and sharing printed multi-volume card catalogs and art periodical indexes. There was also a time when art libraries shared a discovery system named Research Libraries Information Network (RLIN), as well as the shared catalog of auction catalogs, Sales Catalog Index Project Input On-line (SCIPIO). Owing to the desire for world-wide dissemination and, again, economies of scale, both resources were integrated into OCLC, which allowed world-wide discovery of materials held by art museum libraries and contributed to making OCLC the enormous consortium that it is today. OCLC membership, although often taken for granted by many museum librarians, may be beyond the very small art library's budgetary ability. As important as mega-consortia such as OCLC, Europeana, DPLA, and others are to the art museum community, there are other issues that can be better addressed by joining local partnerships. These may include networking on a local level, staff training, cooperative collection development, and, most importantly, shared ILSs to enhance local access and visibility.

It is easy to assume that libraries would naturally gravitate into partnerships composed only of similar institutions. However, a 2012 OCLC survey found that 52 percent of libraries were members of consortia that included diverse types of libraries.[3] Art museum libraries are often geographically isolated from one another; thus collaborating with other types of libraries at the local level may be the only option. A rare exception that must be mentioned in any piece on art museum library consortia is NYARC, a collaboration between three major art museum libraries in the New York City area and made up of the libraries of The Frick Collection, The Museum of Modern Art, and The Brooklyn Museum. These three institutions share a combined catalog and work together to support innovative projects.[4] In the words of Deirdre Lawrence, NYARC allows librarians to "better serve . . . users by providing more resources and aggregated collections to deliver information in the spirit of one-stop shopping."[5] These libraries can take advantage of geographic proximity in order to enhance resource-sharing services, provide leadership in the field, improve access to materials, minimize duplication, support the scholarly mission of each museum, and develop relationships with local academic institutional libraries.

MEMBERSHIP RESPONSIBILITIES, INDIVIDUAL NEEDS

Forming a multi-type local library consortium would be a simple task if all libraries had the same needs and could function under the same protocols. In his essay on automating libraries, Kraig Binkowski observes that "the challenge with any grouping of libraries (particularly multi-type) is to make certain that the individual and specific concerns of a museum library are heard alongside those of larger libraries."[6] As a special library, art museum libraries may hold a collection that is part circulating and part rare or unique, that can include holdings from ephemera to limited edition books to the institutional archives or records. Thus, an important aspect of joining a consortium is that of negotiation. Consortial agreements should allow a certain degree of flexibility or decision-making power for each of their members. After all, it is in every partner's best interest to keep the group together.

Membership benefits and responsibilities are usually described in a renewable contract and any costs (if applicable) will be billed in accordance with a periodically revised fee schedule. Contracts should outline all aspects of participation, including management, billing services, training, and security requirements for members, expected attendance of consortium meetings, equipment, and staffing requirements. Museum management must be aware that membership fees will likely increase with time as costs rise or the consortium may require the purchase of updated equipment or other unexpected expenditures. Consortia participation will very likely require an information professional to be on staff. Will museum management support these necessary expenses in the long term? The decision to leave a consortium can prove expensive.

Consortial agreements are as unique as their members. Through readings and conversations with fellow librarians, it became clear to this author that no museum library partnership functions quite the same.[7] Some local consortia are managed by a city or state institution (perhaps the local public or state library) with consortial charges ranging from none to a designated cost charged to members. Such is the case, for example, of the Indianapolis Museum of Art at Newfields library and the Phoenix Art Museum library. Both are independent, noncirculating collections integrated into their local public library's ILS and easily discoverable by community users. In both cases the art museum libraries' holdings provide public library patrons access to the specialty materials and reference services that public libraries cannot. Both libraries function, to a lesser or greater extent, as a branch library of the local public library.

Other consortia are supported or managed by large institutions such as a university which may absorb a portion (or all) of the costs associated with the partnership as well as provide the technology support to host the shared ILS. The Research Library at the Amon Carter Museum of American Art in Fort Worth makes its collections accessible through the Cultural District Library Consortium managed by Texas Christian University. The museum, in turn, enhances the art history holdings of the university library. A very different museum-university partnership is that of the Cleveland Museum of Art's Ingalls Library, which collaborates with Case Western University. While the Cleveland Museum Library supports its own ILS, the two institutions provide a joint graduate degree that grants some museum library staff adjunct faculty status. The Ingalls Library provides the more specialized art history collection. This partnership has inspired further collaboration in the shape of publications and events.

In other cases, the consortium may include hired staff to provide support to the cooperative at large while each member pays a share of the costs. The William Morris Hunt Memorial Library of the Museum of Fine Arts, Boston, is a member of the Fenway Library Organization, a consortium of thirty-seven academic and special libraries in Massachusetts, which shares an ILS and includes several full-time staff that provide exclusive support to the consortium and manage issues such as group pricing negotiation with vendors and enhanced interlibrary loan services.[8]

SHARING RESOURCES AND
INCREASED PURCHASING POWER

This author's conversations with fellow art museum librarians revealed that many local partnerships for art museum libraries began as a way to address the need for automation which, in many cases, took the form of a shared ILS. A robust ILS is not only expensive to purchase but requires regular upgrades, maintenance, and dedicated systems librarians or information technology professionals, thus placing it beyond the budgets of many libraries and museums. Museum information technology staff members' time is generally stretched, having to maintain the institutional website, content management system, interactive applications, and the many other databases and software used by various museum departments. In many cases, joining a consortium has been the only viable option to have a publicly accessible collection and ILS.

Partnerships can offer better access to research materials available locally. This makes interlibrary loan requests quicker for the museum researcher and friendlier to the environment. Museum libraries may not always provide reciprocal interlibrary loan benefits to partner libraries due to the noncirculating or restricted nature of their collections; however, some libraries extend limited borrowing privileges, such as the Amon Carter Museum library to Texas Christian University faculty. Consortia membership often includes delivery services, which may be subject to additional fees.

Negotiation of database and other e-content contracts and access could be the subject of another chapter but generally consortia members can benefit from collective pricing. Smaller art libraries in local partnerships may have complete or limited access to databases purchased by the larger institutions—that is, depending on the terms of the larger institution's or consortium contract with an independent vendor. In cases such as this, large institutions subscribe to a range of databases covering topics that may fall largely out of scope of the art museum's collection development policy and budget but are sometimes necessary for a curator's interdisciplinary research. In other cases, negotiated access and subscription costs could be divided between partners as negotiated by the consortium's managing body.

Art museum library holdings tend to be unique in a given geographic area, but collaboration still makes it possible for all partners to make better purchasing decisions in order to eliminate all unnecessary duplication. If a title or resource exists locally at a partner library, the art museum librarian can decide whether to purchase or if the library would be better served by borrowing said materials as needed and using funds elsewhere. Museum libraries are prone to receive multiples of certain publications and can provide consortia partners with the added benefit of access to or transfer of their duplicate materials for their own collections.

Lastly, library partners can pool their resources to provide support for certain services such as cataloging or training. This author's local consortium managing institution, for example, regularly invites catalogers in the system to training sessions and webinars. In addition, it provides cataloging assistance (for a small cost) to the many members who have librarians but lack support staff. Cooperative agreements for a shared ILS will likely include a basic cataloging standard to which member libraries agree to conform. These standards should allow some flexibility for the art museum librarian and other special collections to enhance the records as necessary.

THINKING ABOUT THE FUTURE

Museum library holdings have grown to incorporate not only printed books, but in some cases institutional or artists archives, museum records, artist books, and a range of digital materials. This author would venture to say that, in most cases, the library staff has not grown in proportion to the tremendous variety of assets now required to be managed by librarians. Responsible management of electronic collections requires long-term preservation, which increases library staff's workload and need for specialized training. Is partnering with other institutions the answer to limited staffing? The *Horizon Report: 2017 Library Edition* lists cross-institution collaboration under its long-term trends accelerating technology adoption in research and academic libraries.[9] It states that "[s]upport behind technology-enabled learning has reinforced the trend toward open communities and consortia as library leaders, educators, and technologists come together to develop platforms and software that help institutions aggregate and store data, ensuring sustainable access and preservation."[10] As art museum libraries look forward to being more active in digital preservation, participating in consortia will hopefully minimize the cost of storage for maintaining large repositories as well as the desired geographic redundancy for born-digital archives and digitized collections.

Technology will keep changing and so will our profession, but one can only hope that partnerships will simplify our work with the ever-growing formats of art historical scholarship being incorporated into our collections. We should be looking forward to more shared e-content, digitization, web archiving, and whatever else the future brings. With partnerships, this seems attainable.

NOTES

1. James Burgett, John Haar, and Linda L. Phillips, *Collaborative Collection Development: A Practical Guide for Your Library* (Chicago: American Library Association, 2004), 2.

2. Valerie Horton and Greg Pronevitz, *Library Consortia: Models for Collaboration and Sustainability* (Chicago: American Library Association, 2015), 11–26.

3. "A Snapshot of Priorities and Perspectives: U.S. Library Consortia," OCLC Report. Accessed March 10, 2018, www.oclc.org/content/dam/oclc/reports/us-consortia/214986-member -communication-survey-report-consortia-review.pdf.

4. Sumitra Duncan and Karl-Reiner Blumenthal, "A Collaborative Model for Web Archiving Ephemeral Art Resources at the New York Art Resources Consortium (NYARC)," *Art Libraries Journal* 41, Special Issue no. 2 (Art Ephemera) (April 2016): 116–26.

5. Deirdre Lawrence, "New York Art Resources Consortium: A Model for Collaboration," *Art Documentation* 28, no. 2 (Fall 2009): 61.

6. Kraig Binkowski, "Joining the Revolution: A Primer for Small Art Museum Library Automation," in *Art Museum Libraries and Librarianship*, edited by Joan M. Benedetti (Lanham, MD: Scarecrow Press, 2007), 39.

7. I would like to thank Sam Duncan, Patricia Peregrine, Deborah Smedstad, Heather Saunders, Beth Owens, and Louis Adrian for sharing their thoughts and answering my questions about their institutional partnerships.

8. "The History of FLO," Fenway Library Organization. Accessed August 22, 2018, https://libraries.flo.org/home/history.

9. *Horizon Report: 2017 Library Edition,* New Media Consortium. Accessed August 14, 2018, http://cdn.nmc.org/media/2017-nmc-horizon-report-library-EN.pdf.

10. Ibid. 8.

III

PERSONNEL IN THE
ART MUSEUM LIBRARY

14

Entering the Field

Resources for Aspiring Art Museum Librarians

Lauren Gottlieb-Miller, The Menil Collection

For aspiring art museum librarians, breaking into the field seems a daunting task. There is no singular training program for art information professionals as a broader group, nor is there consensus among established art museum information professionals as to what constitutes the best path forward. Established art museum librarians enter the field via a variety of routes and possess varied backgrounds and credentials. Aspiring art museum librarians beginning to look at training programs and established librarians looking to move into museum work are faced with confusing and often times conflicting advice as to what constitutes the best way toward their career goals.

This chapter provides information on core competencies for art information professionals, an overview of graduate programs offering coursework in art librarianship, and paid internships for librarians seeking hands-on experience in art museum environments. It confines its scope to training for museum librarians specifically, though the literature on this topic generally extends to art information professionals as an aggregate. Additionally, this chapter emphasizes a diversity of experiences and training pathways rather than proposing an industry standard for training in our profession and does not seek to elevate one pathway over all others. Although this chapter is not meant to be a step-by-step guide on "how to become an art museum librarian," the author hopes it can be a useful companion to career planning.

CORE COMPETENCIES

When thinking about how to prepare for a career in art museum libraries, we are really asking about what kind of skills are required to be an information professional in an art museum environment. Art museum libraries are as varied as the professionals who staff them, and for this reason a variety of education and experience pathways can pave the way to a rewarding career. For the art museum librarian, core competencies matter just as much, if not more, than credentials. With any specialized field there is a sense from job seekers that the right degrees, internships, and fellowships can guarantee employment in their field of choice; the truth is that many paths can lead to this corner of the profession.

According to the Institute of Museum and Library Services's Museum Universe Data File for the fiscal year 2018, there are approximately 2,620 art museums in the United States[1] and approximately two hundred staffed libraries embedded in art museums and galleries as estimated in the Art Libraries Society of North America (ARLIS/NA) Museum Division crowdsourced list and reported in the ARLIS/NA 2016 white paper, *State of Art Museum Libraries.*[2] Staffing numbers vary and are influenced by the institutional priorities of the larger institution in which the library is embedded, as well as the larger economic realities facing art museums in a given season. Staffing requirements for art museum libraries are multi-factorial, and while recommendations exist, there is no standard set by the Association of Art Museum Directors.[3] Art museum libraries can have staff numbers in the dozens or can be staffed by one person. For this reason, art museum librarians must be flexible professionals, able to wear a variety of hats and embrace new trends in art information management.

What makes a successful art museum librarian and successful candidate for employment in an art museum library is mastery of core competencies. Although graduate work often provides a springboard for developing competency in key areas such as research skills and subject specialization, other competencies, like public service and instruction ability and individual professional practice, can be gleaned through professional practice in a variety of environments and training programs.

The *Core Competencies for Art Information Professionals*, a report authored by Karen Stafford, Maggie Portis, Amy Andres, and Janine Henri and published by ARLIS/NA in 2017, provides aspiring art museum librarians a key text when evaluating where they most need professional development.[4] These core competencies were developed to articulate the skills required of art information professionals that "are above and beyond general competencies"[5] set forth by the American Library Association (ALA) and expected of graduates from ALA–accredited graduate programs in library and information studies (LIS).[6] These standards were determined based on analysis of recent position descriptions in art information and visual resources fields, membership surveys of ARLIS/NA, the Visual Resources Association, and the Association of Architecture School Libraries, interviews with hiring managers, and a literature review.[7] The following core competencies are outlined in the report:

1. Art information professionals have broad and specialized subject knowledge in the fields of art, architecture, design, and related fields.
2. Art information professionals recognize users' information needs and teach users to locate, evaluate, access, acquire, and critically assess the information they need.

3. Art information professionals develop, organize, and manage collections responsive to the mission of their organizations, outreach, and institutional programs.
4. Art information professionals have knowledge of trends in the field of library and information science relevant to arts and visual resources librarianship and are prepared to contribute to the advancement of the art library and visual resources professions.[8]

These core competencies should guide graduate students as they select course-work, complete capstone projects, look for practicum opportunities, and apply for internships. For the established professional seeking to move into an art museum library, this report can help expose areas of strength in one's background and areas to expand through continuing education courses, conference workshops, or additional graduate work.

GRADUATE PROGRAMS

Professional librarians in art museums are expected to be experts at supporting the kind of specialized research taking place in these institutions. At minimum, profes-sional librarians are expected to hold a master's degree in library and information sci-ence from an ALA-accredited institution. It is increasingly common for institutions to indicate a subject master's in art history as either a preference or a requirement.[9] The necessity for graduate degrees in addition to a master's degree in LIS in order to succeed professionally in a given position is at the discretion of hiring committees and dictated by the specific requirements of any given position. Whether additional degrees give job seekers an edge on the market is not established in professional lit-erature. This section confines its discussion to graduate programs in LIS. Pursuing multiple graduate degrees, or completing a PhD, is ultimately up to the individual's interests and financial ability. Although certain positions require additional graduate work, the lack of graduate training beyond a graduate degree in LIS does not exclude qualified job seekers from employment in an art museum library.

As of November 2019, there are sixty-two ALA-accredited graduate library and information science schools.[10] The master's degree in LIS is a generalist degree. There is some variety in course content among these programs when it comes to electives and in-program practicum experiences, but all accredited programs prepare their students for careers in the larger information profession. Students pursuing a career as an art information professional or, more specifically, an art museum librarian, will need to seek out opportunities within the framework of these graduate programs to gain necessary experience to be prepared for the unique opportunities the museum library environment presents.

Several graduate programs in LIS offer exceptional training opportunities for stu-dents seeking a career in art museum librarianship. LIS programs often collaborate with other academic departments at their universities to offer dual degree programs in various disciplines and elective graduate coursework that builds on the foundational work taken toward completing an LIS degree. For instance, concentrations or coursework in special collections, book history and print culture, foreign languages, and the digital humanities are also applicable to art museum environments. Many programs offer coursework in book arts, particularly those programs at universities with robust book arts programs and collections.[11] Many museums, especially smaller museums, employ professionals in dual librarian/archivist roles, so coursework in archival description and management is useful. Of accredited graduate programs, only one, Pratt Institute, explicitly offers an advanced certificate in Museum Libraries for students who have already earned an LIS degree.[12] As of 2016, the University of Kentucky, Pratt Institute, University of North Carolina–Chapel Hill, Indiana University, and the University of Wisconsin–Madison all have established dual degree programs for LIS and art history, and many others offer dual degree programs in a variety of allied disciplines.[13]

Because it is not always obvious what programs offer to support career development for art museum librarians, the Professional Development Committee of ARLIS/NA published *Fine Arts and Visual Resources Librarianship: A Directory of Library Science Degree Programs in North America*[14] in 2016, compiling detailed information on all ALA-accredited library and information science programs in the United States (including Puerto Rico) and Canada. The directory provides detailed information on forty-two of the fifty-nine schools accredited at the time of publication and provides information on programs and specialized courses offered, credit and exemption, internships, campus resources, admission deadlines, and financial assistance available. Most helpful, perhaps, is that it gives a clear picture of how each program's unique mix of course offerings, extracurricular offerings, and established relationships with art museums and campus galleries can support students building careers in art librarianship and seeking experience in art museums in particular.

Graduate coursework is an important component for aspiring art museum librarians, but it is certainly not the only part. Choosing a graduate program is a personal choice and involves many factors, such as geographic location, current employment and family demands, and financial situation. It is not the intention of this chapter to assign value to one type of graduate experience. There are many factors that go into whether to choose on-campus or online learning programs, pursue a dual degree, or enter the job market after earning a library degree. Regularly examining job ads and networking with professionals already working in art museum libraries will give you the best sense of what is desired and required to secure a position as an art museum librarian.

INTERNSHIPS, PRACTICUMS, AND MENTORSHIP

Experience in a museum environment is one of the most valuable experiences for aspiring art museum librarians. Internships provide excellent opportunities for new professionals to explore work in a museum setting before entering the job market and to meet established professionals who can serve as career advisors, mentors, and teachers. Internships and practicums take the abstract concepts and theoretical work from graduate coursework and set it in an applied environment, whereas mentoring relationships can help guide early career librarians as they make their way into the field.

Despite the fact that they share similar internal structures and operational styles with academic and public libraries, art museum libraries are unique information agencies. Art museum librarians work with unique patron groups, from docents and curators to art appraisers and the general public. For students geographically distant from art museum libraries, an internship can provide a career broadening experience.[15] Many paid internships[16] are advertised on ARLIS-L, the listserv for ARLIS/NA, each year. Though most internships are funded by their host institutions, ARLIS/NA offers the Wolfgang M. Freitag Internship Award, which provides financial support for a 150-hour internship in an art or architecture setting for students preparing for a career in art or architecture librarianship or visual resources curatorship.[17]

Practicums are a graduation requirement for most graduate degrees in LIS. These experiences are generally compensated with graduate credit only and are proposed by the student to a relevant host institution. Graduate students looking to augment their generalist coursework can pursue practicum experiences in art museum libraries to gain practical field experience. These opportunities are generally held over one semester or summer for between one hundred to 150 hours, depending on the program. They allow students to pursue areas of professional interest while gaining access to mentorship from professional librarians at the host institution.

Mentoring relationships between new and established art museum professionals can be a mutually beneficial relationships. Insofar as graduate programs provide mentoring in the form of academic advisors and trusted instructors, establishing a mentoring relationship with an established art museum librarian who has navigated the career planning process can open new doors when it comes to entering the job market. ARLIS/NA offers a formal year-long mentoring program in addition to other programming aimed to bring students and early career professionals into the field.[18]

CONCLUSION

Many paths can lead to a career as an art museum librarian, and securing a position as a museum librarian is a function of many factors that may include timing and geography as well as an assemblage of degrees and internships. There is no combination of degrees and experiences that can guarantee someone a position in a museum library, but there are many avenues to secure the skills necessary to excel in an art museum library. By using the *Core Competencies* as a guide while choosing coursework and extracurricular experiences, aspiring museum librarians can set themselves on the right trajectory toward achieving their career goals. Established librarians working in other fields seeking employment in an art museum setting can use the core competencies to think about their existing experiences in other information environments in a new way, or utilize mentoring relationships to build networks in their new field.

NOTES

1. Institute of Museum and Library Services, "Museum Data File," 2018. Accessed November 2019, https://www.imls.gov/research-evaluation/data-collection/museum-data-files #museumdatafile.

2. Anne Evenhaugen, Shaina Buckles Harkness, Alison Huftalen, Nicole Lovenjak, Mary Wassermann, and Roger Lawson, editors, *State of Art Museum Libraries 2016: ARLIS/NA Museum Division White Paper* (Tucson, AZ: Art Libraries Society of North America, 2016). https://www.arlisna.org/images/researchreports/State_of_Art_Museum_Libraries_2016.pdf.

3. The Association of Art Museum Directors provides accreditation to museums and is the organization that museum leadership looks to for standards and guidance: htto://www .aamd.org.

4. Karen Stafford et al., *ARLIS/NA Core Competencies for Art Information Professionals*, (Tucson, AZ: Art Libraries Society of North America, 2017). Accessed November 2019, https://www.arlisna.org/images/researchreports/arlisnacorecomps.pdf.

5. Ibid.

6. American Library Association, "Core Competencies," 2008. Accessed November 2019, http://www.ala.org/educationcareers/careers/corecomp/corecompetences.

7. Stafford et al., *ARLIS/NA Core Competencies*.

8. Ibid. This report is worthwhile reading in full for anyone considering a career as an art information professional.

9. Accessed 2019, https://www.arlisna.org/images/researchreports/arlisnacorecomps.pdf.

10. American Library Association, "Directory of ALA-Accredited and Candidate Programs in Library and Information Studies." 2019. Accessed November 2019, http://www.ala.org /CFApps/lisdir/directory_pdf.cfm.

11. Ibid. Four programs in the report indicate areas of concentration in book arts: University of Alabama, University of California–Los Angeles, Dominican University, and University of Iowa.

12. Pratt Institute, "Museum Libraries." Accessed November 2019, https://www.pratt.edu /academics/information/advanced-certificates/museum-libraries/.

13. Caley Cannon and Stephanie Grimm, editors, *Fine Arts and Visual Resources Librarianship: A Directory of Library Science Programs in North America,* ARLIS/NA, 2016. Accessed November 2019, https://www.arlisna.org/images/researchreports/degree_programs _directory.pdf.

14. Ibid.

15. V. Heidi Hass, in her essay "Internships in Art Museum Libraries," provides a broad exploration of what an internship in an art library can look like and how established art museum librarians can select candidates and construct meaningful experiences. V. Heidi Haas, "Internships in Art Museum Libraries," in *Art Museum Libraries and Librarianship* (Lanham, MD: Scarecrow Press, 2007), 201–4.

16. Though unpaid internships hosted by art museums do exist, it's the author's opinion that art museums benefiting from the labor and knowledge of early career professionals must compensate them. Unpaid internships perpetuate class and race inequality in our profession.

17. Art Libraries Society of North America, "Wolfgang M. Freitag Internship Award." Accessed November 2019, https://arlisna.org/about/awards-honors/68-internship-award.

18. Art Libraries Society of North America, "Mentoring Programs." Accessed November 2019, https://arlisna.org/professional-resources/mentoring-programs.

15

Demonstrating the Value of the Art Museum Library through Strategic Volunteer and Intern Management

Traci E. Timmons, Seattle Art Museum

Volunteerism in museums is on the rise. In fact, the majority of people who work in museums are volunteers.[1] Not unexpectedly, this trend is reflected in a growing number of volunteers in the art museum library.[2] And, although "free labor"—as volunteering is apt to be called—on the surface may appear to be wholly positive, engaging and managing volunteers is far from free and can come with unexpected challenges. However, despite this, the strategic management of volunteers can add value and strengthen the place of the art museum library within the institution.

With instances of staff reductions and mergers, there is a growing fear among art museum library staff that volunteers could be asked to take the place of formerly paid positions.[3] The phenomenon of volunteers replacing paid library staff is a concern initially expressed in the 1970s by public libraries, whose activism ultimately led to the creation of *Guidelines for Using Volunteers in Libraries*.[4] Despite these strides, evidence suggests that these guidelines are being whittled away.[5] Art museum library staff of the early twenty-first century typically lack union status and the bargaining power that accompanies it. Further, there is sometimes a lack of understanding regarding the art museum library's value when revenue generation is prioritized over scholarship, access, and skilled staff assistance for institutional leadership.[6]

In her survey of small art museum libraries, Joan M. Benedetti found that a significant number of librarians were not full time and "in many cases . . . volunteers and interns supplement[ed] paid staff."[7] Further, there are examples of art museum libraries in the United States that have no paid staff and are run solely by volunteers.[8] In the Art Libraries Society of North America (ARLIS/NA) 2016 white paper, *State of Art Museum Libraries*, the authors remark:

> When museums are faced with downsizing, layoffs of library staff have been easier for [an] administration to justify than cuts to development, curatorial, or public relations

staff. Art museum libraries are increasingly required to function with reduced support for staff, and are forced to rely more heavily on volunteers, interns, and temporary contract positions.[9]

Understanding this trend in the 1990s, in its *Staffing Standards for Art Libraries and Visual Resources Collections*, ARLIS/NA's Staffing Standards Committee recommended what public library unions had recommended in the 1970s: "[v]olunteers may be used for special projects but must not take the place of staff positions required for the regular functions of the library."[10]

For art museum libraries that have experienced downsizing, library managers are faced with few options if they desire to continue to maintain a high level of service for their patrons. Confronted with a lack of staff resources, but also having a need to continually show value and deliver mission-critical services, volunteers and interns can be a tremendous resource—but their integration into library workflows must be pursued strategically. And, rather than seeing them as a potential employment threat or a burden on staff time, it is important to think of volunteers and interns as valuable resources that can potentially strengthen the value of the library.

Managing volunteers and interns can take a great deal of time and draws upon one's interpersonal project and time management skills. The successful management of these groups is guided by institutional policies and procedures, but should also be defined by library-specific policies that include the early establishment of strategic project and task assignments and limits for the types of work that can be done by volunteers, smart recruitment and selection, standardized management practices, mechanisms to promote the work being done by these groups, and a means to recognize the important assistance that volunteers and interns bring to the library.

Determining before recruitment what jobs volunteers will do, what projects interns will do, and what duties and tasks will remain solely with paid professional staff is key. Setting these guidelines beforehand will save time and set a standard for what the institution sees as professional work, volunteer work, and internship work in the library. It is also essential to make distinctions between interns (paid and unpaid) and volunteers with respect to what projects or tasks are assigned, as they are very different groups with potentially very different skill sets and goals. It may also be necessary to make differentiations within the group of volunteers, as well, where varying skill sets or backgrounds exist. Importantly, any work done by volunteers and interns should always demonstrate the library's ongoing commitment to the mission and goals of the institution. Tying projects and tasks to a mission statement, strategic plan objectives, or institutional goals will instill a sense of value for the library throughout the institution, as well as for the individuals performing the work.

Interns are typically current graduate or postgraduate students in the library and information science field and, occasionally, undergraduate students. They may also come from related fields of study. Internships are tied to specific projects and limited in duration; they may last an academic quarter or semester, or they may be year-long projects, but they should have a designated beginning and end.[11] Internships may come with additional benefits that volunteers do not have, such as an institutional email address or access to staff programs. Internships will typically lend themselves to stand-alone projects. If they are paid interns, the internship sponsor—a foundation, a donor, or the institution itself—may have stipulations about the type or subject-focus of work done. Keeping all of these things in mind, interns may have a more elevated status and be more like professional employees in the eyes of the institution. Because of this, it is important to have projects for interns that meet the institution's criteria and are in line with the goals of the library, but do not simultaneously undermine the work of paid staff. Internships should benefit the intern by providing a real-world experience and training, and, ideally, produce a tangible end-product that the intern can share.

Creating internship descriptions can be extremely useful. These descriptions can mimic job descriptions and describe a project in detail, but they should also list the responsibilities and, importantly, any skill or educational requirements. Descriptions are an important tool in the recruitment process. Establishing projects and position descriptions ahead of time means the library staff can guide internship work purposefully.[12]

Volunteers are a group whose members may have a wide range of skills, educational background, and experience. Volunteers may be retired librarians, or even currently employed librarians, who want to utilize their skills in an art museum environment. Other volunteers may not have any library background or educational experience, but are interested because they have long been users of libraries or are considering pursuing a library or information science educational program and wish to know more about the field. All of these types of volunteers can potentially provide important assistance. Similar to the creation of projects for interns, establishing tasks or ongoing projects for volunteers ahead of recruiting is critical to guiding volunteer work in the best interest of the library. Projects for volunteers lacking library work experience may be targeted to tasks that are typically more routine or housekeeping in nature: shelving books, making photocopies, wrapping dust jackets, filing, and so forth. Volunteers with strong library skills can provide great assistance in long-term projects that are not appropriate for interns because they are ongoing and offer little opportunity for new skill development. These volunteers can take on tasks that library staff might like to do, but will never have the time to do (e.g., low-priority, ongoing cataloging projects; creating inventories or bibliographies; shelf-read, scan, and check duplicates; box up interlibrary loan requests; check in serials, etc.).

Similar to internships, volunteer position descriptions, including skills required, can be very useful. Because volunteer tasks can be varied, can potentially change when there is a need, and are often ongoing, these position descriptions can be broad and list a sample of possible tasks or simply state that the tasks or duties are assigned by library staff based on current needs. Having several position descriptions—one for library-skilled volunteers and one for those lacking library work experience—may also be useful depending upon each library's situation. Further, including skills and even educational requirements can be helpful in recruiting and selecting the best-fitting library volunteers.[13]

Art museums have a great range of volunteer programs, but despite the size, for-mality, or even existence of a formal volunteer program, the library should strive to participate in the selection process or at least be able to manage volunteers strategi-cally when the selection is done on the library's behalf. In an ideal world, volunteers and interns should complete an application, go through a screening process, and interview with the library employees to whom they'd be reporting; those individuals would ultimately determine the candidates' eligibility.

For those art museum libraries that get recruiting and selection assistance from another department, it is important to share the position descriptions. The goal is to leave as little guesswork as possible for those providing recruitment assistance outside of the library. If library staff is solely responsible for volunteer recruitment, these same position descriptions should be utilized wherever recruiting happens: websites, listservs, online job boards, newsletters, and so forth. Regardless of who is doing the recruiting, targeted marketing of these opportunities should be carefully considered and have library staff input whenever possible.

While there is no one source that will consistently provide the best applicants, general announcements on the museum's website may result in a large number of applicants, including many who may not possess the necessary skills for positions, but that approach is one of the most equitable in that it opens the playing field to anyone. Universities with academic master's of library and information science or similar programs in close proximity may have a large pool of very qualified candi-dates from which to pull. Reaching those candidates may require direct contact with a university staff or faculty member, or it may require posting to a listserv of which one needs to be a member. It may be the case that library staff need to step in on behalf of the volunteer department to facilitate announcements to these groups. Importantly, with the continuous increase in the number of students receiving their master's of library and information science degrees through online programs, there may be an additional unknown set of students in the library's vicinity. This is a group that could especially benefit from internships and volunteer opportunities given that they typically do not have access to the same academic library experiences that those completing residential programs will have.[14]

One of the most time-consuming aspects of managing volunteers and interns is the initial onboarding and training. Rather than bringing people on ad hoc, estab-lishing specific starting dates for groups of volunteers and interns can save time and has the added benefit of being predictable. Starting dates can align with an academic calendar or be seasonal. Communicating the designated shifts and starting dates with others involved in recruitment and including this information with any position descriptions and postings is crucial.

Creating a standardized training plan is a way to save time and make sure that all volunteers and interns receive the same information. Group onboarding allows library staff to do the training once, but it has the added benefit of giving new vol-unteers and interns a chance to meet one another and hear different questions and perspectives. Once the training, common to all starting volunteers and interns, is complete, individual task and project training can begin. And, although individual training is additional and will take time, the amount of time is lessened by not having to repeat the common training information again.

Unlike interns, volunteers may stay with the library for a number of years. These volunteers can have a role in volunteer management that can greatly ease the burden of managing a number of people with limited staff time and resources, but attention must be paid to maintaining the volunteer versus staff role distinctions. Long-time volunteers can fill a particularly useful role as mentors to new volunteers. There are instances of mentorship programs where new volunteers are paired with veteran volunteers, and the veteran or mentor volunteer is able to answer questions and reiterate policies, minimizing frequent interruptions to library staff. Moreover, this creates a much richer experience for new volunteers and provides a well-earned leadership role for volunteers who now have a great deal of art museum library experience. A "lead volunteer" position can also be helpful. Typically held by a long-time volunteer, this role can include assistance with creating the monthly schedule and communications to volunteers, among other tasks. In its *Standards and Best Practices for Museum Volunteer Programs,* the American Association for Museum Volunteers advises, "[f]or some museums, the establishment of an advisory committee of volunteers may be appropriate."[15] Installing a lead library volunteer in museum volunteer committees can play an important role in helping volunteers in other museum departments understand the value of the library. The lead volunteer may have opportunities for information sharing or presenting on behalf of the library at committee meetings.

As volunteers and interns settle in and complete tasks and projects, it is important to communicate that good work is part of an ongoing effort to raise awareness about the library and promote its value to the institution as well as to the outside world. Promotion should strengthen the value of the library and its staff, rather than undermine it, by conveying a sense that volunteers and interns do all of the work. And any promotion should focus on projects or tasks where a connection to institutional goals, strategic plans, or priorities can easily be made. Using the language of the institution's mission and goals within promotion can help instill the library's valuable place within the institution.

Promotion can be done anywhere: on social media, print media, or in person. Requiring a written project summary at the internship's completion can be a useful tool for library promotion. This may take the form of blog posts or reports written by interns. Blog posts are especially useful because the content, now anchored on a website with a shareable URL, can be distributed out to other social media outlets. Additionally, this same content may be used for institutional print publications like bulletins and newsletters. Even though the intern may be developing the content, it is the library staff's role to direct the content internally to marketing, public relations, and other departments responsible for promotion. Presenting these projects and demonstrating their value and correlation with institutional goals and priorities in person can be very powerful.

In conclusion, art museum libraries need to engage with volunteers and interns in a way that ultimately creates value and raises awareness about the work that is done in libraries to support the strategic goals of the larger institution. Recruiting, selecting, and managing volunteers and interns is a formidable task, but good preparation in defining roles and clearly identifying skills and educational backgrounds required can make the task much easier and lessen the chances of volunteers supplanting paid staff. Creating policies and standards for scheduling and training can ultimately help alleviate the staff time taken to do repeated instruction and answer frequently asked questions. Intern and volunteer work clearly tied to the institutional mission and goals can be strategically promoted and marketed to raise awareness and demonstrate the mission-critical value of the art museum library.

NOTES

1. Elizabeth Merritt, "Volunteers and Museum Labor," *Center for the Future of Museums Blog*, October 18, 2016 (9:16 am). http://futureofmuseums.blogspot.com/2016/10/volunteers-and-museum-labor_18.html. See also Philip M. Katz and Elizabeth E. Merritt, *2009 Museum Financial Information* (Washington, DC: American Association of Museums, 2009).

2. For the purposes of this chapter, *paid* interns will be considered part of the general volunteer and intern group mentioned throughout. Although paid, these interns are typically paid less than permanent staff or have a limited term of work.

3. Carolyn Walters, "Fine Arts Library to Close in May 2017," Indiana University, Bloomington, Libraries website, April 4, 2017, https://libraries.indiana.edu/fine-arts-library-close-may-2017. Of the respondents to a survey of art museum library staff, conducted in August 2019, 34 percent said volunteers or interns did the work of traditionally paid staff.

4. Principle 1: Basic to the success of a volunteer program are prior planning and approval on the part of the staff and the governing body of the library. Principle 6: Volunteers should not supplant or displace established staff position spaces. American Library Association, "Guidelines for Using Volunteers in Libraries," *American Libraries*, vol. 2, no. 4 (April 1971): 407–8. The most recent and updated American Library Association work on the subject is Preston Driggers and Eileen Dumas, *Managing Library Volunteers*, second edition (Chicago: American Library Association, 2011).

5. Erica A. Nicol and Corey M. Johnson, "Volunteers in Libraries: Program Structure, Evaluation, and Theoretical Analysis," *Reference and User Services Quarterly* 48 (2008): 157. See also Maureen West, "Volunteers Can Cause Friction with Employees," *The Chronicle of Philanthropy*, October 15, 2009. https://www.philanthropy.com/article/Volunteers-Can-Cause-Friction/173273; and Michael Kelley, "Bottoming Out?" *Library Journal* 136 (1) (January 2011): 28.

6. Anne Evenhaugen, Shaina Buckles Harkness, Alison Huftalen, Nicole Lovenjak, Mary Wassermann, and Roger Lawson, editors, *State of Art Museum Libraries 2016: ARLIS/NA Museum Division White Paper* (Tucson, AZ: Art Libraries Society of North America, 2016), 4–5. https://www.arlisna.org/images/researchreports/State_of_Art_Museum_Libraries_2016.pdf. The authors remark that the "museum community has not actively emphasized the role of art libraries with their professional organizations." This is exemplified by the American Alliance of Museum's resistance to include libraries among the facilities required for museum

accreditation. See Joan M. Benedetti, "Managing the Small Art Museum Library," *The Journal of Library Administration* 39, no. 1 (2003): 25. So much of the art museum library's value is unquantifiable. Such values include providing critical research assistance in helping curators develop exhibitions; making available rare, ephemeral, and focused materials that help visitors understand themes, artists, and ideas connected to museum exhibitions and objects; art museum librarians and archivists bring information organization and knowledge management to inter-departmental projects and initiatives; and many librarians and archivists act as the museum's historian and are the stewards of institutional history.

7. Joan M. Benedetti, "A Survey of Small Art Museum Libraries," *Art Documentation: Journal of the Art Libraries Society of North America* 22, no. 2 (Fall 2003): 32.

8. The Laguna Art Museum's Carole Reynolds Art Research Library is "professionally staffed by volunteers." See "Volunteer Opportunities—Carole Reynolds Art Research Library," Laguna Art Museum. Accessed March 12, 2018, http://lagunaartmuseum.org/get-involved/volunteer/. The Nevada Museum of Art's Center for Art + Environment Research Library and Archives is also staffed by volunteers. "Volunteer Opportunities—Research Library and Archive Support," Nevada Museum of Art. Accessed March 12, 2018, http://www.nevadaart.org/give/volunteer/volunteer-opportunities/.

9. *State of Art Museum Libraries 2016: ARLIS/NA Museum Division White Paper.*

10. ARLIS/NA Staff Standards Task Force, *Staffing Standards for Art Libraries and Visual Resources Collections*, ARLIS/NA Occasional Papers, no. 11 (Raleigh, NC: ARLIS/NA, 1996). https://www.arlisna.org/publications/arlis-na-research-reports/publications-archive/168-staffing-standards-for-art-libraries-and-visual-resources-collections-short-version.

11. As an example, the Washington State Department of Labor and Industries states, "[t]he internship is of a fixed duration, established before the start of the internship." Washington State Dept. of Labor and Industries, *Unpaid Internships 101*, Document F700-173-000 (Olympia, WA: Washington State Dept. of Labor and Industries, 2017), 2. http://www.lni.wa.gov/IPUB/700-173-000.pdf.

12. ARLIS/NA maintains an intern roster that can provide very helpful examples of internship descriptions. See https://www.arlisna.org/professional-resources/internship-roster (accessed January 6, 2020).

13. Volunteer position descriptions are also useful when a volunteer is not a good fit for the needed role in the library and may need to support the institution in another volunteer capacity.

14. SR Education Group's *Guide to Online Schools* gathers all of the online library and information science programs in one place: https://www.guidetoonlineschools.com/degrees/library-science. The American Library Association also offers a comprehensive list of library certificate and degree programs, inclusive of both residential and online programs: http://www.ala.org/aboutala/offices/library-certificate-and-degree-programs. Lastly, Art Library Students and New ARLIS Professionals is another area to reach potential interns: http://arlisnap.arlisna.org/.

15. American Association for Museum Volunteers, *Standards and Best Practices for Museum Volunteer Programs*, revised May 2012. https://aamv.wildapricot.org/Standards-and-Best-Practices.

Part IV

DIGITAL LANDSCAPES IN THE NEW ART MUSEUM LIBRARY

16

Digital Art History and the Art Museum Library

Stephen J. Bury, The Frick Collection

The core definition of digital art history is the use of computational tools or methods with digital data to answer art historical questions. It has been seen as a subset of digital humanities and, indeed, it can employ the same tools (e.g., visualization, geographical information systems, text analysis, data mining, or virtual reality). The predominance of the use of digital images and also of conservation data may make it, in some eyes, distinctive from digital humanities. It also overlaps with digital substitution as in the case of the digital catalogue raisonné or the replacement of the light-box with the digital ARIES (Art Image Exploration Space) tool, a collaboration between the New York Tandon School of Engineering and the Digital Art History Lab at the Frick Art Reference Library.[1] Again, the history of digital art is an appropriate subject of study for digital art historians but it is not exclusive to them. The digital publications of museums are another ingredient. Another approach is not to define art history but to characterize it by activities associated with it: the Getty Foundation Digital Art History program sees the term as "a shorthand reference for the potentially transformative effect that digital technologies hold for the discipline of art history . . . allow[ing] researchers to handle large volumes of digitized images and texts, trace patterns and connections formerly hidden from view, recover the past in virtual environments, and bring the complex intricacies of works of art to light as never before."[2] This chapter will approach digital art history in the widest sense and from all these different and overlapping perspectives.[3]

Many art museum libraries are hard pressed for resources, whether staff, time, or money. Why should they become and remain involved in digital art history? Although digital art history has been slow to take off for various structural and institutional reasons, it is now at a tipping point and has become a core activity of many art institutions. Partly this is because of the widespread adoption of artificial intelligence and the availability of big data repositories, and by advances in other disciplines like medicine,

155

market-trading, transportation, and so forth. Art history would be a curious outlier were it to be unaffected, especially considering that contemporary art is increasingly being produced digitally, whether photography, video, or immersive installations. Last but not least, the increasing amount of digitized content—images and full-text —from museums and art libraries, data in museum and library catalogs, web archives, and so forth, has reached a critical mass, which cries out for new tools and strategies to incorporate it into research being done in the field.[4]

At the same time new cohorts of art history students are emerging from such institutions as Wired! at Duke University, the Yale Digital Humanities Lab and the Edith O'Donnell Institute of Art History at the University of Dallas, Texas, which claims to be "the first art history institute founded in the digital age." The art history undergraduate program at New York University from 2019 teaches a course, Digital Tools for Art History, designed by Pepe Karmel and Deena Engel, where students are taught Photoshop, how to use online image repositories, interpretation of scans, virtual reality and three-dimensional modeling, digital art, Zotero, data transcription and entry, and so forth. These students will be a part, an increasing part, of the next generation of curators. The Digital Art History Lab at the Frick Art Reference Library, The Frick Collection, which started in 2017, is seeing an increasing involvement of students, researchers, and the general public interested in its workshops and lectures. The rest of this chapter focuses on what any museum library, irrespective of resources, could, and perhaps should, be doing. It can be called the four As: awareness, advice, advocacy, and alliances.

The art librarian should never forget that they are primarily in the information business, and those information school introductions to information theory and coding should enable them to understand digital art history.[5] Their other information-seeking and disseminating skills allow them to be a source of information about digital art history and the projects that are taking place internationally in this area. The Art Libraries Society of North America (ARLIS/NA) has both a Digital Humanities Special Interest Group and is preparing a directory of digital art history, which will also form a registry of digital art history projects and datasets.[6] Meanwhile, John Taormina's *Digital Humanities Bibliography* (2019) for Wired! at Duke University and Ellen Prokop's DAHL Zotero Library for the Frick Art Reference Library Digital Art History Lab, which exists in Zotero and static versions, provide good summaries of the literature of and projects in digital art history.[7] Additionally, there is a wider digital humanities guide prepared by the University of Southern California.[8]

There exists an international network in digital humanities research—the Digital Humanities Conference—began in 1989, and the first digital research in the humanities and arts in 1997, and the Computer Vision symposium began at the Frick Collection in 2018. ARLIS/NA, ARLIS/UK and Ireland, and the College Art Association have had sessions or posters on digital art history at conferences in recent years and are good places to discover new projects and to make contacts. *Art Documentation* and *Art Libraries Journal* are good sources for new initiatives. *JAIC: The Journal of the American Institute for Conservation of Historic and Artistic*

Works includes articles on machine learning and other computational approaches to museum conservation. There are also specialist journals—*Computers and the History of Art* began in 1991, and the *International Journal for Digital Art History* began in 2019. Datasets are mostly made available via GitHub: The Museum of Modern Art (MoMA), The Tate, the Carnegie Museum of Art, as well as the Frick Art Reference Library have pages and datasets there. All four institutions have exemplary conditions that define how these datasets can be used.[9]

Drawing the attention of colleagues to what is happening in other museums and organizations is an excellent way to begin advocacy. The Getty Foundation Digital Art History initiative has supported digital mapping, virtual reality, and visualization projects.[10] The "Connections" diagram for the exhibition, *Inventing Abstraction, 1910–1925* (MoMA, New York, December 23, 2012–April 15, 2013) traced the relationships of early twentieth-century artists in a three-dimensional network diagram that demonstrated international connectivity and also the importance of women— "its pioneers were more closely linked than is generally thought."[11] The Exhibition History site created and maintained by the MoMA Archives includes digitized installation photographs and press releases, and additional metadata for exhibitions dating from the museum's founding in 1929. In addition to its presence on the MoMA website, the data was also put into the public domain on GitHub, allowing—actually encouraging—participation in the use of the data by anyone, asking and answering such questions as "which artists are mostly frequently exhibited with another artist?"[12]

An art librarian's participation might begin with personal staff development— learning about digital art history techniques, Linked Open Data, Zotero, structuring data, data mining, and so forth, or organizing a workshop with an outside expert for library staff or a wider internal or public audience. Each institution has a protocol for such events, and these should always be observed: a digital art history initiative should not be perceivable as a rogue event. Consideration should also be given to exploiting an existing electronic resource/database to consider how these existing datasets could be used in a digital art history project. At the Frick Art Reference Library many of the digital art history initiatives arose because of a desire to fully exploit the digitization of 1.2 million photographs of works of art in its Photoarchive. This led to work on computer vision with the ability to recognize similar images without the initial intervention of attribution, the automatic subject description of images for indexing and crowdsourcing for Americans with Disabilities Act (ADA) captioning. It is useful to have a real problem and then to think how the methodologies of digital art history could be usefully and creatively applied. But advocacy should apply to the museum, too, in promoting open access for images, release of datasets, and cooperation with collaborative conservation projects using digital tools.

Conservation departments could be useful allies in institutions where curatorial staff might be focused primarily on connoisseurship: many exhibitions utilize the results of x-rays, reflectographs, infrared, and so forth. An example of interest to the museum institution and the wider public is the Frick Art Reference Library's work with Professor C. Richard (Rick) Johnson Jr. from Cornell University's

Department of Engineering to present evidence from thread counts on Vermeer rolls of canvas or chain lines from the process of seventeenth-century papermaking to determine which Rembrandt prints were related in material terms.[13] Other internal allies are museum development departments, who increasingly use big data and are interested in network diagrams and other visualizations. Publications departments are also interested in non-print forms of publication. Curators in specialist modern or contemporary art museums are generally less resistant to digital art history— MoMA would be one example. Curators in more traditional disciplines may need the example of their fellows and interns, so they are worth cultivating as allies.

If an art museum library is near to or has connections with a local library and information science school, there may be opportunities to collaborate on such activities as data-thons or Wikipedia Edit-a-Thons, testing the potential audience for, and possible support for, further digital art history activities.

It can be argued that as important as financial contributions to an art museum library are, an equally valuable asset is being able to work collaboratively with local, national, or even international technology partners. It is important to have a clear understanding of what your library's needs are for a project—rather than a collaboration for collaboration's sake, the project must advance institutional strategies and agendas. For many art institutions with large digitized image collections, compliance with the ADA (1990), which did not directly address web issues, involves adding alternative text (alt text) for images, but this task is resource consuming. Part of the Frick Art Reference Library's approach was to work with technological partners—in this case with Stanford University's Department of Statistics and Cornell University's Department of Engineering and, in a separate project, with the University of Pennsylvania's School of Engineering—to achieve ADA compliance using artificial intelligence.

There are downsides to digital art history—ethical issues with data and sometimes with the algorithms themselves.[14] It can be resource intensive, expensive, and for each successful project there may be five that were not. Sustainability is another issue. Although data and code can be open source and housed on GitHub, many projects, and in particular digital publications, are difficult to archive and thus to continue to make available. Sustaining a digital project over its lifetime requires a continuity of staffing and funding, and this should be taken into account at the beginning of any initiative. But digital art history does offer the opportunity to ask questions that, in the past, would be difficult to answer or even impossible to ask. And it also makes our collections available for new uses by digital natives in a more democratic manner than before.

NOTES

1. "ARIES: ARt Image Exploration Space," Digital Art History, Projects, The Frick Collection. Accessed October 3, 2019, https://www.frick.org/research/DAHL/projects.

2. "Digital Art History," The Getty Foundation. Accessed October 3, 2019, https://www.getty.edu/foundation/initiatives/current/dah/index.html.

3. Diane M. Zorich, "Transitioning to a Digital World: Art History, Its Research Centers, and Digital Scholarship," Samuel H. Kress Foundation. Accessed October 3, 2019, http://www.kressfoundation.org/research/transitioning_to_a_digital_world/; Johanna Drucker et al., "Digital Art History: The American Scene," *Perspective* 2 (2015): 2–13; *Art History in Digital Dimensions: A Report on the Proceedings of the Symposium Held in October 2016 at The Phillips Collection, Washington D.C. and the University of Maryland, College Park* (New York: Digital Art History Lab of the Frick Art Reference Library, 2017). Accessed October 3, 2019, https://drum.lib.umd.edu/handle/1903/21830; Kimon Keramidas and Ellen Prokop, "Introduction: Re-Viewing Digital Technologies and Art History," *Journal of Interactive Technologies and Pedagogy* 12. Accessed October 3, 2019, https://jitp.commons.gc.cuny.edu/introduction-re-viewing-digital-technologies-and-art-history/.

4. Juilee Decker, editor, *Technology and Digital Initiatives: Innovative Approaches for Museums* (Lanham: Rowman & Littlefield, 2015); Tula Giannini and J. P. Bowen, *Museums and Digital Culture: New Perspectives and Research* (Basel: Springer Nature, 2019); The New York Art Resources Web Archive, for example, contains seven terabytes from museum, gallery, and artists' websites.

5. Claude Elwood Shannon, *Claude Elwood Shannon: Collected Papers* (New York: IEEE Press, 1993).

6. Michelle Wilson and Samantha Deutch, editors, *Directory of Digital Art History (DAHD)*. Accessed October 3, 2019, https://www.arlisna.org/organization/featured-projects/1475-directory-digital-art-history-dahd.

7. John Taormina, editor, *Digital Humanities Bibliography* (Durham, NC: Duke University, 2019). Accessed October 3, 2019, https://s3-us-west-2.amazonaws.com/dukewired/wp-content/uploads/2019/02/11171028/DH-bibliography-2.19.pdf; Ellen Prokop, DAHL Zotero Library. Accessed October 3, 2019, http://bit.ly/1SUHQc1, and static version at http://www.frick.org/research/bibliography_digital_art_history.

8. *Digital Humanities*. Accessed October 3, 2019, https://libguides.usc.edu/digitalhumanities.

9. *Age of Vermeer* Frick Collection [dataset]. Accessed October 3, 2019, https://github.com/frickcollection/age-of-vermeer/blob/master/README.md.

10. The Getty Foundation Digital Art History. Accessed October 3, 2019, https://www.getty.edu/foundation/initiatives/current/dah/index.html.

11. *MOMA: Inventing Abstraction: Connections 1900–1925.* Accessed October 3, 2019, https://www.moma.org/interactives/exhibitions/2012/inventingabstraction/?page=connections.

12. *MoMA Exhibition History*. Accessed October 3, 2019, https://www.moma.org/calendar/exhibitions/history/about?locale=en.

13. The Vermeer Project. Accessed October 3, 2019, https://www.youtube.com/watch?v=wtekI-agtys; see also Walter Liedtke, C. Richard Johnson Jr., and Don H. Johnson, "Canvas Matches in Vermeer: A Case Study in the Computer Analysis of Fabric Supports," *Metropolitan Museum Journal* 47 (2012): 99–106. Accessed October 3, 2019, https://people.ece.cornell.edu/johnson/LiedtkeMMJ.pdf; Charles R. Johnson, "The Watermark Identification in Rembrandt's Etchings Project at Cornell," The Rembrandt WIRE Project). Accessed October 3, 2019, https://www.youtube.com/watch?v=HgeIVwWQPmY.

14. Michael Kearns and Aaron Roth, *The Ethical Algorithm: The Science of Socially Aware Algorithm Design* (New York: Oxford University Press, 2020).

17

The Changing Ecologies of Museum Metadata Systems

Jonathan Lill, Museum of Modern Art

Librarians are trained to be experts in metadata whether or not they spend time creating that metadata as catalogers or systems librarians. In art museums, metadata is created in curatorial departments, archives, and elsewhere across the institution to describe artworks, institutional records, and other valuable materials. Librarians are experienced in creating well-structured, consistent metadata, implementing name authority files and controlled vocabularies, and applying complex classification schemes, and they can use their skills to increase discovery and access to museum collections and scholarship. Gaining a holistic view of all the metadata created by an institution contextualizes the work the library does, and, as shall be demonstrated, paves the way for new methods of access and discovery. This chapter will discuss the who, what, where, and whys of metadata creation inside an organization and will go on to examine museums that are exploiting the commonalities among their metadata systems for new projects. Finally, this chapter will briefly examine linked open data (LOD) and demonstrate how the principles embedded in LOD are guiding many of these solutions.

ENVIRONMENTAL SCAN: METADATA AND SYSTEMS

As a first step to thinking about metadata, it is useful simply to understand where it is kept, by which departments, and for what purposes. Large institutions typically have several distinct systems for the library, the artwork collection, digital resources, and archival systems. Smaller institutions may try to minimize costs by making one type of software fit diverse needs. Institutions of all sizes often utilize simpler tools such as Excel spreadsheets or Google Docs; if such documents play a role in how one creates and stores metadata for discovery and access, then they too should be

161

understood as important systems in their own right. For a good overview of the larger systems frequently seen in museums, archivist, developer, and preservation expert Ashley Brewer has maintained a public spreadsheet comparing commercial and other metadata systems used by art museums. The spreadsheet currently lists sixty-eight different systems.[1] In museums, the systems managed by the library and those library staff, who have privileges to use, can vary widely.

Diagramming the systems used by an institution is the second step to understanding the metadata ecology of which the museum library is a part. In 2018, Duke University Libraries diagrammed their current metadata creation and discovery systems and found it had enormous utility in orienting current and new staff to where their work fits into the overall ecology.[2] Like Duke, the Art Institute of Chicago produced the diagram in figure 17.1 to understand better how to streamline their systems.[3] As it illustrates, metadata created in the library has the possibility of ending up in many different places alongside metadata from many other systems.

As metadata flows from where it is created to where users access it, does it overlap with information about the same item created somewhere else? At the Museum of

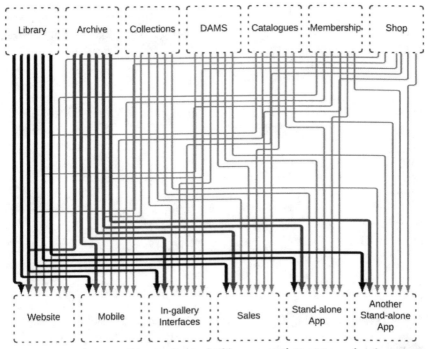

Figure 17.1.   Diagram of Art Institute of Chicago metadata systems showing where metadata is created and stored (top), and where it is displayed and accessed (bottom). After Illya Moskvin and Nikhil Trivedi, "Building a Data Hub: Microservices, APIs, and System Integration at the Art Institute of Chicago," *MW19: MW* 2019. [Redrawn by Jonathan Lill.]

Modern Art (MoMA), for instance, when an item in the library—which already has a bibliographic record in the library catalog—is loaned out for exhibition, it is put into the same workflow as artwork loans and thus requires creating a record for the item in the museum's collection management system. At the same time, a high-resolution image of the item is made and stored in a digital asset management system with attendant descriptive metadata. Thus, three systems have metadata describing the same object. If an institution wants to connect the three records (or easily ascertain that they described *exactly* the same item), it can make sure that a single unique identifier is copied from system to system, such as a call number, barcode, or bibliographic system record identifier. For added convenience, the new identifiers might be copied from the collection management system and digital asset management system back to the original bibliographic record, or a spreadsheet outside of any system can contain all the information.

One object may be represented in more than one system, but the picture broadens when one considers the possible overlap among types of objects across systems. Libraries may own books that are rare or artist-made. Do the institution's curatorial departments also accession books as part of the museum's art collection? What about posters and other graphic works, photographs, or ephemera? What steps would be needed to produce a list of all examples of one class of items regardless of which department holds them? One step could be to ensure that wherever that metadata lives, the items are classified consistently (e.g., a "poster" is called a poster in every system in which a poster is described). This can be achieved by adopting a consistent, controlled vocabulary across all the systems, or more simply by maintaining a crosswalk for reference where different terms in each system are matched to each other.

If types of materials overlap among departments and systems, it is certain that there is overlap among creators—authors, artists, curators—across systems. Museum libraries will have books about (or by) artists whose artworks are hanging in the galleries. When the same names appear in both the library system and the museum's collection management system, the names aren't often in the same format, so how can they be tied together? The best answer may be to match the names to each other and store a unique identifier for one in the record for the other, or to store in each place with a unique identifier from an external authority file. This way it does not matter if different systems refer to the artist as "Basquiat, Jean-Michel, 1960-1988,"[4] "Jean-Michel Basquiat, American, 1960–1988,"[5] or "Samo" (the artist's early pseudonym); systems can recognize that the records refer to the same person because of the system identifiers or because all three records match to an external authority identifier such as the Getty's Union List of Artist Names ("Basquiat, Jean-Michel [American painter and sculptor, 1960–1988]," identifier 500093239).

These are the types of linkages that make it possible for a search result to show *everything* made by or concerning a specific artist, format, or medium: finding the similarities among an institution's metadata systems and encoding those points of congruence in the metadata itself. Only then can a museum respond to such a query with a display that can include correspondence from the archives, artist files, recent monographs, as well as artworks in the collection.

MAKING CONNECTIONS

Many art museums are aligning their metadata to produce more detailed and unified online displays of cross-departmental holdings. An exemplary case is The Georgia O'Keeffe Museum in Santa Fe, New Mexico, which launched a beta version of a new "Collections Online" site in fall 2019.[6] The site unites metadata from the museum's collections system, library catalog, archival finding aids, and digital asset management system into a single search interface. The website clearly indicates that all these materials come from different departmental collections, but treats them like a single group in order to search for any materials—artworks, correspondence, photographs—by their common charateristics, including date of production, creator, or subject. The site fully exploits the varieties of roles individuals have to objects. O'Keeffe was for a time married to noted photographer Alfred Stieglitz, but "Collections Online" allows a user to discover photographs where he is the subject rather than the photographer, while also leading the researcher to letters where he is the writer or the recipient, all in addition to his photographs. Whereas O'Keeffe's paintings were already readily available on the museum's website, the "Collections Online" initiative is a vast improvement in discoverability for library and archives materials. Furthermore, by establishing webpages for creators like Stieglitz and thousands of other names, the O'Keeffe Museum's website provides a place to communicate information about those persons, and a place from which to link to additional resources—Wikipedia, ULAN—for learning more.

The O'Keeffe Museum is not the only museum building with such a project. In summer 2019, the director of web content for the Victoria and Albert Museum announced a similar initiative, saying,

> Yet—right now—it's difficult, nigh on impossible, for us to answer the question, *"Can you show me everything you have about William Morris?"* . . . This is because the V&A's information on William Morris exists across seven different systems—our collections management system, our content management system, our blog, our library catalogue, our archive, our image licensing website and online shop. There are probably others.[7]

In spring 2019, the Philadelphia Museum of Art inaugurated its Art Information Commons project in order to overcome the information silos that "make it more difficult to find relevant items, such as a preparatory drawing, letter from the artist, historic installation photography, and scholarly publication that all pertain to the same work of art."[8] Part of the project's goal is to achieve "the holistic management of its collections related to data" and the creation of an information culture "that spans the entire organization and will benefit data creation, access, and preservation for years to come."[9] It is as yet unclear what kind of interfaces the project will produce, but it certainly aims to change how metadata producers across the museum understand the context of their work.

More museums are expanding their websites in ways that do not necessarily feature rich metadata-fueled search environments but still improve online discoverability and access to library materials. In 2016 the MoMA published thousands of new webpages, one for each exhibition in their then eighty-seven-year history (figure 17.2). Those pages were built on historical exhibition data developed by the MoMA archives. The exhibition data was connected on spreadsheets to checklists and installation images from the archives, press releases from the library, and newly scanned exhibition catalogs matched to their MARC metadata from the MoMA library catalog.

Figure 17.2. Homepage of MoMA historical exhibition pages aligning metadata from library, archives, collections, and web systems in one place, https://www.moma.org/calendar/exhibitions/history.

LINKED OPEN DATA

These projects could not happen without understanding the metadata systems—collection management system, library catalog, spreadsheets—aligning the metadata by their points of commonality—artist name, role, exhibition, format—and embedding that information in the metadata. Such activities are also the basic steps toward implementing LOD. Very simply, LOD is a set of strategies and standards for encoding and publishing metadata online in a manner that makes it much easier for other computers and systems to find it, understand what it is, and integrate it with metadata from other institutions. LOD is not now, and perhaps will never be, a substitute for current institutional metadata systems (or whatever current systems become). The core concept of LOD is that anything one wants to describe—an artwork, an artist, or anything else—can be assigned a place on the web, a uniform resource identifier (URI).[10] In addition, whatever one wants to say about that entity, such as title, or medium, or creator, is also defined by its own URI and that, finally, as many of the values as possible are given URIs as well. The result would be a place on the web given not only to a specific painting (e.g., *Starry Night*),[11] the medium itself, oil on canvas,[12] and the creator, Vincent Van Gogh,[13] but also to the concept of painting, the concept of medium, and the concept of a creator. As museums work to connect and interlink metadata across their institutions for better access, LOD promises to help do the same across the entire internet.

If that seems like an impossibly distant goal, Tim Berners-Lee, the person who formulated the major concepts of LOD, helpfully laid out steps on how to get there with his five-star linked data scheme:

☆ Data is available on the web, in whatever format, but with permissions for anyone to access and use it.
☆☆ Available as machine-readable structured data, such as in a spreadsheet rather than a Word document or PDF.
☆☆☆ Available in a non-proprietary format (i.e., CSV, not Microsoft Excel).
☆☆☆☆ Published using open standards from the W3C and establishing URIs for things so people can point to them.
☆☆☆☆☆ All of the above and actively linking to other LOD.[14]

As this list shows, it is not difficult to achieve three-star LOD with a little effort, but the question arises as to what data a museum might want to make public. Data about artworks owned by the museum is certainly an obvious choice, and collection data has been the focus of LOD initiatives for several years.[15] The MoMA posts collection data on GitHub as well as a separate dataset of the artists in its collection and another of its exhibition history.[16] The Rijksmuseum, leading the field, recently launched "Rijks Data," which hosts separate datasets for not only their collection data, but also for the controlled vocabularies they use in the museum as well as their entire library catalog.[17]

Other museums may decide not to go quite that far, but in thinking about what data to make public, they can reframe the questions asked earlier in this chapter. As one might want to be able to see all the artists' books in the museum regardless of what department they are in, so too might one ask to see, all at once, artists' books from many institutions. For institutions where such a goal would be useful, making a spreadsheet of only artists' book data available to the public can be an important step to take. If the library's artist files contain significant materials on artists in the collection or important to the local community, then making that data public can be a significant way of drawing attention to the collection and making the information about the materials more useful. Matching those artist file names to artworks in the collection, Wikipedia pages, or ULAN records, makes the data more valuable and ties data from an institution more fully into a future LOD universe.

Metadata is much more than MARC records in a bibliographic catalog. By understanding the different places metadata resides across an institution, one can start identifying areas where the metadata overlaps, and, by exploiting these connections, provide new ways for users to discover and access collections in the library, in the museum's collection, and elsewhere. The same techniques used to accomplish this internally can also set one well on the path toward LOD. Eventually, the metadata for *all* the materials art museums preserve and promote might be fully integrated (or able to be integrated) with the metadata from the international community of museums, uniting the local ecology of the institution with that of the broader world.

NOTES

1. Ashley Brewer, "The Collection Management System Collection," *Ashley Brew Blog Progress Process*, August 9, 2017. Accessed March 25, 2020, https://bits.ashleyblewer.com/blog/2017/08/09/collection-management-system-collection/.

2. Maggie Dickson, "Mapping Duke University Libraries' Discovery System Environment," *Bitstreams: Notes from the Digital ProjectsTeam*, March 18, 2018. Accessed March 25, 2020, https://blogs.library.duke.edu/bitstreams/2018/03/18/mapping-duke-university-libraries-discovery-system-environment/.

3. Illya Moskvin and Nikhil Trivedi, "Building a Data Hub: Microservices, APIs, and System Integration at the Art Institute of Chicago," *MW19: MW 2019*, January 15, 2019. Accessed March 25, 2020, https://mw19.mwconf.org/paper/building-a-data-hub-microservices-apis-and-system-integration-at-the-art-institute-of-chicago/.

4. "Basquiat, Jean-Michel, 1960–1988," Library of Congress Linked Data Service Name Authority File. Accessed December 6, 2019, http://id.loc.gov/authorities/names/n85819387.

5. For a typical formulation of the name on a museum's wall label; see "Jean-Michel Basquiat," The Museum of Modern Art. Accessed December 6, 2019, https://www.moma.org/artists/370.

6. "Collections Online Beta," The Georgia O'Keeffe Museum. Accessed December 6, 2019, https://collections.okeeffemuseum.org/.

7. Kati Price, "Redesigning the V&A's Collections Online," *V&A Blog*, May 30, 2019. Accessed March 25, 2020, https://www.vam.ac.uk/blog/digital/redesigning-the-vas-collections-online.

8. Philadelphia Museum of Art, "The Philadelphia Museum of Art, Art Information Commons Mellon Foundation Proposal," 2018. Shared with the author, 2.

9. Philadelphia Museum of Art, but also quoted in Bree Midavaine, "Setting the Scene: An Environmental Scan for the Art Information Commons Initiative at the Philadelphia Museum of Art" 2019, 1. Accessed March 25, 2020, https://artinformationcommons.github

.io/uploads/Art%20Information%20Commons%20Environmental%20Scan%20White%20
Paper.pdf. The same webpage includes a link to the Google sheet compilation of projects and
endeavors around the world that the Philadelphia Museum considers to be working in the
same space.

10. For most purposes, a URL (Uniform Resource Locator) or webpage is interchangeable
with the concept of the URI. See "Naming and Addressing: URIs, URLs, . . ." W3C Architecture Domain. Accessed December 6, 2019, https://www.w3.org/Addressing/.

11. "The Starry Night," Wikidata. Accessed December 6, 2019, https://www.wikidata
.org/wiki/Q45585. While *Starry Night* has a webpage at the site of the museum who owns
it, https://www.moma.org/collection/works/79802, that page doesn't have any adequately
structured data about the painting, so another authority system might be preferred. And the
Wikidata record contains the MoMA work identifier, from which the link to the museum
webpage can be constructed.

12. "Art and Architecture Thesaurus Online," The Getty Research Institute. Accessed
December 6, 2019, https://www.getty.edu/research/tools/vocabularies/aat/. For oil paint, the
URI is http://vocab.getty.edu/page/aat/300015050, and for the canvas support it is http://
vocab.getty.edu/page/aat/300014078.

13. "Union List of Artist Names Online," The Getty Research Institute. Accessed December 2019, http://vocab.getty.edu/page/ulan/500115588. Unlike terms relating to visual arts,
in which the Getty's AAT is by far the most comprehensive authority file, museums have a
wider array of name authority files to choose among and match to, and in this example there
is no special reason to prefer ULAN.

14. "5 Star Linked Data," W3C. Accessed December 6, 2019, https://www.w3.org/2011/gld
/wiki/5_Star_Linked_Data.

15. The American Art Collaborative is a notable past project (see http://americanartcol
laborative.org/), whereas Linked.Art, https://linked.art/, is another ongoing effort.

16. "The Museum of Modern Art," Github. Accessed December 6, 2019, https://github
.com/MuseumofModernArt.

17. "Rijks Data," The Rijksmuseum. Accessed December 2019, https://data.rijksmuseum
.nl/bibliographic-data/.

18

Digitization and Digital Repositories

Bryan Ricupero, University of Wyoming,
and Sophie Jo Miller, University of Wyoming

This chapter examines key components in the digitization and repository processes and systems related to two-dimensional objects in art museum libraries. These include policies for building collections in digital repositories, digitization processes and workflows, platforms used for sharing various collection types, Americans with Disabilities Act (ADA) accessibility standards, and long-term preservation strategies.

While viewing a digitized version does not entirely replace the impact of the physical object, it does offer unique, new ways for the public to discover and experience it, while also reducing wear and tear on the originals. Furthermore, "digitization allows the (virtual) integration of (physically) separated information and objects in collections, even if these objects are from different departments. Digitization would further solve the concern of defining where the collections are to be managed, by the museum or by the museum library, reducing the problem of the artificial division of collections."[1] Although at present most museums commit a very small percentage of their budgets—on average, less than 10 percent—to building digital collections, it is hoped that this allocation will increase as funding agencies for cultural heritage institutions realize the value of high-quality digital surrogates for both preservation and accessibility.[2]

DIGITAL COLLECTION POLICIES

The authors of this chapter created a survey to capture the digitization policies and practices in use in libraries. The survey was shared through the three listservs in August 2019: the Art Libraries Society of North America, American Alliance of Museums, and the Mountain Plains Library Association. A total of ninety-four responses were received; of these, thirty-one were complete enough to analyze. Twenty-seven of these identified as museum libraries, five as academic, and one as a historical society; two institutions identified as both museum and academic. Nearly 35 percent of respondents have five or fewer full-time employees, whereas 30 percent report having one hundred or more full-time employees. Some institutions are currently developing digital collection policies with plans to implement them soon, whereas others choose to utilize existing analog collection policies.[3]

Institutions having digital collection policies have developed common characteristics, including:

- Digitization methods, primarily photography;
- Storage, ranging from cloud-based to local servers with IP address limitations;
- Findability, with some institutions making digital objects findable by catalog number; and
- Funding, with specific references to digitizing "as grants become available."[4]

Some institutions align their digital collection policies to existing object collection policies.[5] Guidelines offered by the Northeast Document Conservation Center[6] and the Council on Library and Information Resources[7] can be usefully applied across a wide range of institution types and collections. The transformation of museums, libraries, and archives toward digital asset creation and management is discussed at length in the *Best of Both Worlds: Museums, Libraries, and Archives in a Digital Age.*[8]

Subject and Content Collection Focus

The majority of respondents to the survey conducted by this chapter's authors reported having a subject or collection content focus at their institutions, with concentrations spread between art, geographic locations, and anthropology and paleontology. A total of 60 percent of respondents reported having a subject or collection focus without a digital policy, whereas the remaining 40 percent were divided with 20 percent having both a subject focus and a digital policy, 15 percent having no subject focus or policy, and 5 percent having no subject focus but having a digital policy. Having a subject or collection focus can diminish the need to have a standardized policy for digital collections, as consistency will be maintained within the subject or collection focus.

Workflows and Digitization Techniques

Approximately 80 percent of respondents reported that around 75 percent of their digitization happens in-house. Roughly half of that group reports 100 percent digitization happening in-house. All but one of the respondents who submitted details about their digital collection policies are in the 80 percent who primarily digitize materials in-house.[9] The choices that institutions make regarding workflows and digitization processes heavily depend on the collection size, budget, and number of dedicated staff assigned to these projects. Considering these factors, it makes sense that survey respondents generally referred to methods that have a relatively low startup cost. This is consistent with research done outside of the survey, which will be addressed later in this section.

The Federal Agency Digitization Guidelines Initiative established a standard used by many institutions for digitization. These guidelines emerged in 2007 as a way to address the need for standardized best practices around "digitized and born digital historical, archival and cultural content"[10] and apply to specific digitization needs, including bound and unbound documents, newspapers, photographs and photographic negatives, non-print two-dimensional art (such as paintings and graphic arts), and microfilm.[11] These guidelines are comprehensive but can be difficult for institutions— even those with ample staff and financial resources—to implement because of the complexity of this work and because they are applicable only to specific object types.

The most common techniques used by survey respondents for digitizing physical holdings are digital photography and flatbed scanning. These methods are relatively inexpensive and have a low learning curve, making them easy to learn and to train others to do. Another benefit is that cameras and scanners, when well cared for, can last several years, providing a high return on investment.

The widespread use of digital photography and flatbed scanning among respondents is common in institutions with limited resources. Eric Michael Wolf and Lauren Gottlieb-Miller (both of The Menil Collection) discuss approaches to digitization adopted by smaller institutions, using their museum as a case study.[12] They first began work on digital projects in 2015 with one full-time and one part-time staff member and a similarly small budget. Their initial focus was on making born-digital content, specifically gallery guides, available through both their local catalog and through OCLC WorldCat. They began digitizing some of the historic books in their collection using a digital single-lens reflex (DSLR) camera to which they already had access and eventually were able to expand the digitization program by adding a flatbed scanner and increasing their staff to two full-time librarians. The Menil Collection offers an example of how even a small institution lacking a large budget can begin a digitization program using resources already at their disposal.

Several survey respondents also reported using photogrammetry to generate three-dimensional (3D) images. Although photogrammetry requires specific software and computing power to run software for image assembly and cleanup, photogrammetry can utilize an existing digital photography station and equipment. For institutions that already have this infrastructure, it may be able to be used in both stand photography and to generate 3D data and modeling. "Photogrammetry modelling begins with a series of photographs taken from varying angles. Common features are matched within overlapping photographs, relevant depths are extracted, and a virtual 3D model is created."[13] Several free programs such as AgiSoft and COLMAP can be used as alternatives to more expensive software that requires ownership and licensing. The Minneapolis Institute of Art's 3D modeling efforts provide a good look at the use of photogrammetry techniques in an art library setting.[14]

Reflectance transformation imaging (RTI), mentioned by a small number of survey respondents, and it also provides a highly accessible technique for near-3D digitization. In an Ithaka S+R report on research service needs, RTI was described as a method "which allows scholars to view an object with a variety of different light sources, something that might not have been available to them in a traditional museum setting."[15] This is an example of digitization fulfilling needs that cannot be filled through traditional methods. Like photogrammetry, RTI has a relatively low cost for institutions already making use of digital photography. However, in order to achieve results that can be used for research purposes, light and camera position must be carefully controlled.[16] To help make this method more affordable, Cultural Heritage Imaging offers a free image building tool for RTI captures, as well as robust documentation for the entire RTI process.[17] RTI offers a way for institutions already working with digital photography to expand their digitization options without purchasing additional expensive photographic equipment.

Platforms and Hosting

The most common scenario for hosting, organizing, and presenting collections; long-term storage for master images; and contributing to a large-scale aggregation point is content management software used in concert with a digital asset management system. Among survey respondents, the most common in use was PastPerfect. All responses indicating the use of PastPerfect were from museums and art libraries. The second most common system was LUNA, followed by CONTENTdm. The open source web-publishing platform Omeka was also mentioned by several responding institutions as their primary tool for creating digital exhibits.

There are many factors to consider when implementing or migrating to new systems. Survey respondents noted both institutional and product-specific limitations that can impact repository management. These are some of the themes that emerged in the survey responses that can also be used to help analyze how available systems can support the unique needs of art museum libraries:

- User privileges can be an issue; one cannot protect master images and still allow access to derivatives.
- Some products focus on fine art and visual resources, whereas others focus on material culture.
- The user interface and back end interface require workarounds and redundant steps.
- Some systems may have no web component.
- Users cannot download materials for their own use.
- Rights management may not exist in some systems.
- Maintaining relationships between records can become challenging.
- Metadata can't be edited in bulk without a complicated scripting program.

- These systems are difficult for institutions with a small staff or limited funds to implement.
- Artist/estate copyright presents a financial limitation to using reproductions as liberally as an institution would like.

Hosting location, either in-house or through a vendor or partner institution, was a near even split. A small majority of respondents, 56 percent, host in-house, and the remaining 44 percent rely on a vendor or cooperating institution for hosting. A practical cost-cutting solution is the use of consortial or shared efforts in hosting and managing digital content. In selecting a platform or a hosting arrangement, there is no perfect solution. "Your library may already have an existing repository, but try to evaluate prospective new platforms independently of whether or not they are 'better' or 'worse' than your current platform. In many ways, a new platform will likely just be different—and that's going to be a combination of positive and negative."[18]

Americans with Disabilities Act Accessibility

Any assessment of a digital platform should consider its adherence to established ADA accessibility guidelines. In order to be fully compliant, a website has to meet several basic criteria such as video captioning and keyboard-only navigation. The World Wide Web Consortium aims to develop and establish web standards that lead to near- and long-term improvements in web usability, including accessibility. The consortium is run by a full-time staff and receives input from a variety of member organizations throughout the world. This international approach allows the World Wide Web Consortium to create web accessibility standards that have a positive impact on a global scale. The overview for the current version (2.1 as of this writing) covers requirements for ADA-compliant web interfaces divided into four categories:

Perceivable
- Provide text alternatives for non-text content.
- Provide captions and other alternatives for multimedia.
- Create content that can be presented in different ways, including by assistive technologies, without losing meaning.
- Make it easier for users to see and hear content.

Operable
- Make all functionality available from a keyboard.
- Give users enough time to read and use content.
- Do not use content that causes seizures or physical reactions.
- Help users navigate and find content.
- Make it easier to use inputs other than keyboard.

Understandable
- Make text readable and understandable.
- Make content appear and operate in predictable ways.
- Help users avoid and correct mistakes.

Robust
- Maximize compatibility with current and future tools.[19]

Institutions may struggle to implement these characteristics for accessible web interface design because of limitations imposed by software, funding, or expertise.[20] However, every step taken toward improving web accessibility makes content available to more users. Institutions should strive to meet as many of the requirements as possible.

Survey responses regarding ADA accessibility are evenly split, with approximately 53 percent reporting "no" and 47 percent reporting "yes" to whether their collections are displayed on an ADA-compliant interface. Half of the respondents lacking compliant interfaces recognize the importance of accessibility and acknowledge the need to improve ADA compliance. About 25 percent of respondents provided reasons for not implementing improved accessibility ranging from lack of time and funding to a need for increased awareness about what ADA compliance entails. One respondent stated that ADA compliance is "not really applicable as the collection is available on the web." It is possible that several respondents view ADA compliance as relating only to physical barriers and are unaware of digital barriers to access, such as incompatibility with screen readers, interfaces with poor visibility, and lack of transcripts for audio and video.

Digital Preservation

Having a digital preservation policy ensures that preservation systems and protocols are part of the project from the beginning, ensuring long-term access and sustainability. Digital preservation is integral to the digitization workflow and a first step in this process is to create a digital preservation policy identifying the goals and strategies for digital preservation within an institution. In their case study "Better Together," Rafferty and Pad discuss the process of creating a digital preservation policy for the Baltimore Museum of Art, where Rafferty works as the head librarian and archivist.[21] Although they primarily discuss art museums in this case study, several of their points reflect issues similar to those brought up by survey respondents who participated in a study by this chapter's authors. One of the key issues they address (specifically in relation to art museums) is that the vast majority of digital preservation policies come from academic libraries and archives, which might have collections with "needs that are related, but not entirely the same."[22]

Rafferty and Pad state that, "Digital preservation is not simple, regardless of the size of an institution, and taking these first steps can seem out of reach for small and even midsized museum."[23] For many art museums (especially small museums with limited staff and funding), creating a strong digital preservation policy may be seen as a lofty task, especially with the majority of examples coming from non-museum institutions. According to a Library of Congress digital preservation policy analysis, only two of the thirty-three policies they analyzed came from museums.[24]

Implementing preservation workflow can seem like a daunting process, and approaches vary depending on budget and technical infrastructure in place at each institution. Three survey respondents indicated that they used Amazon Web Services for long-term storage of master copies, and four respondents reported sharing digitized content through the Internet Archive. Although digital preservation is about more than just keeping a copy of a file, off-site back-up of master copies is a first step for many institutions.[25] Another preservation strategy is a turnkey repository platform that offers the benefit of additional preservation and access services; some examples include DSpace, Archivematica, Arctos, VertNet, eMuseum, Laserfiche, MDID, and Preservica. Cost, security, and access are all important factors to consider when evaluating digital preservation options, whereas turnkey solutions may remove many of the technical barriers to preservation, their cost may make them prohibitive to small institutions. Some preservation platforms may include public interfaces to allow collections to be shared, but many institutions share digitized materials and collections through aggregators and external hosts like the Digital Public Library of America, the Getty Research Portal, Hathi Trust, and the Internet Archive. Digital preservation is a complex topic and an integral facet of the broader digital workflow with many case studies and broad overviews to support further learning in this area.[26]

CURRENT USES OF DIGITIZATION AND FUTURE POSSIBILITIES

Digitization and digital preservation programs are still relatively new among art museum libraries, and an institution's size, collecting priorities, budget, and the technological resources available necessarily impact the ways in which institutions approach digitization. Methods pioneered by larger institutions offer possibilities for what smaller institutions may be able to do in the future as the means become available.

Some institutions simply use digitization to provide another means of examining objects that cannot be shared through more traditional methods such as interlibrary loan. For example, the Getty Research Institute (GRI) has developed a portal that allows users to search and access the digital art history books and journals for free. In addition to managing this portal, the GRI also contributes to it, digitizing and sharing out-of-copyright books from their collections. In some cases, books are digitized and uploaded upon demand by researchers, thus simultaneously making them available to the general public. According to their blog *The Iris*, they are able to digitize most books in under an hour and make them publicly available in less than a day—quicker than they would be able to ship a physical volume, assuming the volume was even in good enough condition to ship.[27]

While the GRI is primarily digitizing books, other institutions are using digitization to present and preserve visual images and archival content related to exhibitions. The Museum of Modern Art in New York offers a digital "Exhibition History" on their website starting with the museum's first exhibitions in 1929 and continuing to those currently on display. Users can search exhibitions and programs by type and decade, and individual entries offer a variety of content, including images of the works of art exhibited and installation views, artist profiles, press releases, and content checklists. In this case, digitization offers the public a way to see not only the art, but also some of the historic context in which it was displayed, creating a dynamic user experience.[28]

Digitization of art museum library collections allows for art libraries to share materials beyond the physical boundaries of their building to increase the visibility of their collections and extend the impact of their mission to a global audience. Sharing these collections ensures that art library collections continue to be a vibrant part of the scholarly discourse that is moving increasingly online. It also shows the unique and adaptable skill sets of art librarians, who are increasingly required to fluidly navigate between physical and digital information environments.

NOTES

1. Trilce Navarrete and John Mackenzie Owen, "Museum Libraries: How Digitization Can Enhance the Value of the Museum," *Palabra Clave (La Plata)* 1, no. 1 (October 2011): 12–20.

2. The size of responding institutions varies widely. Nearly 33 percent report having five or fewer full-time employees, whereas 30 percent report having one hundred or more full-time employees.

3. Fifteen (plus one) respondents answered "No" when asked if they had a digital collection policy. Five answered "Yes," and ten respondents did not answer this question. One respondent did not answer "Yes" or "No," but explained in the comments that they only create digital surrogates and did not feel they needed a policy for this purpose. Their response is considered a "No."

4. This quote comes from a respondent who works for a state repository focusing on anthropology, archeology, and paleontology. Their institution has a digital collection policy, which was referred to in their response. The full quote reads: "Transfer of digital records from archaeologists must meet our curation guidelines. For new acquisitions, we have a photo policy for objects, and for digital records that are archived. Material from old 35mm slide libraries are digitized as grants become available. We seek [financial] support from federal agencies who own some of the archaeological collections. Object images are searchable by catalog number."

5. Of these respondents, one refers to this as having a digital collection policy, whereas others refer to it as not having a digital collection policy. The primary difference is that the respondent who views this as a digital collection policy discussed extending standard object policy to include digital objects.

6. Janet Gertz, "Reformatting: 6.6 Preservation and Selection for Digitization," *Northeast Document Conservation Center*. Accessed April 10, 2020, https://www.nedcc.org/free-resources/preservation-leaflets/6.-reformatting/6.6-preservation-and-selection-for-digitization.

7. Council on Library and Information Resources, "Identification, Evaluation, and Selection," *CLIR Publications*. Accessed April 10, 2020, https://www.clir.org/pubs/reports/pub101/section2/.

8. G. Wayne Clough, *Best of Both Worlds: Museums, Libraries, and Archives in a Digital Age* (Washington, DC: Smithsonian Institution, 2013). https://permanent.access.gpo.gov/gpo41908/BestofBothWorldsSmithsonian.pdf.

9. One institution reported that 75 percent to 99 percent of their digitization is outsourced. This respondent states that their digitization policy is an extension of their standard collection policy. The connection between in-house digitization and developing digital collection policies should be researched further.

10. *FADGI Guidelines*. Accessed August 7, 2020, http://www.digitizationguidelines.gov/.

11. Information and Document Management International, "Part Two: Is FADGI for Everyone?" *Gale General Onefile*, 2018. Accessed November 11, 2019, https://link.gale.com/apps/doc/A565450035/ITOF?u=wylrc_uwyoming&sid=ITOF&xid=dcf9945c.

12. Eric Michael Wolf and Lauren Gottlieb-Miller, "The Small Easy: Budget-Neutral Digital Projects at Small Libraries," *Art Documentation: Journal of the Art Libraries Society of North America* 36, no. 2 (September 1, 2017): 332–44.

13. James Miles, Mike Pitts, Hembo Pagi, and Graeme Earl, "New Applications of Photogrammetry and Reflectance Transformation Imaging to an Easter Island Statue," *Antiquity* 88, no. 340 (June 2014): 596–605.

14. Minneapolis Institute of Art, "3D Modeling of Mia Collections," *Minneapolis Institute of Art Website*. Accessed April 10, 2020, https://new.artsmia.org/art-artists/research/case-studies/3d-modeling-of-mia-collections/.

15. Matthew P. Long and Roger C. Schonfeld, "Preparing for the Future of Research Services for Art History: Recommendations from the Ithaka S+R Report," *Art Documentation: Journal of the Art Libraries Society of North America* 33, no. 2 (September 1, 2014): 192–205.

16. Ibid.

17. Cultural Heritage Imaging, *Reflectance Transformation Imaging (RTI)*. Accessed November 15, 2019, http://culturalheritageimaging.org/Technologies/RTI/index.html.

18. Hillary Corbett, Jimmy Gaphery, Lauren Work, and Sam Byrd, "Choosing a Repository Platform: Open Source vs. Hosted Solutions," in *Making Institutional Repositories Work*, edited by Burton B Callicott, David Scherer, and Andrew Wesolek (West Lafayette, Indiana: Purdue University Press, 2016), 3–14.

19. Shawn Lawton Henry and Wayne Dick, "WCAG 2.1 at a Glance," *W3C Web Accessibility Initiative*. Accessed April 10, 2020, https://www.w3.org/WAI/standards-guidelines/wcag/glance/.

20. In such cases, a common interim practice is to have an accessibility statement soliciting user feedback.

21. Emily Rafferty and Becca Pad, "Better Together: A Holistic Approach to Creating a Digital Preservation Policy in an Art Museum," *Art Documentation: Journal of the Art Libraries Society of North America* 36, no. 1 (March 1, 2017): 149–62.

22. Ibid, 150.

23. Ibid, 158.

24. Madeline Sheldon, *Analysis of Current Digital Preservation Policies: Archives, Libraries, and Museums. The Signal*, Library of Congress, August 13, 2013. Accessed November 13, 2019, http://www.digitalpreservation.gov/documents/Analysis%20of%20Current%20Digital%20Preservation%20Policies.pdf.

25. Han Yan, "Cloud Storage for Digital Preservation: Optimal Uses of Amazon S3 and Glacier," *Library Hi Tech* 33, no. 2 (January 1, 2015): 261–71. https://doi.org/10.1108/LHT -12-2014-0118.

26. Additional sources on digital preservation: Jeremy Myntti and Jessalyn Zoom, *Digital Preservation in Libraries: Preparing for a Sustainable Future* (American Library Association, 2019); Digital POWRR, "From Theory to Action: 'Good Enough' Digital Preservation Solutions for Under-Resources Cultural Heritage Institutions," August 2014. Accessed August 24, 2020, https://commons.lib.niu.edu/bitstream/handle/10843/13610/FromTheoryToAction_POWRR_WhitePaper.pdf?sequence=1&isAllowed=y; Smithsonian Institution Archives, "Digital Preservation Challenges and Solutions." Accessed August 24, 2020, https://siarchives .si.edu/what-we-do/digital-curation/digital-preservation-challenges-and-solutions.

27. Tristan Bravinder, "The People behind the Getty Research Portal," *The Iris: Behind the Scenes at the Getty*, August 6, 2018. Accessed April 10, 2020, https://blogs.getty.edu/iris /the-people-behind-the-getty-research-portal/.

28. Museum of Modern Art, *Exhibition History*. Accessed April 10, 2020, https:// www.moma.org/calendar/exhibitions/history?locale=en&utf8=%E2%9C%93&q=&sort _date=closing_date&constituent_id=&mde_type=All&begin_date=1980&end_date=1989& location=both&page=&direction=.

19

The Rise of Wikimedia in GLAM Institutions

*Sarah Osborne Bender, National Gallery of Art, and
Carissa Pfeiffer, Black Mountain College Museum + Arts Center*

Organizing information, providing access, increasing engagement, and leveraging technology to support research and preservation of intellectual content are priorities for GLAM institutions, using the popular acronym for galleries, libraries, archives, and museums. Over the last several decades, these principles have also intersected with a broader societal shift characterized in part by open access, shared authority, and cooperative digital peer production.[1]

Wikimedia and its associated projects (such as Wikipedia, Wikimedia Commons, and Wikidata, to name those of most consequence to the GLAM sector) are key players in the collaborative effort to thread those priorities through mission-driven efforts serving collections and communities.

HISTORY OF GLAMS IN WIKIMEDIA

Collaborations between GLAM institutions and Wikimedia projects go back more than a decade, with the first "GLAM-Wiki Conference" in Australia in August 2009 laying the foundation for the future. The conference concluded with the publication of a list of recommendations for GLAM institutions, Wikimedia, and the Australian government to facilitate closer collaboration, addressing concerns ranging from the legal (copyright and licensing) to the technological (metadata, stable URLs, and more). One actionable request was for GLAMs to "investigate ways of supporting Wikimedians who work on the institution's subject matter in a similar way to the institution's existing real-world volunteer community."[2] From hosting edit-a-thons to adding content, the Wikimedia-related activities that GLAMs engage in today were popularized and piloted thanks largely to sustained internal museum efforts of residents dedicated to the work of improving Wikipedia, Wikidata, and other Wiki-media projects, beginning shortly following the conference in Australia.

The first Wikipedian-in-Residence was a volunteer position conceived and held by Liam Wyatt in the summer of 2010 at the British Museum. Wyatt spent five weeks working with staff and volunteers to improve Wikipedia content on pages relating to the museum's collections.[3] Since then, more than two hundred people have served as Wikimedians-in-Residence at institutions ranging from museums to libraries, archives, and galleries, and even corporate entities.[4] As residencies have become more common, relationships between institutions and their residents or staff engaged in Wikimedia-related work continue to vary widely. Residencies have been volunteer or paid positions, short-term or long-term, depending on local context and the needs of the organization,[5] and regular GLAM employees have also found themselves collaborating with Wikimedia, either formally or ad hoc. Whatever the work looks like, common characteristics and expectations have emerged to ensure that it meets the needs of both GLAM and Wikimedia communities without compromising the values of either.

Specifically, this manifests as an emphasis on connecting three (sometimes overlapping) groups: GLAM institutions, Wikimedia communities, and the broader public served. Those working with Wikimedia projects on behalf of institutions are *not* primarily editors of Wikipedia articles; rather, they facilitate collaboration and use professional expertise to enrich and link content. This model helps to avoid the potential for a conflict of interest, and invites reimagining the role of institutional authority as lateral with the role of the communities served, bringing together the established expertise and authority that GLAM institutions have long emphasized with the cultural principles of the open web: participation by all, iterative and user-centric approaches, transparency in decision-making, and shared standards, to name just a few.[6]

ENGAGING COMMUNITIES WITH WIKIPEDIA EDIT-A-THONS

As public participation in the digital realm has become commonplace, Wikipedia offers a well-known and relatively accessible platform for community engagement practices centered on information literacy strategies and knowledge construction. One of the most common and low-barrier strategies for engaging external communities is to host Wikipedia Edit-a-Thons: facilitated opportunities for new and seasoned editors alike to learn communally and make contributions to Wikipedia (and sometimes other Wikimedia projects as well), often centered around a theme. They are typically organized as in-person events, but may also include remote participants.

Many librarians and researchers are already familiar with Wikipedia's front-end. Edit-a-thons are designed to provide the training, encouragement, and resources to allow them to become active participants in constructing the site. Moving past the front-end is also a way for users to discover and practice digital literacy concepts such as verifying information, evaluating sources, identifying bias, providing citations, and even learning about copyright. Institutions generally make their own library resources available to editors for finding new information or citations to add to articles. In this way, edit-a-thons help participants gain confidence using library services and materials for research, while also expanding information literacy, technology, and writing skills. Recent opportunity papers from the International Federation of Library Associations and Institutions[7] and the Association of Research Libraries[8] have noted that connecting sources to Wikipedia articles teaches critical research skills to academic and public patrons alike.

In the broader landscape of contemporary librarianship, Wikipedia is not only a new platform for library instruction and discovery, but also part of a civic and social landscape in which librarians facilitate community-driven knowledge creation beyond their home institution. Writing about their work with edit-a-thons in 2015, Siân Evans, Jacqueline Mabey, and Michael Mandiberg define "networked librarianship" as a logical and digitally enabled extension of embedded librarianship, the main feature of which is a more collaborative and intimate relationship with patrons than has traditionally been expected.[9] Similarly, Lori Byrd-McDevitt's (previously Byrd Phillips) 2013 discussion of open authority in museums advocates making use of museum expertise collaboratively to validate, filter, and navigate content that includes the insights and experiences of a broader set of audiences.[10] The expertise of museum librarians and the reputable resources they provide, together with the shared knowledge and perspectives of individuals who benefit from connecting with this expertise, form a compelling example of how museum libraries can share authority with those they serve.

CORRECTING THE RECORD

The civic and social aspects of this relationship also expand the role of the librarian as an "information activist" who strives to decrease barriers between people and information.[11] This includes addressing technology access and promoting participation among groups and individuals who are impacted by structural inequity. Many edit-a-thons are connected to initiatives aimed at increasing representation of marginalized groups on Wikipedia and other Wikimedia projects, both as subjects of articles and as editors.

A 2011 survey from the Wikimedia Foundation generated the now frequently cited statistic that only about 9 percent of contributors to Wikimedia projects at the time identified as women. The gender gap also manifests in content: as of March 2020, about 18 percent of the biographies on English Wikipedia were about people assigned a female "sex or gender" statement on Wikidata.[12] Campaigns such as Women in Red and Art+Feminism address this structural gender bias, and similar endeavors are focused on anti-racist and decolonization efforts through campaigns such as AfroCROWD, Black Lunch Table, and the UN's International Year of Indigenous Languages.

In keeping with the theme of networked communities and collaboration, edit-a-thons may be affiliated with one or more of these or other initiatives. Art museum libraries over the past several years have found an especially fitting partner in Art+Feminism, founded in 2014 by Evans, Mabey, Mandiberg, and Ptak. Art+Feminism is focused on improving content related to the arts, gender, and feminism across Wikipedia, as well as training new editors of all genders. GLAM institutions of all sizes, from the largest to some of the smallest, have hosted events affiliated with Art+Feminism.[13]

In addition to edit-a-thons, art museum librarians and their institutions have numerous other ways to engage professionally with Wikipedia and related projects. In her 2013 article "The Temple and the Bazaar: Wikipedia as a Platform for Open Authority in Museums," Lori Byrd-McDevitt positions edit-a-thons as just the tip of the iceberg for museum professionals using Wikipedia and expresses a desire to see experts in the future contributing beyond these events to reach a more global audience, for instance, by contributing directly to article discussion pages.[14] Librarians based in museums are well-aligned to make such contributions, and indeed, there are also campaigns and events in the Wikipedia universe designed to get more librarians involved. Since 2016, the #1Lib1Ref ("One Librarian, One Reference") campaign has served as a low-barrier entry point for librarians of all types to familiarize themselves with Wikipedia while improving its quality, specifically by adding references to articles that lack citations.[15]

BEYOND WIKIPEDIA: GLAM INSTITUTIONS AS CONTENT CONTRIBUTORS

Many GLAM institutions are working to expand the exchange of data and images among collecting cultural heritage institutions and the public through open access and Creative Commons principles and practices. Wikimedia Commons and Wikidata are the largest, most widely adopted platforms for these activities, and a growing number of institutions are incorporating components of them into workflows for cataloging, digitization projects, and registrarial duties. The impact of this work at the institutional level, created or contributed at a critical mass, can transform existing concepts of custodianship and access into linked content with global reach and elastic function.

Collection Images in Wikimedia Commons

Results of an ongoing jointly authored online survey, "Survey of GLAM Open Access Policy and Practice," begun by Andrea Wallace and Douglas McCarthy, showed 637 international GLAM institutions that make open data available on their "website and/or external platforms such as Github, Europeana, German Digital Library and Wikimedia Commons"[16] in October 2019. Although Wikimedia Commons is not the only platform fulfilling open-access goals, it has advantages over others in its ubiquity and relative ease of use. GLAM institutions contributing public domain images to Wikimedia Commons gain access to arguably the largest image-seeking audience on the web. As of October 2019, Wikimedia Commons included over forty-seven million media files available for free reuse,[17] both within Wikipedia by embedding and linking in related articles and through file download.

Contributing institutions see positive results from opening up collection images and information on Wikimedia platforms: for instance, increased traffic back to collection webpages from links included in the Wiki entry. William Blueher, metadata and collections librarian, Thomas J. Watson Library at The Metropolitan Museum of Art, reported in 2014 that a linking project between digitized library content from the Watson Library and Wikipedia pages resulted in a page view increase of 1,600 percent at the library's website.[18] Additionally, providing accessible and downloadable quality images (that are in the public domain) and their associated metadata from Wikimedia Commons lessens the burden on incoming requests for institutional rights and reproduction services that generally collect only modest administrative fees for providing these open images to requestors. The direct access to publication-quality content for reuse is a boon for scholars, or anyone, looking to illustrate work using GLAM collection objects.

Assessment of reuse of contributed images to Wikimedia Commons is a difficult metric to generate. Some work has been done using reverse image lookup methods to track how and where Wikimedia Commons images are used online.[19] Tools such as BaGLAMa2 and the Wikimedia REST API generate pageview data, but they have limitations.

Institutionally contributed images in Wikimedia Commons are typically of higher quality than images of those same art objects sourced through general online image searches because they are generally pulled from the same files the museum uses for object representation on their website. The owning institution has the opportunity to influence the visual veracity of the reproduced artwork on the web, where representational control is impossible to achieve. The proliferation of discolored, low-quality online digital representations of Johannes Vermeer's *The Milkmaid* (1657–1658) in the collection of the Rijksmuseum came to be known as the "Yellow Milkmaid" and was used as an argument for that institution taking control of their collection images (see figure 19.1). The museum has cited that image's poor reproductions as "the trigger for us to put high-resolution images of the original work with open metadata on the web ourselves. Opening up our data is our best defence against the 'yellow Milkmaid.'"[20] For a GLAM institution with fewer resources than the Rijksmuseum, loading collection images into Wikimedia Commons achieves the goal of providing open access to high-quality images with accompanying metadata without having to develop webpages and maintain image services on their own website.

Figure 19.1. "The Yellow Milkmaid Syndrome," illustrated by eight different versions available on the internet of *The Milkmaid* by Johannes Vermeer, circa 1660, in the collection of the Rijksmuseum, Netherlands. The Rijksmuseum, purchased with the support of the Vereniging Rembrandt.

Wikidata and Library Metadata

Just as Wikimedia Commons has grown into a resource larger than any single institution could generate alone, the structured data environment of Wikidata is a rapidly developing source for unique identifiers that represent items (real-world objects, concepts, and events).[21] These identifiers are already being utilized in MARC records in some libraries, but best practices and workflows have yet to be fully proposed or widely adopted. In the meantime, a number of initiatives from leading library organizations have shared recommendations for introducing Wikidata-based uniform resource identifiers into the library catalog. The Project for Cooperative Cataloging has examined Wikidata (described as an "external platform")[22] as a possible source of identifiers for use in authority record work. The report entitled *ARL White Paper on Wikidata: Opportunities and Recommendations*[23] positively acknowledges the low barrier to participation in the world of linked and open data with Wikidata, but doesn't see it replacing the core responsibilities of library collection management systems. Taking the broad view of linked data within the lifecycle of creating metadata and providing discovery access, Stanford University's Linked Data for Production project, funded by the Mellon Foundation, is a cohort of seventeen Project for Cooperative Cataloging member libraries. This group, which invites participation through affinity groups, online meetings, and web forums, supports "transition from the current MARC-based system to linked data-based workflows"[24] focusing strongly on Wikidata.

The transcendence of traditional structures justifies these initiatives. Wikidata could enhance or transform systems of creating, managing, and accessing library collection metadata. It is system independent, and it supports creation of linked open data which moves seamlessly between local systems and networked platforms. Representing over three hundred languages, Wikimedia projects have natural inclusivity as a globally distributed concept management resource. The vast collaborative efforts to employ these identifiers have brought GLAM institutions together to develop standards and best practices previously unreachable.

These resources can raise concerns as much as opportunities. The globally distributed creation and editing ability on Wikimedia platforms is an environment of flux, unlike traditional centralized authority resources backed by an established institution or governing body such as Library of Congress Name Authority File, Getty vocabularies, and Virtual International Authority File. Wikidata's perpetual potential for editing and lack of authoritative ownership of identity management entries is a new concern for collection catalogs typically maintained by highly skilled catalogers and registrars. As Martin Malmsten has noted, in the linked open world of Wikidata, "the matter of control then becomes a matter of trust rather than technology."[25] Librarians must decide how to adapt to those risks while embracing the vast possibilities.

Leveraging GLAM-Wiki Content

As this mass of GLAM object images and their metadata grows, the creative possibilities also multiply. Testing the concept of trust in collectively generated content, some museums and libraries are experimenting with leveraging the content in Wikipedia (which carries a Creative Commons Zero "No Rights Reserved" license) to enhance resources on their own websites. The Museum of Modern Art has developed a dynamic operation that pulls the lead paragraph from artist articles on Wikipedia to display on artist webpages in the MoMA website. In this way, the museum is able to present more detail for many of the approximately ten thousand artist pages that previously had little more than a brief biographical entry (as identified after a 2014 redesign of the museum's website) with content that is up-to-date and written at an accessible level and style. For artists of lesser prominence, this Wikipedia entry makes up the chief content of the page. For other high-profile artists, the Wikipedia content is an element presented alongside MoMA's own biographical entry written by curators. Explicitly illustrating the link between the museum's site and Wikipedia, the Wikimedia identifier is displayed alongside a link to "view or edit the full Wikipedia entry," thereby inviting the reader to be a part of the knowledge lifecycle.[26] The Tate art galleries are also including Wikipedia biographical entries on their website.

In Wikimedia Commons, work on improving structured metadata will result in enhanced conceptual connectivity between museum objects. The Wikimedia Commons template for artwork metadata includes a property labeled "exhibition history." When employed, the property could take a researcher on a path through exhibitions in which an art object has appeared, and it is possible to envision the ability to virtually re-create historic exhibition checklists within Wikimedia Commons. Further expanding the representation and findability of media, a pilot project is underway to generate automated structured metadata from existing media files, with a focus on content from the GLAM sector.[27]

CONCLUSION

In a 2013 article about linked open data, Becky Yoose and Jody Perkins wrote that GLAM institutions "have accumulated an embarrassment of riches in the form of unique digitized resources and structured data as well as unmined unstructured content, all of which are lying fallow inside a Web of documents and untapped relationships."[28] Since then, tremendous potential for open, linked, and activated collections data and object images has been realized, and momentum continues. Librarians in the GLAM sector have also used Wikimedia projects for cross-institutional collaborations and public engagement, including participatory practices alongside communities that are shaping their own representation within Wikipedia's "working draft of history."[29] Not only are the reach and impact of these global platforms far greater than any one institution can achieve, but they also provide a forum for the voices of both institutions and individuals to contribute meaningfully to the shared cultural record.

NOTES

1. Yochai Benkler, *The Wealth of Networks: How Social Production Transforms Markets and Freedom* (New Haven: Yale University Press, 2006).

2. "GLAM-Wiki Recommendations," *GLAM-Wiki: Finding the Common Ground*, conference held at the Australian War Memorial, Canberra, August 6–7, 2009, convened by Liam Wyatt. Accessed October 18, 2019, https://meta.wikimedia.org/wiki/GLAM-WIKI_2009 _report.

3. Andrew Lih, "What are Galleries, Libraries, Archives, and Museums (GLAM) to the Wikimedia Community?" in *Leveraging Wikipedia: Connecting Communities of Knowledge*, edited by Merrilee Proffitt (Chicago: ALA Editions, 2018), 9.

4. Full list of past and present WiRs," from the article "Wikimedian in residence," last modified December 3, 2020, at 23:21. Accessed December 7, 2020, https://meta.wikimedia .org/wiki/Wikimedian_in_residence.

5. Alexander D. Stinson, Sandra Fauconnier, and Liam Wyatt, "Stepping Beyond Libraries: The Changing Orientation in Global GLAM-Wiki," *Italian Journal of Library, Archives, and Information Science* 3, no. 9 (2018): 21–22.

6. These principles, and the ways they extend into practice in archives, are nicely summarized by Kate Theimer, "What Is the Meaning of Archives 2.0?" *American Archivist* 74, no. 1 (2011): 58–68.

7. International Federation of Library Associations and Institutions, "Opportunities for Academic and Research Libraries and Wikipedia," 2016. Accessed October 20, 2019, https://www.ifla.org/files/assets/hq/topics/info-society/iflawikipediaopportunitiesforacademicand researchlibraries.pdf; and "Opportunities for Public Libraries and Wikipedia," 2016. Accessed October 20, 2019. https://www.ifla.org/files/assets/hq/topics/info-society/iflawikipediaand publiclibraries.pdf.

8. Association of Research Libraries, "ARL White Paper on Wikidata: Opportunities and Recommendations," April 18, 2019. Accessed October 20, 2019, https://www.arl.org/wp-content/uploads/2019/04/2019.04.18-ARL-white-paper-on-Wikidata.pdf.

9. Siân Evans, Jacqueline Mabey, and Michael Mandiberg, "Editing for Equality: The Outcomes of the Art+Feminism Wikipedia Edit-a-Thons," *Art Documentation: Journal of the Art Libraries Society of North America* 34, no. 2 (2015): 197.

10. Lori Byrd Phillips, "The Temple and the Bazaar: Wikipedia as a Platform for Open Authority in Museums," *Curator: The Museum Journal* 56, no. 2 (2013), 222.

11. Anthony G. Molaro, "On My Mind: Information Activist," *American Libraries* 40, no. 12 (2009): 37. Cited in Evans, Mabey, and Mandiberg (2015): 200.

12. "Wikidata Human Gender Indicators (WHGI)," open data set. Accessed March 5, 2020, http://whgi.wmflabs.org. Cited in Wikipedia:WikiProject Women in Red, last modified March 3, 2020, at 06:35. Accessed March 5, 2020, https://en.wikipedia.org/wiki/Wikipedia:WikiProject_Women_in_Red.

13. A selection of institutions that have hosted edit-a-thons in collaboration with Art+Feminism can be found on the nonprofit's website, http://www.artandfeminism.org.

14. Phillips, "The Temple and the Bazaar," 230.

15. Zoë McLaughlin, "#1Lib1Ref: An Easy Gateway to Wikipedia Editing," *ACRLog*, January 29, 2019. Accessed October 20, 2019, https://acrlog.org/2019/01/29/1lib1ref-an-easy-gateway-to-wikipedia-editing/.

16. Douglas McCarthy and Dr. Andrea Wallace, "Survey of GLAM Open Access Policy and Practice." Accessed October 18, 2019, https://tinyurl.com/y6b9vokw.

17. Wikimedia Foundation. Accessed October 18, 2019, https://wikimediafoundation.org/.

18. William Blueher, "Watson Library Collaborates with Wikipedia," *In Circulation* (blog), Metropolitan Museum of Art, July 30, 2014. Accessed October 20, 2019, https://www.metmuseum.org/blogs/in-circulation/2014/wikipedia.

19. See Isabella Kirton and Melissa Terras, "Where Do Images of Art Go Once They Go Online? A Reverse Image Lookup Study to Assess the Dissemination of Digitized Cultural Heritage," in *Museums and the Web 2013*, edited by N. Proctor and R. Cherry (Silver Spring, MD: Museums and the Web, March 7, 2013).

20. Harry Verwayen, Martijn Arnoldus, and Peter Kaufman, *The Problem of the Yellow Milkmaid: A Business Model Perspective on Open Metadata*, White Paper No. 2 (Paris: Europeana, November 2011). Accessed October 11, 2019, https://pro.europeana.eu/files/Europeana_Professional/Publications/Whitepaper_2-The_Yellow_Milkmaid.pdf.

21. Wikidata:Glossary, last modified October 20, 2019, at 15:55. Accessed October 20, 2019, https://www.wikidata.org/wiki/Wikidata:Glossary.

22. *PCC Task Group on Linked Data Best Practices, Final Report*, September 12, 2019. Accessed October 18, 2019, http://www.loc.gov/aba/pcc/taskgroup/linked-data-best-practices-final-report.pdf.

23. Association of Research Libraries, *ARL White Paper on Wikidata: Opportunities and Recommendations* (Association of Research Libraries and WikiData, April 18, 2019).

Accessed October 20, 2019, https://www.arl.org/wp-content/uploads/2019/04/2019.04.18
-ARL-white-paper-on-Wikidata.pdf.

24. Stanford Libraries, "Stanford Libraries announces Linked Data for Production (LD4P)
Cohort Members and Subgrant Recipients," news release, November 1, 2018.

25. Martin Malmsten, "Cataloguing in the Open: The Disintegration and Distribution
of the Record," *JLIS.it, Italian Journal of Library, Archives, and Information Science* 4, no. 1
(2013): 417.

26. Fiona Romeo, "Bringing [Art] Knowledge to Everyone Who Seeks It," Digital @
MoMA—Medium, January 7, 2016. Accessed October 20, 2019, https://medium.com
/digital-moma/bringing-art-knowledge-to-everyone-who-seeks-it-899ec257a55c.

27. "Commons: Structured Data/GLAM/Projects, Wikimedia Commons," last modified
June 13, 2019, at 07:29. Accessed October 18, 2019, https://commons.wikimedia.org/wiki
/Commons:Structured_data/GLAM/Projects.

28. Becky Yoose and Jody Perkins, "The Linked Open Data Landscape in Libraries and
Beyond," *Journal of Library Metadata* 13, no. 2-3 (2013): 197–211.

29. Lih, "What are Galleries, Libraries, Archives, and Museums (GLAM) to the Wikimedia Community?" 7.

20

Getting a Seat at the Table

Art Museum Libraries as Open Access Stakeholders

Heather Saunders, The Cleveland Museum of Art

Open access (OA), which is defined as "[b]arrier-free access to online works and other resources,"[1] has taken the research community by proverbial storm, and the trend of OA is expected to continue apace. In the realm of art museums, the past decade has seen the Rijksmuseum in Amsterdam become the first to embrace OA in 2011, with others following, including the Cleveland Museum of Art in 2019. Releasing a digital collection of images, exhibition catalogs, massive open online courses, and other content to the public as OA moves museums away from the staid gatekeeper model and tends to yield spectacular press coverage. Substantial executive support is necessary across departments to implement OA initiatives, and this can serve as an opportunity to showcase the diverse skills of library staff members. Art museum executives may regard OA as concerning mostly departments outside the library, such as curatorial, collections management, and information technology. However, as museum professional Kristin Kelly noted in a 2013 study for the Andrew W. Mellon Foundation on OA in art museums in the United States and the United Kingdom, "Libraries . . . have been in the vanguard of the open access movement."[2] This chapter contains advice for how library administrators can position the library as a vital stakeholder.

WHAT IS OPEN ACCESS?

Maryam Fakouri, attorney and Scholarly Publishing Outreach Librarian at the University of Washington, Seattle, defines OA as "when creators and researchers make their work available to anyone online at no cost."[3] Another key characteristic is the exclusion or mitigation of limits on use. At its most open, OA allows users to share, remix, and reuse public domain content for scholarly, commercial, and non-commercial purposes.[4]

In the case of art museums, OA involves sharing both cultural and information resources. What is shared is at the discretion of the museum. For example, releasing provenance information is relatively unusual, whereas releasing images is typical. Approaches vary: for example, in going OA, a museum can determine the size and resolution of images and the degree of permissions, controlling details like whether attribution should be required or requested merely as a courtesy.[5]

OA users range from educators to artists. In terms of the creation of artworks, the value of releasing OA images is substantial, given the popularity of appropriation as a strategy in contemporary art. For art historical research, OA is invaluable; as Martin Paul Eve, editor of an OA journal notes, the academic reproduction of images is thorny, with "enormous problems and costs [involved] in securing rights."[6]

The belief that "creativity requires the reuse of preceding work" led to the creation of Creative Commons (CC) licenses,[7] which are the most frequent way to reduce or remove barriers to access.[8] CC licenses are "not a replacement for copyright but a superstructure atop it that undoes many of the provisions that stop others from using work."[9] They have proven effective in courts of law throughout the world.[10] In fact, copyright authority Peter Suber[11] writes:

> They are . . . lawyer-drafted, enforceable, understood by a large and growing number of users, and [are] available in a large and growing number of legal jurisdictions. Moreover, each comes in three versions: human-readable for nonlawyers, lawyer-readable for lawyers and judges, and machine-readable for search engines and other visiting software.[12]

As an example of OA, this excerpt was published under a CC license so there is no need to be concerned about its length; according to the license, there is only a need to credit the author. In contrast, his biography, excerpted verbatim in the endnote, arguably does not need to be cited because it contains solely facts, which aren't subject to copyright. If this book had not been released as OA, a case could be made that reproducing a modest amount of text in this chapter falls under "fair use." Because the reproduction is for the purpose of scholarship, it could be argued that it is fair. Otherwise, it would be necessary for this chapter's author to pay royalties to Suber or to wait until the publication's copyright expires and enters the public domain.[13]

Regardless of whether art museums go OA, museum personnel, including library administrators and others likely to encounter copyright questions, should familiarize themselves with best practices in fair use.[14] The reason is that fair use can be used in certain circumstances to justify making a copy when OA is not an option, and the Association of Art Museum Directors considers relying on fair use to be a right in order to support museum missions.[15]

One step beyond the CC licenses, which include a range of restrictions (or, stated more positively, a range of openness), is an "un-license" available to owners of copyright, including artists, with zero restrictions. This un-license, called Creative Commons Zero, is described by Katie Zimmerman, Massachusetts Institute of Technology Scholarly Communications and Licensing Librarian, as "volunteering for the public domain," as opposed to waiting for works to age into the public domain.[16]

Essentially, as Suber states, OA is "compatible with copyright law."[17]

What Is Copyright?

In virtually any jurisdiction around the world, copyright is an "automatically conferred, time-limited, exclusive right to distribute an original work."[18] In the United States, the 1787 constitution references copyright as pertaining to "the progress of Science and useful Arts."[19] Thus, copyright is about moving forward, not stalling. And yet, as Dwayne Butler observes, there is a "fear of replication."[20]

Carla Myers, Miami University Libraries assistant professor and Coordinator of Scholarly Communications, states, "too often in copyright, we think there has to be one right answer," which can forestall progress.[21] As to how that can relate to OA in art museums, Elizabeth Saluk, Registrar for Exhibitions and Rights and Reproductions at the Cleveland Museum of Art, explains that the necessary details to make a determination about the status of public domain for artworks aren't always available, and not every work is as simple to assess as a Renaissance painting or a contemporary work. At the crux of the issue, she finds a fascinating, "legal [and ethical] tightrope walking" of balancing the need to release as many images as possible as OA while respecting the copyright of the original creators.[22]

As Kenneth D. Crews, attorney and international copyright consultant, observed of copyright, "change in attitude or awareness . . . happens slowly."[23] The same is true of OA. At the 2018 Challenges in the Scholarly Publishing Cycle symposium in London, England, Helen Blanchett, a scholarly communications subject specialist at the not-for-profit company Jisc Netskills, stated about OA, "Everything is changing all the time." A symposium participant quipped that travel by automobile has long replaced travel by horse, but at one point in time, the idea of trading in horseshoes was unpalatable.[24] Jane Alexander, chief digital information officer at the Cleveland Museum of Art, likens copyright to a glass wall and OA as a means to come out from behind it. She elaborates, "We [museums] need to be the source of truth and give it away."[25] Brewster Kahle, founder of the Internet Archive, a digital library powerhouse,[26] identifies the need for courage when pursuing OA; he described it as essential because, "Sometimes the weight of 'no' outshouts the mission."[27]

To Go OA or Not to Go OA?

OA is a paradigm shift, and inevitably, art museums will have some trustees, leaders, or staff who are nervous. For example, they may express concern about losing revenue from image rights. However, a Europeana Foundation study of the Rijksmuseum's OA initiative found that the loss of image sales was balanced by an increase in goodwill, both through profile enhancement via others' use of its content and refinement of its sponsorship program.[28] Also, not everything can be measured:

Saluk calls the gains against which the Cleveland Museum of Art leveraged anticipated losses "unquantifiable."[29] Minimizing inquiries about image rights frees up staff for other tasks and initiatives; consider that as of the writing of this chapter, in the nine months following the Cleveland Museum of Art's launch of OA, image rights questions dropped anecdotally by two-thirds in both the collections management and library departments. The former processed image requests for 201 works in that time period—a stark contrast to 552 such requests the previous year.[30]

There are many reasons to pursue OA. Bobby Glushko, head of the Scholarly Communications and Copyright Office at the University of Toronto Libraries, and Rex Shoyama, online development manager at Thomson Reuters, identify OA as being appealing for its capacity to increase audience recognition for the author(s), advance the collective nature of scholarship, democratize publishing by empowering authors, challenge the package subscription model that requires academic libraries to pay for the same content multiple times even after the respective institutions have paid to support the generation of said scholarship, and equalize access to information.[31] The final point, which Glushko and Shoyama call the social justice rationale, is germane to art museums.

When contending with copyright, Crews recommends "keep[ing] your eyes on the mission of the institution and be[ing] flexible."[32] Ian Gill, documentation associate at the San Francisco Museum of Modern Art, found in his thesis for the San Francisco State University museum studies master of arts program, that there is "consensus on . . . a general perception of Open Access as benefitting the public, promoting scholarship, and aligning with the museum mission."[33] For example, the Cleveland Museum of Art's mission is "to create transformative experiences through art, for the benefit of all the people, forever." Because open content is typically shared online, it has a global reach. An example is HoloLens Hyland consuming the Cleveland Museum of Art's application programming interface to allow people from around the world to view and interact with art in an augmented space, as shown in figure 20.1. Barriers within OA continue to exist, however, namely for people with disabilities, lack of access to the internet, and lack of English reading knowledge.[34] Lest it seem that OA is exclusively left-wing, OA invites associations ranging from Marxism to neoliberalism.[35]

Where Does the Library Fit?

With such diverse possible applications for OA, it is unsurprising that there is not a clear understanding of who should and should not be involved, or at what stage, in an art museum. Most likely, every institution embarking on an OA initiative will take a different approach, but the process might look like the following: at least a year in advance, museum leadership will explore the idea of going OA and establish a core team. The team will present examples of peer institutions that have gone OA to the board of trustees. To make OA relatable, the core team will liaise with those institutions and with leaders from organizations such as CC. Once the project is

Figure 20.1.   Russ Klimczuk (Assistant Treasurer–Finance, center) using a Microsoft HoloLens device. Photography by Scott Shaw Photography.

sanctioned, the team will identify the ideal scope for content to share as open and confer with legal counsel. Lastly, the team will determine what amount of content will be released and when, with the option of releasing content in stages, and will seek the involvement of various departments and potential community partners leading up to a high-profile launch (see figure 20.2).

Once library administrators have been alerted about the plan to go OA, they can position themselves as logical partners by explaining that OA has an established presence in the library profession, with OA having flourished as a solution to prohibitively expensive academic journal package subscriptions. They can share "good news stories" such as OA articles being cited more often than non-OA articles—even those within the same issue, because a broader audience increases the likelihood of being cited,[36] and they can provide a bibliography about OA. Library administrators can also draw parallels to existing library initiatives within their respective institutions that qualify as OA, such as uploading scans of books in the public domain to the Internet Archive. In addition to highlighting the past and present state of affairs, library administrators can help art museum leadership look toward the future by positioning themselves as internal and external advocates for the merits of OA. For example, they can attend a meeting of curators to explain what OA entails and to allay concerns, because misunderstanding OA is its primary obstacle, according to Suber.[37] Lastly, library administrators can promote OA publicly through existing channels with which they are more likely to be familiar than executives, such as Open Access week and Wikipedia Edit-a-Thons.

Support of OA can be facilitated at all levels of the library. Andrea Bour, collections information data analyst at the Cleveland Museum of Art, explains that top priorities for populating metadata are the fields for the date of creation of an artwork, the artist's name, and the artist's death date.[38] The reason is that, as Zimmerman generalizes about copyright across the globe, what is of interest is the life of the creator plus a particular number of years.[39] Library staff are well-suited to conduct such data entry accurately because they are generally detail-oriented and potentially familiar with resources like the Getty Union List of Artist Names and MARC records from which data can be extracted. They are also adept at interpreting and formatting citations, and they can expand bibliographies to showcase publications containing reproductions or mentions of museum artworks; this step can be taken in anticipation of a potential increase in research requests following a spike in online discovery. Circulation staff can page and return new publications for curators, their assistants, and their interns, who can assist with a backlog of citation entry into the museum's system. Additionally, reference and instruction personnel can enhance staff and users' copyright literacy, field questions about citing and using OA content, and advise patrons on how to publish their own content openly based on their familiarity with the publishing industry. As Zeller and Stenberg write:

> Library staff have long been a trusted source of information for academic creators on a variety of issues. Copyright, licensing, and intellectual property issues are areas in which

Figure 20.2. Jane Alexander (Chief Digital Information Officer, left) and William Griswold (Director and President, right) announcing the launch of open access at the Cleveland Museum of Art, January 23, 2019. Photography by Scott Shaw Photography.

academic creators increasingly expect their libraries to be able to provide information and support. As we move into the twenty-first century, more library staff members will be developing knowledge and expertise on the particulars and technicalities of law and policy in these areas.[40]

Once museum staff have a cursory understanding of OA, protocols and workflows need to be established in consultation with legal counsel, documented, and disseminated internally to appropriate parties. In keeping with best practice in project management, all stakeholders should have a clear understanding of their roles. For example, if the library has a recommendation for a different approach to data entry based on cataloging standards, it is helpful to know what mechanism to funnel the recommendation through and who will make the final decision. If regular liaising proves helpful for clearing up confusion, standing drop-in meetings may be helpful.

From start to finish, the art museum library can play a vital supporting role for OA, although it could be argued that the work is never complete because digital collections are in a state of continual growth.

Nothing in this chapter is intended as legal advice.

NOTES

1. Peter Suber, *Open Access* (Cambridge, MA: The MIT Press, 2012), 175.

2. Kristin Kelly, *Images of Works of Art in Museum Collections: The Experience of Open Access—A Study of 11 Museums* (Council on Library and Information Resources, 2013), 22. https://clir.wordpress.clir.org/wp-content/uploads/sites/6/pub157.pdf.

3. Maryam Fakouri, "What We Talk About When We Talk about Open Access," *ACRL Presents*, webinar, 48:02, October 25, 2017. https://www.youtube.com/watch?v=7erd303P0Mg.

4. Heather Saunders, "Paradigm Shift: Open Access at the Cleveland Museum of Art," *The Thinker* (blog), The Cleveland Museum of Art, January 25, 2019. Accessed April 28, 2020, https://medium.com/cma-thinker/paradigm-shift-open-access-at-the-cleveland-museum-of-art-482938442a84.

5. For examples of how approaches differ to releasing images as OA, see Kristin Kelly.

6. Martin Paul Eve, *Open Access and the Humanities: Contexts, Controversies and the Future* (Cambridge, UK: Cambridge University Press, 2014), 97.

7. Ibid., 103.

8. Ibid., 20.

9. Ibid., 20–21.

10. Creative Commons, "Case Law," last updated August 9, 2017. http://wiki.creative commons.org/Case_Law.

11. Peter Suber is director of the Harvard Open Access Project, a faculty fellow at the Berkman Center for Internet and Society, and senior researcher at the Scholarly Publishing and Academic Resources Coalition.

12. Peter Suber, *Open Access*, 70.

13. For an overview of the complexity of copyright expiration, see Peter B. Hirtle, Cornell University Library Copyright Information Center, "Copyright Term and the Public Domain

in the United States," 2004–2020, last updated January 3, 2020. https://copyright.cornell
.edu/publicdomain.

14. Creative Commons USA defines fair use as "a provision of copyright law that allows
the use of copyrighted work without permission from the copyright holder under specific
circumstances." "What Is the Difference between Fair Use and CC?" July 18, 2018. https://
creativecommonsusa.org/index.php/ufaqs/what-is-the-difference-between-fair-use-and-cc/.

15. Association of Art Museum Directors, *Guidelines for the Use of Copyrighted Materials
and Works of Art by Art Museums* (Association of Art Museum Directors, October 11, 2017), 5.
https://aamd.org/sites/default/files/document/Guidelines%20for%20the%20Use%20of%20
Copyrighted%20Materials.pdf.

16. Katie Zimmerman, Miami University Libraries Oxford Copyright Conference, "Finding the Public Domain: Practical Rights Review for Mid-century Collections," September 26,
2019.

17. Peter Suber, *Open Access*, 21.

18. Martin Paul Eve, *Open Access and the Humanities*, 17.

19. "Transcript of the Constitution of the United States (1787)," *Our Documents*, n.d.,
Section 8, paragraph 7. https://www.ourdocuments.gov/doc.php?flash=true&doc=9&page=
transcript.

20. Dwayne Butler, "How'd We Get Here? The Evolution of Copyright Law," September
25, 2019.

21. Carla Myers, introductory remarks, Miami University Libraries conference, September
25, 2019.

22. Elizabeth Saluk, personal communication, September 18, 2019, and November 14,
2019.

23. Kenneth D. Crews, "Policy Making and Interpretation," Miami University Libraries
conference, September 26, 2019.

24. *Research Information* magazine, Challenges in the Scholarly Publishing Cycle symposium, hosted in partnership with Info International, London Art House, London, England,
December 3, 2018.

25. Jane Alexander, personal communication, September 18, 2019.

26. The Internet Archive—through its "highly significant mass digitization project" and
establishment of the Open Content Alliance—is "a transparent open source alternative to the
closed doors of corporate and commercial initiatives" like Amazon and Google. *The Politics of
Mass Digitization*, 12, 13. Brewster, Kahle personal communication during visit by Advancing Art Libraries and Curated Web Archives symposium attendees to Internet Archive, San
Francisco, February 12, 2019.

27. Advancing Art Libraries and Curated Web Archives symposium visit to Internet Archive, San Francisco, February 12, 2019.

28. Joris Pekel, *Democratising the Rijksmuseum: Why Did the Rijksmuseum Make Available
Their Highest Quality Material without Restrictions, and What Are the Results?* (Europeana
Foundation, November 14, 2014), 14. https://pro.europeana.eu/files/Europeana_Professional
/Publications/Democratising%20the%20Rijksmuseum.pdf.

29. Elizabeth Saluk, personal communication, September 18, 2019.

30. James Koehler, department coordinator, Photographic and Digital Imaging Services,
personal communication, October 31, 2019.

31. Bobby Glushko and Rex Shoyama, "Unpacking Open Access: A Theoretical Framework for Understanding Open Access Initiatives," *Feliciter* 61, no. 1 (2015): 9–10.

32. Kenneth D. Crews, "Policy Making and Interpretation."

33. Ian Gill. "Assessing the Impact of Open Access on Museum Image Use Policy," Western Museums Association, n.d., paragraph 7, Re. May 2017 thesis. https://westmuse.org/articles/assessing-impact-open-access-museum-image-use-policy.

34. Peter Suber, *Open Access*, 27.

35. Martin Paul Eve, *Open Access and the Humanities*, 7.

36. Steve Hitchcock, "The Effect of Open Access and Downloads ('Hits') on Citation Impact: A Bibliography of Studies," *The Open Citation Project*, last updated June 25, 2013. http://opcit.eprints.org/oacitation-biblio.html.

37. Peter Suber, *Open Access*, x.

38. Andrea Bour, personal communication, October 2, 2019.

39. Katie Zimmerman, "Finding the Public Domain."

40. Micah Zeller and Emily Symonds Stenberg, "Faculty Require Online Distribution of Student Work: Enter the Librarian," in *Open Access and the Future of Scholarly Communication: Implementation*, Kevin L. Smith and Katherine A. Dickson, eds. (Lanham, MD: Rowman & Littlefield, 2017), 27.

Index

About the Editors
and the Contributors

ABOUT THE EDITORS

Amelia Nelson is the head of library and archives at the Spencer Art Reference Library in The Nelson-Atkins Museum of Art. Prior to joining the Nelson-Atkins, she worked in academic and public libraries. She is inspired by the innovative work that art libraries and archives do to share unique resources in this rich information landscape. She works with colleagues to support public services, develop inspiring collections, and create digital initiatives. She has published and presented on integrating museum teaching techniques into information literacy classes, collaborations with faculty using special collections in art history classes, and development of a wide range of programs built on the library's extensive collections. She is a member of the Art Libraries Society of North America (ARLIS/NA) and has served as the ARLIS Central Plains Chapter chair and newsletter editor, peer-reviewer for *Art Documentation*, and as development coordinator for the 2020 St. Louis ARLIS conference. She earned a BArch from Kansas State, an MA in library science from the University of Missouri, an MA in art history from the University of Missouri–Kansas City, and a Museum and Free-Choice Learning/Informal Education Certificate from Oregon State, Professional and Continuing Education.

Traci E. Timmons is senior librarian at the Seattle Art Museum. In her role, she oversees two research libraries and one satellite library collection. Prior to joining the Seattle Art Museum, she worked in academic and special libraries, museums focused on contemporary art, and the tech industry. For more than twenty years, she ran Vecellio.net, a website devoted to the sixteenth-century Venetian artist and costume and lace book author Cesare Vecellio. The site was used in art history classrooms throughout the United States. She has contributed research in the areas of early printed European books, artists' books, digital collections, classification theory, and is a regular contributor to the Seattle Art Museum Blog. As a member of ARLIS/NA, she has served as the George Wittenborn Memorial Book Award Chair, Joint Conference Local Arrangements Co-Chair, and Northwest Chapter Chair. She has been awarded several 4Culture grants, and most recently, a National Endowment for the Humanities Collections and Reference Resources Grant for her work on time-based media digitization, preservation, and access. She earned her MA in art history from the University of South Florida and her MLIS from the University of Washington.

ABOUT THE CONTRIBUTORS

Courtney Becks is the librarian for African American studies and the Jewish studies bibliographer at the University of Illinois at Urbana-Champaign. Her research interests include African American art and aesthetics; style/fashion; media; and material culture. Becks is one of three ethnic studies subject specialists at the University of Illinois Libraries. As the African American studies librarian and Jewish studies selector, she supports the research of all faculty, staff, and students on campus with interests in any aspect of these fields, develops the collections, and provides reference assistance and library instruction.

Sarah Osborne Bender is the head of library technical services at the National Gallery of Art in Washington, DC. Her professional interests are in developing collection metadata and creative connections within metadata to tell new stories about the history of art. She has worked with library and cultural heritage metadata in a number of museums, both large and small, and has been an active member of the Art+Feminism initiative since its inception.

Stephen J. Bury is the Andrew W. Mellon Chief Librarian at the Frick Art Reference Library, The Frick Collection. Formerly, he was the head of learning resources at Chelsea School of Art, and then the head of European and American maps, music, and philatelic collections at the British Library.

Lee Ceperich has served as director of the Margaret R. and Robert M. Freeman Library at the Virginia Museum of Fine Arts since 2010, and has been a rare book librarian since 2005. Prior to her arrival at the Virginia Museum of Fine Arts she worked in special collections at the Library of Virginia and the Archives of American Art, Smithsonian Institution. She has served as a consultant for institutional special collections, a reviewer for National Endowment of the Humanities grant programs and as an adjunct faculty member teaching a graduate course in art librarianship for Catholic University of America in Washington, DC. Ceperich received an MLIS degree from Catholic University, an MA in museum studies from Virginia Commonwealth University, and a BA in art history from James Madison University. She is currently serving on the executive board of LYRASIS. Other professional affiliations include ARLIS/NA, ALA (CALM, ACRL, RBMS) AAM, and VAM. Ceperich's areas of interest and specialization include illustrated books, applied arts, design, and ornamentation in all media. She has lectured on early twentieth-century design portfolios, artist-illustrated books, binding designs and special collections.

Sumitra Duncan is head of the web archiving program at the Frick Art Reference Library. In this role she manages the web archiving program of the New York Art Resources Consortium (NYARC), which consists of the Frick Art Reference Library and the libraries and archives of the Brooklyn Museum and The Museum of Modern Art. She cofounded and co-coordinates the Web Archiving Special Interest Group (SIG) of the ARLIS/NA and the Archive-It New York Users Group. She holds an MSLIS from Pratt Institute and a BA in English from Virginia Commonwealth University.

Anne Evenhaugen is the head librarian for the Smithsonian American Art and Portrait Gallery Library, and head of the Art Department of the Smithsonian Libraries. She manages the day-to-day operations of a large research library, and staff and special projects across the five art libraries at the Smithsonian Institution. With her particular interest in artists' books, Evenhaugen was central in the effort to make the Smithsonian's large collection of artists' books more searchable online. She has worked for a variety of arts organizations, including Moderna Museet and the Fotografiska Museum in Stockholm, the American Alliance of Museums, and the National Gallery of Art in Washington DC. She holds degrees in art history, library science, and art curation from Mary Washington College, the University of Maryland, and Stockholm University in Sweden, where she curated her first large show on artists' books, *Reading the Object*, at Moderna Museet in 2011.

Alba Fernandez-Keys is the head of libraries and archives at the Indianapolis Museum of Art at Newfields. She earned her bachelor's degree in art history and MLS from the University of Arizona in Tucson. She is a member of the Art Libraries Society of North America where she has served in various leadership roles. Fernandez-Keys has led the Library and Archives Department at Newfields since 2010, oversaw the establishment of the institutional Archives, and has led several digitization projects, including the National Endowment of the Humanities–funded "Documenting Modern Living: Digitizing the Miller House and Garden Collection." Her current projects relate to cataloging ephemera and institutional knowledge management.

Lauren Gottlieb-Miller is the librarian at the Menil Collection in Houston, Texas. In this role she oversees the museum's research library, special collections, and archives. Prior to joining the Menil Collection in 2016, she worked in a variety of academic, museum, and special libraries including the Kohler Art Library at the University of Wisconsin–Madison and the Hirsch Library at the Museum of Fine Arts, Houston.

As a member of ARLIS/NA she has served as the museum division moderator, secretary for the ARLIS Texas Mexico Chapter, and on the Wittenborn Book Award Committee. Her contributed research centers on visibility, access, and preservation for special and unique collections. She received her MA in library and information studies from the iSchool at the University of Wisconsin–Madison in 2014 and a graduate certificate in the history of the books and print culture in 2016.

Jonathan Lill is the head of metadata and systems for the archives, library, and research collections, at The Museum of Modern Art (MoMA). Previously he led the MoMA Archives' exhibition history project, which included publishing the full history of MoMA and MoMA PS1's exhibitions online linked to related artists, documents, and library materials. He continues to explore how data from across the GLAM sector (galleries, libraries, archives, and museums) can be deployed to increase access to archives and library resources, connect institutions, and promote scholarship.

Dan Lipcan is the head librarian of the Phillips Library at the Peabody Essex Museum, the oldest continuously operating museum in the United States. He oversees a talented staff charged with stewarding and sharing the library's extensive collection of books, archives, ships' journals, broadsides, and ephemera. He joined the Peabody Essex Museum in May 2019 after a sixteen-year tenure at The Metropolitan Museum of Art's Thomas J. Watson Library. At The Metropolitan Museum of Art, Dan managed the library's systems, technology, and digitization initiatives to support the core activities of staff, library volunteers and interns, and thousands of researchers.

Doug Litts is information services librarian at West Point Military Academy. He was formerly the executive director of the Ryerson and Burnham Libraries at the Art Institute of Chicago overseeing the largest art museum library in the Midwest. Previously, he was the head librarian at the Smithsonian American Art Museum/National Portrait Gallery in Washington, DC, and before that, as library director at the Corcoran College of Art + Design and Gallery and as assistant librarian at the Virginia Museum of Fine Arts. He is an active member of ARLIS/NA and has served on the executive board and as an editor of *ARLIS/NA Reviews*. He received his MS in library and information science from the University of Illinois at Urbana-Champaign and his MA in history of art and archaeology from New York University.

Janice Lea Lurie began her thirty-year art museum library career at the Albright-Knox Art Gallery in Buffalo, New York, as an assistant librarian/archivist and then was later promoted to head librarian. For nearly the past nineteen years, Lurie has been working as head librarian at the Minneapolis Institute of Art, where she has overseen several preservation and accessibility initiatives involving the documentary collections of the Minneapolis Institute of Art's Library and Archives. In 2014, she earned her digital archives specialist certificate from the Society of American

Archivists and was recertified in 2018. She was a Roberta Mann Innovation Award recipient in 2017. Lurie graduated from Syracuse University with an MA in art history and an MLS from the School of Information Studies. Lurie served two terms as chapter chair of Art Libraries Society of North America–Twin Cities and also served as co-chair of the Silent Auction Committee for the Art Libraries Society of North America 2011 joint national conference held with VRA in Minneapolis.

Gwen Mayhew is the head of collection access at the Canadian Centre for Architecture in Montreal. In her role, she oversees reference, cataloging, circulation, and systems, and collaborates with staff across the institution to provide access to the collection in the Canadian Centre for Architecture's study room and online. Prior to that, she spent ten years working at the Thomas J. Watson Library in The Metropolitan Museum of Art where she focused on volunteer instruction, interlibrary loan, and reference. In 2019, Mayhew gave a presentation on reference books at the ARLIS/NA conference in SLC with former colleague Annalise Welte, and in 2016 she presented a poster at the ARLIS/NA-VRA conference in Seattle with former colleague Naomi Niles on story time in The Metropolitan Museum of Art's libraries. She holds an MLS from Queens College, an MA in art and museum studies from Georgetown University, and a BFA in art history from Massachusetts College of Art and Design.

Sophie Jo Miller is a library specialist in digital collections at the University of Wyoming and a communication instructor at Laramie County Community College. Her work in libraries is focused on maintaining and adding content to the institutional repository. She has worked with a variety of collections from departments and museums across campus, ranging from stereoviews, to historic clothing, to geological samples. She earned her MA in communication from Eastern New Mexico University.

Beth Morris is an independent librarian, preservation specialist, book conservator, and scholar. Prior to this, she was librarian at the Yale Center for British Art from 2011 to 2020, growing from Librarian I to Librarian III while specializing in preservation and conservation of books, paper, and special collections. She has worked in numerous areas of libraries and museums with a focus on collections, instruction, outreach, development, project management, preservation, and conservation. While working in these areas she regularly uses and develops techniques for assessment, organizational models, online environments for knowledge dissemination, and learning and institutional training. Morris's research interests are focused on advancing collections management, preservation, conservation, research, community, and social services. Morris has presented and published on conservation and preservation strategies in libraries.

Carol Ng-He is an award-winning art museum educator and library professional. Prior to her role as the exhibits coordinator at Arlington Heights Memorial Library in Illinois, she was the school and community program manager at the Oriental Institute of the University of Chicago. She founded the Chicago Area Archivists' Curating and Exhibitions Interest Group, and has served on several committees at the ARLIS/NA. Her publications on the intersections of art, cultural heritage, and informal learning have appeared in the *Journal of Museum Education, Teaching Artist Journal,* and *Visual Inquiry,* among others. She is a coauthor of a manuscript in progress, *Exhibits and Displays: A Practical Guide for Librarians* (Rowman & Littlefield Publishers, 2021). Carol earned her MA in art education from the School of the Art Institute in Chicago and a certificate in Museum Studies at Northwestern University. She is an MLIS candidate at San José State University.

Carissa Pfeiffer is part of a small but mighty team of four at Black Mountain College Museum + Arts Center, where her role encompasses collections, development, and visitor experiences. She enjoys finding the ways that collections connect to the world beyond the museum and inspire people to share their own stories.

Kristen Regina is the Arcadia director of the library and archives at the Philadelphia Museum of Art. She joined the museum in 2015, leading the expansion of the library and archives as the nexus for stewarding analog and digital knowledge resources. She oversees the DAMS initiative, an Art Information Commons—linked data project supported by The Andrew W. Mellon Foundation, and Duchamp Research Portal, a National Endowment for the Humanities—supported collaboration with the Centre Pompidou and Association Marcel Duchamp to aggregate and web-publish sixty thousand archival records and works. She was the project director of the Institute of Museum and Library Services–funded National Digital Stewardship Residency for Art Information professionals. She served as president of ARLIS/NA in 2015. Prior to working in Philadelphia, Regina was head of archives and special collections at the Hillwood Estate, Museum and Gardens in Washington, DC, and has an MA in art history from the University of Maryland.

Alexandra Reigle is the reference librarian at the Smithsonian American Art and Portrait Gallery Library and serves as the manager of the library's art and artist files. Born and raised in Washington, DC, she is happy to work for an institution that taught her so much in a profession that she shares with her late mother. Alexandra enjoys discussing how artist's file collections are vital resources for understanding artists and the art world. She often wishes she had more time to appreciate every piece of ephemera.

Bryan Ricupero is the metadata librarian in digital collections at the University of Wyoming's William Robertson Coe Library. He is focused on providing metadata support for both the digital and institutional repositories, and metadata preparation for the Digital Public Library of America. Ricupero is one of two principal investigators for Wyoming's National Endowment for the Humanities-funded National Digital Newspaper Project, is the principal investigator on a State Historical Records Advisory Board stereograph digitization and image augmentation grant, and provides digitization and metadata support for the High Plains American Indian Research Institute's National Endowment for the Humanities–funded Elk Culture Project in cooperation with the Eastern Shoshone and Northern Arapahoe tribes. Prior to his work at the University of Wyoming, Ricupero held positions in technical services departments at Northwestern University and the University of Louisville. Ricupero completed his undergraduate studies in political science at Boston University and his master's of science in library science at the University of Kentucky.

Heather Saunders is the former director of the Ingalls Library at the Cleveland Museum of Art. Previous places of work include Purchase College (State University of New York, Purchase, NY), where Saunders worked as faculty art librarian, and Nipissing University (North Bay, ON, Canada) where she worked as manager of reference and information studies and later manager of digital resources and information services, as well as part-time art history faculty. She holds master's degrees from the University of Toronto in the history of art and library and information studies. She is an artist and author of the blog, *Artist in Transit* (2009–2019).

Jenna Stout is the museum archivist at the Saint Louis Art Museum's Richardson Memorial Library. She holds a PhD in public history from Middle Tennessee State University, an MLIS degree from the University of North Carolina at Greensboro, and an MA degree in American history from Western Carolina University. Prior to joining the St. Louis Art Museum, Stout worked at a county archives in Tennessee and interned at the Biltmore Estate archives. She is currently documenting the institutional history of the Saint Louis Art Museum. Her other research interests focus on the built environment of tuberculosis medical tourism and early twentieth-century sleeping porch design. In her spare time, she is restoring a 1927 frame bungalow in the City of Saint Louis.

Simon Underschultz is the special collections officer at the National Gallery of Australia Research Library and Archives. While studying his Graduate Diploma in Records Management and Archives at Curtin University, he interned at the National Film and Sound Archive in Canberra. Previously, Simon has published an article in *Art Libraries Journal* (United Kingdom) and presented talks at the Australian Society of Archivists 2017 Conference and the ARLIS/ANZ 2018 Conference. In his current role, he answers reference questions, catalogs books, and manages the art and artist files. His background is in philosophy and film studies. His interests include movies, books, and writing horror stories, hoping one day to become a published fiction writer.

Annalise Welte is a reference librarian at the Getty Research Institute. She works with Getty staff and researchers worldwide to promote discovery, access, and connections to the collections of the Getty Research Institute. In addition to providing research support, she works with a range of groups to facilitate library use through tours and training sessions. Previously, she was senior library associate at the Thomas J. Watson Library in The Metropolitan Museum of Art, working in nearly all departments of the library and ultimately focusing on reference and reader services. Annalise is an active member of ARLIS/NA, serving as the 2019–2020 co-moderator for the Intersectional Feminism and Art Special Interest Group. She received a BA in classics from Trinity College (Connecticut), an MA in the history of art and design, and an MA in information and library science from Pratt Institute.

Tony White is the University Librarian at OCAD University, Toronto. Previously he was the Florence and Herbert Irving Associate Chief Librarian, Thomas J. Watson Library, The Metropolitan Museum of Art. Before coming to The Metropolitan Museum of Art, he was director of Decker Library, Maryland Institute College of Art; prior to the Maryland Institute College of Art, he served as head of the fine arts library, Indiana University–Bloomington, where he was also the director of the specialization in art librarianship. He was the first appointed field editor for Artists' Books and Books for Artists for the College Art Association's online reviews journal. He is a founding board member of the College Book Art Association, and the founder of the Contemporary Artist's Books Conference held each fall at Metropolitan Museum of Art's PS1 (2007–2017), as part of the New York Art Book Fair. For several years he served on the editorial board of the *Journal of Artist's Books*, guest editing issue 25. He teaches a course at the University of Virginia's Rare Book School titled The History of Artists' Books since 1950. He has a post-MLS certificate in preservation management for libraries and archives from Rutgers University, an MLS from Indiana University–Bloomington with a concentration in art librarianship, and an MFA from the School of the Art Institute of Chicago.